P9-DLO-919

THE THRIFTY INVESTOR
Penny-Wise Strategies for Investors on a Budget

CRAIG L. ISRAELSEN

McGraw-Hill

New York   San Francisco   Washington, D.C.   Auckland   Bogotá
Caracas   Lisbon   London   Madrid   Mexico City   Milan
Montreal   New Delhi   San Juan   Singapore
Sydney   Tokyo   Toronto

Library of Congress Cataloging-in-Publication Data

Israelsen, Craig L.
    The thrifty investor : penny-wise strategies for investors on a budget / Craig L. Israelsen.
      p. cm.
    ISBN 0-07-136158-8
    1. Investments. I. Title.

   HG4521 .I853 2000
   332.06—dc21

                                                          00-030549

McGraw-Hill

A Division of The **McGraw·Hill** Companies

1 2 3 4 5 6 7 8 9 0 AGM/AGM 0 9 8 7 6 5 4 3 2 1 0

ISBN 0-07-136158-8

This book was set in New Century Schoolbook by North Market Street Graphics.

Printed and bound by Quebecor Martinsburg.

This publication is designed to provide accurate and authoritative information in regard to the subject matter covered. It is sold with the understanding that the publisher is not engaged in rendering legal, accounting, or other professional service. If legal advice or other expert assistance is required, the services of a competent professional person should be sought.
             —From a declaration of principles jointly adopted by a committee of the American Bar Association and a committee of publishers.

This book is printed on recycled, acid-free paper containing a minimum of 50% recycled de-inked fiber.

McGraw-Hill books are available at special quantity discounts to use as premiums and sales promotions, or for use in corporate training programs. For more information, please write to the Director of Special Sales, Profession̶̶ ̶ ̶ ̶ ̶ ̶ ̶ McGraw-Hill, Two Penn Plaza, New York, NY 10121-2298. Or contact your local bookstore.

CONTENTS

APPENDICES

INTRODUCTION

This is a book about investing, written specifically for people who would like to be *thrifty* investors. Thrifty investors focus on long-term value and intelligent investment integration, rather than short-term, speculative strategies. Therefore, this book won't discuss get-rich-quick stock market schemes or day-trading tactics. Rather, in the broadest sense, thrifty investing might be compared to running a marathon. Sprinting at the start of the race provides a fleeting moment of glory, but the race belongs to the runners who are willing to follow a disciplined plan from start to finish and who endure to the end. In like manner, investing rewards those who endure the ups and downs of the stock market experience.

A thrifty investor is also a person who is provident, or in other words, economically wise. But all the wisdom in the world won't get the job done unless wisdom is combined with action. Thrifty investors must have a willingness to actually start the process of investing. Too many wannabe investors fret about what they wished they had invested in, or endlessly study the many investing possibilities without ever choosing one. This is referred to as "paralysis by analysis." My advice: study your options and then get on with it. Do your homework and then make things happen. A mediocre investment is a lot better than no investment. Waiting for the perfect investment will be a long wait!

This book's main purpose is to help you begin an investment program that meets the constraints of even the thriftiest investor. If you have already started investing, it can help you fine-tune your investment strategies.

Investing is a burden to some and a fascination to others. Truth be known, it's probably a little bit of both to most people. Many people invest because they feel a *need* to do so, not because they really *want* to. Others, energized by phenomenal stock market gains in recent years, actually look for additional investment opportunities. And, there are many who simply haven't begun the process of saving for the future (i.e., investing) for a variety of reasons: not enough money to start (they think), not knowing what to invest in or whom to contact to obtain unbiased information, the "paralysis by analysis" thing, and so on. If any of those concerns sound familiar, then this book is for you.

The Thrifty Investor will identify investments (stocks and mutual funds) that can fit your budget—no matter how large or small. It will also provide the needed information to help you understand different investing alternatives, and then outline the steps involved in actually starting an investment account—whether for you or a child . . . or both. Let me say again: *This book focuses on investments that can fit anyone's budget.*

ACKNOWLEDGMENTS

To wonderful parents who continue to teach me. To Tammy, a most supportive and gracious spouse, and to loving parents who taught her. To our children, Sara, Andrew, Heidi, Mark, Nathan, Emma, and Jared. It is our little ones that give us a reason to invest—of money and of ourselves, both here and forever. Finally, to Kelli Christiansen and Pattie Amoroso at McGraw-Hill. Their support both assisted and encouraged me.

1

The Investment Thing

Here's the deal: We invest money because we believe our investments will grow in value. We might invest for future retirement, for children's education, you name it. Or we believe that we should invest to protect our money from the effects of inflation. Or perhaps we agree that . . .

The most powerful force in the universe
is compound interest.

Albert Einstein (1879–1955)

Now, I trust that Einstein made that comment with a wink. Nevertheless, he was referring to a mathematical principle known as exponential growth. Exponential growth is good when it applies to investments! But exponential growth takes time. The most important ingredient in a successful investment plan is TIME. If given enough time, invested money grows exponentially, and that's what makes investing worthwhile, particularly in the long run. Investment periods start becoming "long run" investments after 10 years or so.

An obvious question is: "What should I invest in?" A complete answer gets complicated real fast. Here's a short answer. If you can commit your money for at least five to seven years, you should consider investing in **stock mutual funds** and possibly individual **stocks.** Thus, the objective of this book is to help you learn more about:

1. Investing in stock mutual funds
2. Investing in Direct Stock Purchase Plans (purchasing stock directly from a company)

3.   Investing in common stock via Internet-based invest-
     ment services

WHY INVEST IN STOCK?

Purchasing stock is a very common way for people to invest in
corporations. There are thousands of corporations to choose from,
both in the United States and abroad. Purchasing shares of
stock, or shares of mutual funds that invest in stock, represents
a method of obtaining ownership in a corporation. Stock mutual
funds are collections (or portfolios) of stock. The number of stocks
held in a mutual fund portfolio can range from less than 10 to
over 4000. People invest in mutual funds by purchasing shares of
the fund. As an investor in a corporation (either by purchasing
stock directly or through a mutual fund), your investment increases in value as the price of the stock increases. However, if
you purchase stock of a company that goes bankrupt, you could
lose your entire investment. The likelihood of that occurring is
small if investments are chosen wisely and if your investment
portfolio is *balanced*. More about the idea of balance later.

WHY DO CORPORATIONS SELL STOCK?

Companies sell stock to investors (such as yourself) to raise
money. Money gained from selling stock is used to finance corporate activities: to construct more buildings, buy more trucks, hire
more people, etc. When a company sells stock, it shares ownership of the business with investors. Rather than selling stock to
raise money, companies can borrow money from banks or sell
bonds to investors. By selling bonds, a company does not share
ownership; it pays interest to the buyers of their bonds. When a
company sells stock, it shares ownership with investors, but does
not necessarily have to pay interest to shareholders. When a
company does make a payment to shareholders, it's called a **dividend.** Companies pay dividends as a way of sharing the corporate profits with shareholders. Plus, it keeps shareholders happy.
Happy is good.

Not all companies pay dividends. Generally speaking,
younger, smaller companies are less likely to pay dividends. Start-
up companies will typically plow their earnings back into the company to facilitate growth. Over time, as the company grows, the
board of directors may decide to begin paying dividends to shareholders. However, despite not paying dividends, such small com-

panies can offer the potential for dramatic growth in stock prices. For example, between 1972 and 1987 the return from holding stock in a small company named *Wal-Mart* was over 6200 percent. The price per share of a new company's stock can double or triple, or more, in one year. Unfortunately, it's not uncommon for the stock of a new company to decline, sometimes disappearing from the financial pages as the company goes out of business.

WHAT CAUSES THE PRICE OF A STOCK TO GO UP OR DOWN?

The price of stock is determined in "stock markets" where the actual buying and selling of stock takes place. The New York Stock Exchange (NYSE) is one such market. The price of a particular stock goes up when more people want to buy it than sell it, and goes down when there are more sellers than buyers. Think of stock markets as behaving like (1) auctions and (2) fickle friends.

Consider the auction analogy. Very simply, stock is purchased by the highest bidder. If the future prospects of a company appear bright, the price per share of that company's stock will often be bid up by investors wanting to purchase shares from people who already own shares. So, just as at an auction, shares of the "hot" stock end up in the hands of the highest bidder—the highest bidders obviously being the most optimistic buyers.

If, on the other hand, a company is not doing well (or is *forecasted* to perform poorly in the future), the price of its stock may plummet as shareholders attempt to sell their shares before the price falls further. Inasmuch as not everyone in the marketplace shares the same view, the falling price of the "doomed" stock attracts the attention of investors who see the declining stock price as a potentially good value. Falling stock prices are somewhat similar to products being sold at "sale" prices, and "sales" usually attract the attention of shoppers (i.e., investors). Investors who begin to gobble up shares of the depressed stock at bargain prices can start a wave of buying, and if it gains momentum, a bidding war can ensue and the price of the stock begins to rise. It is this up and down movement of a stock's share price that resembles the dynamics of a fickle friendship with its characteristic on-again-off-again dynamic.

So, there you have a simple view of why stocks exist in the first place and why the price per share of a corporation's stock rises and falls over time. Understanding that the price of any given stock will fluctuate takes some of the confusion out of investing.

> We are *certain* that a stock's price will fluctuate.
> We are *hopeful* that the price will fluctuate around an upward trend.

What is the advantage of investing in stock (and stock mutual funds) compared to putting your long-term investment money in a savings account or certificate of deposit? Very simply: Return. Performance. Gain. For the highest annual returns (over the long run), stocks are clearly the best choice. *Annual return* is the percentage gain, or loss, of an investment over a one-year period. *Average annual total return* is the average return per year over a multiyear period with dividends reinvested into the account. The "total return" advantage of stocks, compared to bonds or "cash" (savings accounts or certificates of deposit) over several time frames during the last 30 years is shown in Table 1.1.

HOW DOES ANNUAL RETURN TRANSLATE INTO ACTUAL DOLLAR GAINS?

Let's look at the average annual return of the Dow Jones Industrial Average during the decade of the 1990s as an example. During that 10-year period, the DJIA had an average return per year of 18.4 percent. A $500 investment that earns an average of 18.4 percent per year for 10 years would have an ending account value of $2700. After 11 years it would be $3200. After 20 years, $14,650. After 30 years, $79,345. After 40 years, $429,570. After 50 years, $2,325,700. After 51 years, $2,753,600.

Remember the concept of exponential growth mentioned a few pages ago? Well, you're looking at it. Notice that the change in account value between years 50 and 51 ($427,900) is much larger than the change in account value between years 10 and 11 ($500). The longer the investment period, the larger the potential increase in account value from year to year. That's precisely why it's important to start investing as soon as you can. That way you can experience the gains from year 50 to 51 while you're still around to enjoy them.

The key to investing is not picking the exactly correct stock. Rather, it is picking a good sample of stocks and then patiently waiting. Good things often come to those who wait.

The U.S. stock market is measured by indexes, and there are dozens of them. A stock market index is a subset of stocks within the overall stock market. Indexes are created to measure the per-

TABLE 1.1 Historical Returns of Major Investment Assets

Stock Market Index	Measures the performance of...	Average Annual Total Return **5 Years** 1995 - 1999	Average Annual Total Return **10 Years** 1990 - 1999	Average Annual Total Return **30 Years** 1970-1999
Dow Jones Industrial Average (DJIA)	30 Huge U.S. Companies	27.0%	18.4%	13.5%
Standard & Poor's 500 Index (S&P 500)	500 of the Largest U.S. Companies	28.5%	18.2%	13.7%
Standard & Poor's Mid-Cap 400	Medium-sized U.S. Companies	23.0%	17.3%	N/A
Ibbotson Small Company Index	Small U.S. Companies	18.5%	15.1%	14.1%
Russell 2000	2,000 Smallest U.S. Companies	16.7%	13.4%	N/A
Morgan Stanley Capital International EAFE	Large, non- U.S. companies in Europe, Australasia, & the Far East	13.1%	7.3%	13.2%
Government Bonds	Long Term Bonds	9.4%	8.9%	9.0%
Treasury Bills	Short Term Cash Investments (e.g. CD's, Money Market Accounts)	5.2%	4.9%	6.7%

formance of the stock market as a whole or just certain segments of the market. The most commonly cited stock market index by the news media is the **Dow Jones Industrial Average.** The DJIA measures the stock performance of 30 huge U.S. companies. As shown in Table 1.1, the 30 stocks of the DJIA provided an average annual total return of 27 percent over the five-year period ending December 31, 1999. The average annual total return over the past 30 years is a more realistic 13.5 percent per year.

The 30 companies that comprise the Dow Jones Industrial Average (as of January 2000) and their average annual total returns over three different time frames are listed in Table 1.2. Notice that

TABLE 1.2   The 30 Stocks of the Dow Jones Industrial Average (as of January 2000)

DJIA Companies	Total Percentage Return			
	1 Yr Return 1999	3 Year Avg. 1997-1999	5 Year Avg. 1995-1999	10 Year Avg. 1990-1999
	27.2%	23.3%	27.0%	18.4%
Alcoa	125.9%	39.8%	33.2%	18.8%
American Express	63.4	44.6	43.3	21.5
AT&T	2.4	25.5	20.3	13.2
Boeing	28.7	-6.9	13.5	9.6
Caterpillar	4.7	10.0	13.7	14.6
Citigroup	70.1	41.8	52.6	35.1
Coca-Cola	-12.2	4.4	19.0	21.3
Du Pont De Nemours E.I.	26.9	14.3	21.6	15.9
Eastman Kodak	-5.6	-3.8	9.4	14.1
ExxonMobil	12.6	21.0	25.3	16.9
General Electric	53.6	48.4	46.1	28.4
General Motors	26.5	22.9	21.4	12.8
Hewlett-Packard	67.7	32.5	36.7	26.7
Home Depot	69.0	84.0	46.9	44.3
Honeywell International	31.8	21.5	29.6	23.6
IBM	17.6	42.7	43.7	19.3
Intel	39.1	36.2	59.8	44.2
International Paper	28.5	14.0	10.8	9.8
J.P. Morgan & Co.	24.3	12.7	21.9	15.5
Johnson & Johnson	12.5	24.9	29.6	22.3
McDonald's	5.44	21.8	23.2	17.6
Merck	-7.48	21.0	31.2	20.6
Microsoft	68.36	78.1	72.5	57.9
Minnesota Mining & Mfg.	41.08	8.3	16.9	13.3
Philip Morris Companies	-54.66	-11.5	8.4	9.7
Procter & Gamble	21.56	28.5	30.8	22.5
SBC Communications	-7.41	26.4	22.7	16.0
United Technologies	20.96	27.0	35.2	20.1
Wal-Mart Stores	70.4	83.5	46.4	29.3
Walt Disney	-1.7	8.7	14.6	12.8

even though the DJIA averaged 27 percent over the period from 1995 to 1999, many of the corporations within the index had very different returns. Some companies had, over the five-year period ending in 1999, average returns much higher than 27 percent: American Express at 43.3 percent, General Electric at 46.1 percent, Intel at 59.8 percent, and others. Conversely, some companies underperformed the DJIA average, such as Boeing at 13.5 percent, Eastman Kodak at 9.4 percent, and Phillip Morris at 8.4 percent.

The returns over the 10-year period ending in 1999 demonstrate the same phenomena, some companies overperforming the average return of the DJIA index and some underperforming.

While this insight might be obvious to some, it is important to remember that the returns reported for major stock market indexes are just that—*averages*. The performance of individual companies within a stock market index can vary greatly. This is particularly noticeable for the year 1999. The total return for the DJIA during 1999 was 27.2 percent, but the range of returns among the 30 individual companies was from –54.66 percent to 125.9 percent. Six DJIA companies had negative returns during 1999, despite the return of the index being a very impressive 27.2 percent.

> Stock market indexes are only general indicators.
> Just like theories, they often end up hiding as much as they reveal.

As you can see in Table 1.2, the 30 companies in the DJIA are all BIG corporations. Because the Dow Jones Industrial Average only includes a very small number of companies (and there are thousands of companies in the stock market), and focuses only on very large companies, it is *not* the best "general" indicator of the performance of the aggregate U.S. stock market. But inasmuch as it is the most publicized index, it's important to understand what it basically represents.

Another index of large U.S. companies is the **Standard & Poor's 500 Index** (S&P 500). It is a more reliable measure of the entire U.S. stock market because it tracks 500 stocks rather than just 30. Table 1.1 included the average annual total return of the S&P 500 over the past 5, 10, and 30 years. You will notice that the returns of the S&P 500 have been quite similar to those of the DJIA. Both indexes focus on large U.S. stocks.

The actual companies in the S&P 500 Index are listed in Appendix B. A table listing each company's historical performance can be found in Appendix C. The interested reader will probably enjoy learning which companies are in this important stock market index. If you look through the list, you'll no doubt recognize many of the names.

> The S&P 500 represents an excellent list of stocks to choose from when you decide to start investing in individual stocks.

In fact, there are many S&P 500 companies with direct stock purchase plans (as will be shown in a later chapter). The S&P 500 Index is the most prominent U.S. stock market barometer among researchers and academicians.

There are other important equity indexes that assess the aggregate U.S. stock market: the **S&P SuperComposite 1500,** the **Russell 3000,** and the **Wilshire 5000.** Their web address:

S&P Indexes: http://www.spglobal.com/statstotalret.html
Russell Indexes: http://www.russell.com/indexes/
Wilshire Indexes: http://www.wilshire.com

There are over 6000 small companies and nearly 1000 medium-sized companies in the U.S. stock markets, and their performance is often quite different from the 500 companies classified as large companies, hence different indexes are needed. Some small companies trade on the **New York Stock Exchange,** but most are traded in the **NASDAQ** market (also referred to as the Over the Counter market) or on the **American Stock Exchange.**

Small- and medium-sized companies in the U.S. market are tracked by a number of different indexes. Two small company stock indexes are the **Russell 2000** and the **Ibbotson Small Company Stock Index.** Medium-sized companies, or "mid-caps," are tracked by the **Standard & Poor's MidCap 400 Index.** Table 1.1 contains historical return information for each of these three indexes. Neither the Russell 2000 nor the S&P MidCap 4000 have been in existence for 30 years, hence data for that period are not available.

As shown in Table 1.1, medium and small companies have not performed as well, on average, as large company stocks in recent years. However, the 30-year average return for small stocks (as reflected in the Ibbotson Small Company Stock Index) exceeds that of the DJIA or S&P 500.

The performance of stocks outside the U.S. is measured by the Morgan Stanley Capital International Europe, Australasia, Far East Index (or **MSCI EAFE**). As seen in Table 1.1, international stocks have underperformed U.S. stocks in recent years, but have provided comparable returns over longer time periods. The EAFE Index does not attempt to include every non-U.S. country. Morgan Stanley Capital International has many other indexes that target the stock markets of other countries and international regions. The MSCI Indexes can be accessed on the Internet at http://www.mscidata.com.

WHY WOULD A PERSON WANT TO INVEST IN NON-U.S. STOCKS?

Nokia. This Finnish company makes little phones that fit in your shirt pocket. Better yet, they don't have to be plugged in to work. Ah, the cellular phone! Nokia stock produced a 250 percent return in 1998 and 220 percent in 1999. That's a pretty decent return. A $500 investment in Nokia stock on January 1, 1998, was worth $5600 by the end of 1999. The Swedish company Ericsson Telephone, also a maker of mobile phones, had stock returns of 56 percent in 1996, 25 percent in 1997, 30 percent in 1998, and 174 percent in 1999. These are just two examples of the many profitable companies outside the United States. So, why invest in non-U.S. stock? Return. Performance. Gain. The same exact reasons why we invest in U.S. stock. The countries represented in the EAFE Index are shown below.

Countries Included in the MSCI EAFE Index

Australia	Hong Kong	Norway
Austria	Ireland	Portugal
Belgium	Italy	Singapore
Denmark	Japan	Spain
Finland	Luxembourg	Sweden
France	New Zealand	Switzerland
Germany	Netherlands	United Kingdom

The average return of the EAFE Index has been 13.1 percent per year between 1995 and 1999, 7.3 percent during the nineties, and 13.2 percent per year over the 30-year period from 1970 to 1999. Over the long run (30 years) non-U.S. stock has performed comparably to U.S. large stock, U.S. mid-caps, and U.S. small stock.

> Investing in stock (U.S. or non-U.S.) has provided a "stock" return of about 13 to 14 percent per year over the past 30 years.

Regardless of the index chosen, U.S. stocks have had a lot more years with positive returns than negative returns. This is clearly demonstrated in Figures 1.1 and 1.2, which cover the period from 1926 to 1999. In both graphs, *up lines* represent positive annual returns, while *down lines* indicate a negative annual return.

During the 74-year period depicted in Figure 1.1, there were 20 years with negative returns and 54 years with positive returns

FIGURE 1.1 Large Stocks

Annual Returns of S&P 500: 1926–1999

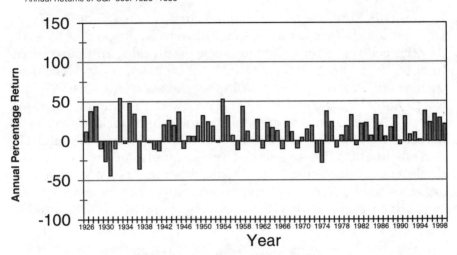

in the U.S. stock market (as measured by the S&P 500). That means that nearly 75 percent of the time, large U.S. stocks provided a positive return. U.S. small stocks (Figure 1.2) generated positive annual returns just over 70 percent of the time. So, despite volatility in stock returns, the end results have been positive in 7 out of every 10 years! Those odds are infinitely better than the chance of making money at the nearest casino. And the odds get better the longer you stay invested.

FIGURE 1.2 Small Stocks

Annual Returns of Small Stocks: 1926–1999

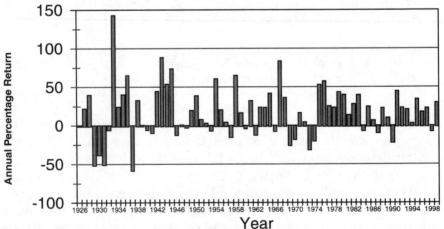

Bottom line: There have been a lot more "up" years than "down" years in the U.S. stock market over the past 74 years. That's really what long-term investing is all about—investing for a long enough period to allow the general upward trend to reward you. Again, patience rears its lovely head.

CHAPTER 2

Risk

Let's talk about the risks of investing. Risk means different things to different people. Generally speaking, investment risk represents the possibility of losing money. That's a perfectly acceptable definition, but for our purposes we will think of risk as the amount of volatility in annual returns for any given investment. The greater the annual deviations from the "average" return, the greater the risk. By this definition, small stock is a more risky investment than large stock. However, and this is the really important point: *Risk is a double-edged sword.* Investments with greater risk usually have the potential for greater gain as well.

The information in Table 1.1 provided annual averages over time, and they were encouraging. While that is important to know, it isn't enough. To assess the risk of an investment, we must understand the annual fluctuation around its average return. Figures 1.1 and 1.2 provided a visual picture of exactly that.

Let's take the case of large stocks (Figure 1.1). The average return per year for large U.S. stocks (Standard & Poor's 500 Index) between 1926 and 1999 has been just over 11 percent. From Figure 1.1 you'll also notice that in many years the return of large U.S. stocks was nowhere near 11 percent. In fact, the annual returns of large U.S. stocks have ranged between negative 40 percent (in 1931) and positive 54 percent (in 1933). The economic disaster of 1931 and the subsequent economic euphoria of 1933 provide the "bookends," the historic high and low, for U.S. large stocks since 1926. Those high and low returns are far from the average of 11 percent, which is one definition of risk—namely, fluctuation of annual returns, which causes fluctuation in your account value. You've got to be able to deal with that type of risk, otherwise investing can emotionally drain you.

If you want an even more exhilarating ride, invest in U.S. small stocks (Figure 1.2). As you can see, they produce higher highs (over 140 percent return in one year) and lower lows (more than a 50 percent loss in one year on three separate occasions). As was the case with large U.S. stocks, the high and low years for small U.S. stock performance occurred between 1929 and 1937—generally considered the Depression era. However, small stocks have averaged about a 12.5 percent return per year over the same 74-year period (1926–1999). Small U.S. stock presents more year-to-year volatility of return than large U.S. stock, but has produced a similar average return over the long run.

In three separate years small stocks lost 50 percent or more, while the worst year for large stocks was just over a 40 percent loss. But in 10 different years between 1926 and 1999, small U.S. stocks had over 50 percent gains, and large stocks, being less *risky,* have only had two years since 1926 with annual returns of over 50 percent. It's important to remember that these return figures are derived from major indexes like the S&P 500, Russell 2000, and the Ibbotson Small Company Stock Index, and not from individual stocks over the 74-year period. If individual large and small stocks were compared, the differences in performance would be *much* larger.

The key point is this: Despite the differences in risk, over long time frames (i.e., over the past 30 years) the returns of large and small stocks are reasonably similar. Since 1970 the average annual return of large U.S. stocks has been about 13.7 percent, and for small U.S. stocks it's been 14.1 percent. So, despite differing levels of year-to-year risk, *long-term* returns for large and small U.S. stocks are quite similar. Over *shorter time* periods, say 10 years or less, the differential in return between large and small stock has been more pronounced.

As seen in Figures 1.1 and 1.2, there *is* volatility when investing in U.S. stock, *but* the volatility typically involves POSITIVE returns. In other words, most investors can't be too irritated if their stock investment or stock mutual fund generates a positive return nearly 75 percent of the time despite the fact that the return each year is variable.

WHY IS THE PERFORMANCE OF SMALL COMPANY STOCK MORE VOLATILE THAN LARGE COMPANY STOCK?

Because, many small companies don't survive. This is what makes investing in small companies riskier than investing in medium or large companies. However, it's worth remembering that Wal-Mart was a small company in the early 1970s. Dell Computer and America Online were small companies in the early 1990s! Small companies represent investment opportunities with the potential to significantly outperform large companies. But large companies are a lot less likely to go bankrupt. So, as is generally the case in the world of investing (and in life), greater potential reward carries with it greater risk.

What does all this teach us about volatility of stock returns, or the *risks of investing?* Several lessons emerge:

Lesson 1:   The annual performance of large stock is generally less volatile (i.e., risky) than small stock.

Lesson 2:   Very few years produce annual returns that are identical to the long-term averages. Stock market averages, therefore, only provide a general guideline of what to expect *over time,* not what to expect in any particular year.

Lesson 3:   Volatility of annual return is not as troubling when the long-term average returns are positive.

Lesson 4:   What goes up also goes down. And what goes down goes back up. Patience and perspective are cardinal virtues of thrifty investors.

Lesson 5:   Investors who patiently and intelligently invest over a long period of time end up being rewarded by volatility rather than hurt by it. This happens by using Lesson 4 to your advantage. Armed with a long-term perspective, thrifty investors have the courage to purchase stock during down-market cycles. They also have the gumption to sell stock (if necessary) during up-markets. In other words: Buy low and sell high. Don't panic when stock prices decline for a period of time. Think of the price decline as "stocks going on sale," so stock up!

In discussing both the returns and risks of investing, I've made references to large, medium (mid-cap), and small companies. (This appears to be a setup for a Three Bears analogy, but it really isn't.) The size of the company you invest in has an impact on the amount of risk you take. Let's look at some examples.

The following are *large* companies: General Electric, Microsoft, Johnson & Johnson, Ford Motor, Duke Energy, Ralston Purina, Minnesota Mining & Manufacturing (3M), McGraw-Hill, McDonald's, Dell Computer, and about 400 others. The 30 stocks in the Dow Jones Industrial Average are all large companies. Among the 500 stocks of the S&P 500 Index as of January 2000, roughly 40 percent were large companies, 50 percent medium companies, and 10 percent small companies. The possibility that a large company will suddenly go out of business is quite low. That's why investing in the stock of large companies is less risky. However, there is no guarantee that the stock of a large company will provide high returns each year.

Examples of *medium*-sized companies include Quaker Oats, The Limited, Dollar General, Mattel, Southwest Airlines, Goodyear Tire & Rubber, Liz Claiborne, and about 850 others. The Standard & Poor's MidCap 400 Index measures the performance of medium-sized companies in the U.S. stock market.

Small companies represent the largest group of stocks in the U.S. stock market. As of December 1999 there were over 6000 small companies with publicly traded stock. Examples include Talbots, Briggs & Stratton, Cooper Tire & Rubber, Tootsie Roll Industries, Barnes & Noble, Spiegel, Ethan Allen Interiors, Snap-On Tools, Papa John's International, Casey's General Stores, Midwest Express Holdings, Avis Rent A Car, Scotts, Pier 1 Imports, and a whole lot more. The Ibbotson Small Company Index and the Russell 2000 Index are two indexes that track the performance of small stocks such as these.

As seen in Table 2.1, the *best performing stock* during the decade of the 1990s was Dell Computer. A $500 single lump sum investment in Dell Computer at the start of 1990 was worth about $425,000 by the end of 1999. In 1999 Dell Computer was classified as a large stock, but in 1990 it was a small stock. So, was the best performing stock during the nineties (Dell) a large stock or a small stock? Both. But it's probably most accurate to define Dell by what it was at the beginning of the decade, and that was as a small stock. Over the 10-year period from 1990 to 1999, the annual return of Dell stock averaged 96.3 percent. In stark contrast, a $500 lump sum investment in Smith Corona,

TABLE 2.1 Best and Worst of the Nineties

INVESTMENT of $500

Ten Year Investment Period: 1990 - 1999

		Average Annual Return	Ending Acct Value of $500 Investment
Best Stock	Dell Computer	96.3%	$424,789
Worst Stock	Smith Corona	-38.7%	$ 4
Best Mutual Fund	Fidelity Select Electronics	37.1%	$ 11,731
Worst Mutual Fund	U.S. Global Inv. Gold Shares	-21.4%	$ 45
Market Indexes.	S&P 500	18.2%	$ 2,662
	S&P MidCap 400	17.3%	$ 2,466
	Russell 2000	13.4%	$ 1,758
	EAFE (non-U.S. stocks)	7.3%	$ 1,011

one of the decade's *worst performing stocks,* left the investor with an ending balance of $4 at the end of 1999. The average return per year for Smith Corona during the nineties was –38.7 percent.

A $500 lump sum investment in the *best mutual fund* at the start of 1990 was worth about $11,731 by year's end 1999. The *worst mutual fund* over the same 10-year period reduced $500 to $45. These examples can be generalized by saying that:

> In any given year, the best individual stock will always outperform the best mutual fund. And the worst individual stock will always be worse than the worst performing stock mutual fund.

Inasmuch as losses stop at zero (i.e., complete loss of investment producing an account balance of zero), the performance of individual stocks versus stock mutual funds will be more similar at the low end of performance than at the upper end. In other words, dollar losses stop when your account hits zero, but there is no upside limit to gains. Losses are limited, gains are virtually unlimited.

As summarized in Table 2.2, mutual funds (as a group) have outperformed individual stocks (as a group) in recent years. This demonstrates the value of mutual funds in reducing risk through diversification (investing in a large number of stocks rather than

TABLE 2.2 Individual Stocks vs. Equity Mutual Funds

Individual U.S. Stocks

	1 Year 1999	3 Years 1997-99	5 Years 1995-99	10 Years 1990-99
Number of Stocks in Existence Over the Specified Time Period	6,242	5,323	4,122	2,397
Average Annualized Return (%)	42.7	6.0	10.3	9.5
Median Annualized Return (%)	-3.9	2.0	9.5	9.3
Highest Return (%)	11,060	476.0	219.8	97.0
Lowest Return (%)	-99.97	-90.8	-79.7	-42.9
Standard Deviation of Annualized Return (%)	229	37	25	14
Number of Stocks with Negative Annualized Return	3,343	2,432	1,280	521
Percentage of Stocks with Negative Annualized Return	54	46	31	22

U.S. Equity Mutual Funds

	1 Year 1999	3 Years 1997-99	5 Years 1995-99	10 Years 1990-99
Number of Funds in Existence over the Specified Time Period	2,448	1,877	1,414	737
Average Annualized Return (%)	27.7	20.4	21.4	15.0
Median Annualized Return (%)	18.0	18.5	20.8	14.7
Highest Return (%)	493.7	119.4	58.2	37.5
Lowest Return (%)	-29.6	-17.6	-17.1	-8.6
Standard Deviation of Annualized Return (%)	37.3	12.6	7.7	4.6
Number of Funds with Negative Annualized Return	311	46	5	3
Percentage of Funds with Negative Annualized Return	13	2.5	0.35	0.4

just one). Diversification stabilizes stock returns, and mutual funds are diversified investment portfolios.

Mutual funds that invest in U.S. stock (only those funds with a full 10 years of performance history) averaged a return of 15.0 percent during the 10-year period from 1990 to 1999. The 10-year average return for individual stocks was 9.5 percent. The variation of return (or what's called the **standard deviation of re-**

turn) among mutual funds was considerably less than the variation among individual stocks over the 10-year period: 4.6 percent for funds and 14 percent for individual stocks. Standard deviation of return is a measure of dispersion around the average. The larger the standard deviation, the greater the risk, because the less accurately mean describes the return of the group.

These performance comparisons illustrate an important reality: Investing in individual stocks can be extremely profitable. It can also be a loser. The extremes, both high returns and large negative returns, are more pronounced when investing in individual stocks compared to investing in stock mutual funds.

In each time period in Table 2.2, stocks had higher high returns and lower low returns than mutual funds. Moreover, 46 percent of the 5323 stocks in existence for the full three years between 1997 and 1999 produced a negative annualized total return. By contrast, only 2.5 percent of the 1877 equity mutual funds with at least three years of performance history had a negative annualized total return over the same time frame. During this three-year period (1997–1999) the DJIA averaged 23.3 percent and the S&P 500 averaged 27.6 percent. So, despite the market indexes registering good returns, nearly one-half of the market's stocks had negative returns over the three-year period. In 1999, 54 percent of the 6242 U.S. stocks tracked by Morningstar had a negative return. Among the 2448 stock mutual funds in existence during 1999, only 13 percent had a negative return.

> Investing in stock mutual funds reduces the chance of experiencing negative returns compared to investing in individual stocks.

U.S. stock mutual funds, as a group, had higher average annualized returns than aggregate U.S. stocks during the three-, five-, and 10-year periods ending in 1999. Mutual funds are often described as an investment product that primarily acts as a risk-reduction tool. In fact, mutual funds add value to investors by reducing the risk of loss.

Ultimately, the issue of investing in stocks versus mutual funds is a matter of perspective based upon personal experience with risk and reward. The returns of mutual funds look pretty bad if, 10 years ago, you had invested in Dell Computer, EMC,

Emulex, Microsoft, Charles Schwab, or 17 other companies that averaged over a 50 percent return during the 1990s. If, however, at the start of 1990 you had invested in Gantos, XCL, Smith Corona, or any of the 42 other companies whose stock had 10-year average annual returns of –20 percent or worse, the returns of mutual funds—any mutual fund—would look quite attractive.

So, given the potential risks, is investing worth it? Sure. Does it matter what you invest in? Sure. Is it possible to predict what the next "Dell Computer" will be? No. That's one of the reasons a lot of people invest in stock mutual funds. Diversifying their investment across a large array of stocks assures investors that they probably won't lose everything. But they won't quadruple their investment in three months either. But to the thrifty (and patient) investor, solid growth in your investments over time is the primary goal. And because of that, stock mutual funds represent the foundation of the thrifty investor.

3

Mutual Funds

We need to talk . . . about mutual funds. For many investors, large or small, mutual funds represent the foundation of their investment plan. Mutual funds are a wonderful tool. When mutual funds are intelligently integrated into a purposeful portfolio the results are rewarding. Let's have this discussion in a question and answer format.

What is a mutual fund?

A mutual fund is an investment company—a company that makes investments on behalf of individuals and institutions. Mutual funds pool investors' money and purchase dozens or even hundreds of stocks, bonds, or other securities. Mutual funds give small investors the opportunity to invest in a diversified portfolio, which is usually safer than investing in just one stock or bond.

How many mutual funds are there?

In January 1980 there were 446 stock and bond funds. In January 1990 there were 1851 stock and bond mutual funds. As of December 31, 1999, there were 10,931 stock and bond mutual funds. The majority of funds (63 percent) invest primarily in stock; the remainder invest in either corporate, government, or municipal bonds. Of the 10,931 total mutual funds, 9269 of them (or 85 percent) came into existence during the 1990s. The decade witnessed a literal explosion in the growth of mutual funds.

How much money have people invested in mutual funds?

As of December 1999, over $4.3 trillion were invested in stock and bond mutual funds. This amount does not include the $1.6

trillion held in money market mutual funds as of year-end 1999. Therefore, total mutual fund assets were nearly $6 trillion at the start of the year 2000.

Are all mutual funds the same?

No. Mutual funds vary by level of investment risk, type of securities held in the fund (i.e., stocks, bonds, real estate, precious metals, etc.), expenses and commissions, and management style.

Are mutual funds a new investment opportunity?

No, the basic concept of mutual funds began in the eighteenth century in Britain. The first U.S. mutual fund was formed in Boston in 1924.

Who can invest in mutual funds?

Anyone and everyone—from a one-year-old . . . to a college student . . . to a professor . . . to employees of a huge corporation . . . to you!

How much money is needed to invest (i.e., purchase shares) in a mutual fund?

Mutual funds require an initial investment, often between $250 to $2500. Subsequent investments can be smaller in almost all cases. Many funds waive the initial investment requirement for investors who start an **Automatic Investment Plan.** An AIP consists of authorizing the mutual fund company to automatically withdraw money from your checking or savings account and purchase shares of a mutual fund. An investment of $50 per month is a common AIP minimum requirement.

Does money have to be invested at regular intervals to maintain an account?

No. If the account is not set up with an AIP, most mutual funds allow total flexibility in terms of the amount and timing of investments into the fund and withdrawals from the fund. (The rules for withdrawal from retirement accounts are different than nonretirement accounts.) Investing on a regular basis is encouraged by financial advisers.

When can money be taken out of a fund?

Money can be taken out of a mutual fund at any time, unless the fund has been set up as a tax-deferred retirement account—such as a 401(k), 403(b), or IRA. Money going into and coming out of tax-deferred accounts is subject to different rules. I suggest that before tinkering with your retirement account, you visit with the employee benefits office at your place of employment. If you are self-employed, you should consult with a qualified tax adviser or a certified financial planner.

After investing in a mutual fund, how does a person go about taking some or all of the money out of the fund?

To redeem money from a mutual fund account, an investor simply contacts the mutual fund company and instructs them to sell part or all of the shares. The mutual fund company buys the shares back from the investor (thus the investor sells their shares back to the mutual fund company) at the market value on the day of the redemption, and mails the proceeds to the investor.

How much commission (or sales load) is charged to purchase shares of a mutual fund?

Commissions range from zero to 8.5 percent. Funds that charge no sales commissions are referred to as **no-load funds.** In recent years, many mutual funds have lowered or eliminated front-end loads and moved the load to the back end. A back-end load (or deferred load) is a commission paid by the investor upon redeeming money from the mutual fund account. Some mutual funds which charge a small front-load commission (3 percent or less) are often referred to as low-load funds. Funds that charge no commission of any kind are permitted to refer to themselves as "pure no-load funds."

Are there other expenses associated with investing in mutual funds?

Yes. All funds assess an annual management fee, also referred to as the annual expense ratio. The average annual management fee for stock mutual funds is about 1 percent, or $1.00 per $100 invested. Bond funds typically have a slightly lower annual management fee. For example, The Vanguard Group is a mutual fund company that is well-known for two things: low expense ratios and lots of index funds to choose from. Index funds are mutual funds designed to mimic one of many different stock market indexes. (More about Vanguard funds a bit later.) The most popular index being mirrored by mutual funds is the Standard & Poor's 500 Index. Index funds typically have very low annual expense ratios.

How does someone go about selecting and investing in a mutual fund?

Financial sources (such as *Forbes, Kiplinger's Personal Finance Magazine, Barron's, Money Magazine, The Wall Street Journal,* etc.) regularly publish information regarding mutual fund performance. After doing your homework, call the fund (usually a toll-free phone call) and ask to receive a prospectus and account application. Information is also available via the Internet. Many mutual fund companies have excellent web sites, such as T. Rowe Price (www. troweprice.com), Invesco (www.invesco.com), and Strong (www. strongfunds.com). This book will also prove to be a valuable resource in helping you select appropriate and affordable mutual funds.

What is a mutual fund prospectus?

It is an informational booklet provided by the mutual fund company which outlines all the details of the fund, such as the fund's minimum initial investment requirement, investment objectives, annual expense ratio, historical return data, and so on.

Must a person invest after requesting a prospectus and application?

No, requesting a prospectus does not obligate a person to invest in a mutual fund. The prospectus should be studied before any money is invested in the fund.

Can a person invest in more than one fund simultaneously?

Yes. There is no limit to the number of different mutual funds a person may invest in. Having a portfolio of more than 10 mutual funds is probably overkill. Investing in three to six mutual funds will typically meet the needs of most investors. However, a "portfolio" of one mutual fund is an excellent starting point!

Do mutual fund companies offer more than one mutual fund?

Yes, many fund companies provide investors with a broad array of mutual fund portfolios ranging from cash reserve funds (money market mutual funds) to high-risk portfolios that invest in small, start-up companies (such as an aggressive growth mutual fund). However, there is no compelling reason to only invest in mutual funds within the same mutual fund company.

Can a person shift money from one portfolio to another within the same mutual fund company?

Yes, this is a common practice. However, the exchange is treated as a sale and a subsequent purchase, so consider the tax ramifications beforehand. The convenience of being able to move money from one fund to another might be attractive, but it must be remembered that doing so incurs tax consequences if the funds involved are not retirement accounts—i.e., 401(k), 403(b), or IRA accounts.

How do investors monitor the performance of their fund(s)?

The mutual fund company in which you have invested money will provide you with performance reviews during the year. Financial magazines, daily newspapers, and many web-based resources also allow you to track your fund. Three excellent financial sites on the worldwide web for tracking the performance of investments are www.quicken.com, www.morningstar.com, and www.bloomberg. com. In addition, most mutual fund companies have web pages that provide information, downloadable account applications, etc. A particularly good web resource for general information about investing is www.vanguard.com.

Can someone invest in mutual funds even if they already have an IRA account and/or a tax-sheltered 401(k) or 403(b) retirement account through their employer?

Yes, personal investment accounts are always permissible regardless of other tax-sheltered accounts an investor may have. Establishing an account for yourself, your spouse, and your children is an excellent way to save money for future needs.

Does an investor pay taxes each year on the dividends and capital gains paid to them by the fund?

Yes, if your fund pays out dividends and/or capital gain distributions they are taxable—unless your account is set up as a tax-sheltered retirement account. Dividends and capital gains in regular accounts (i.e., nonretirement accounts) are taxable whether or not you receive them. Repeat: Even if you have them reinvested into the fund, dividends and capital gains are taxable.

Can I establish mutual fund accounts for my children?

Yes, for your own children or any child (niece, nephew, etc.). These type of accounts are referred to as **UTMA accounts,** or Uniform Transfer to Minors Account. They are very easy to set up. A UTMA account is established for a child with an adult acting as the custodian of the account. Though the child cannot be the legal owner of the account until they reach the age of majority (between 18 and 21 according to state law), *the money in the account becomes the property of the child at the time the account is established.* The custodian manages the account for the minor child, but the money belongs to the child and should therefore only be used for expenses that directly benefit the child. Therefore, taxation of dividends and capital gains generated by the UTMA account is the child's responsibility, not the custodian's. As of 1999, minor children could receive up to $700 in unearned income (i.e., dividends, interest, or capital gains) without owing tax. Obviously, some parents see this as a tax advantage because if the investment account were in their name (and in a non-tax-deferred account), the interest, dividends, and capital gains would be taxable at the parents' tax rate. A potential down side of UTMA accounts is the college financial aid issue. Under current policy, investment monies in a child's own account are weighted more heavily than parental financial resources when considering if the child (i.e., student) qualifies for financial aid.

What is the "best" way to invest in a mutual fund?

Many financial advisers recommend investing on a regular basis, such as $50 or more per month. *If your budget allows $10 per month, that works too!* If the stock market declines, your monthly investment will buy more mutual fund shares each month. This investment method is commonly referred to as **dollar-cost averaging,** or DCA.

Refer back to Table 2.1 (Best and Worst of the Nineties). The information in that table was based upon a lump sum (i.e., one-time) investment of money. Let's take a look at what would have happened if, rather than depositing a lump sum, money were invested monthly. Table 3.1 shows the returns achieved utilizing the dollar-cost averaging (or DCA) approach.

It's worth noting (in Table 3.1) that the dollar-cost averaging approach usually produces results that are at least comparable, and in several cases superior, to lump sum investing. In other words, investing on a regular basis (say, monthly) is a genuinely good investment technique. (More about DCA in Chapter 5.)

Is now a good time to invest?

That depends on what your goals are and how long your investment horizon is. "Now" is always a good time to invest if you choose the "right" stock during the "right" market cycle. But how

TABLE 3.1   Best and Worst of the Nineties

Investment of $50 Per Month: 1990–1999

		Average Annual Return	
		DCA	**Lump Sum**
Best Stock	Dell Computer	95.5%	96.3%
Worst Stock	Smith Corona	-21.7%	-38.7%
Best Mutual Fund	Fidelity Select Electronics	41.8%	37.1%
Worst Mutual Fund	U.S. Global Inv. Gold Shares	-23.0%	-21.4%
U.S. Market Indexes	S&P 500	21.6%	18.2%
	Russell 2000	15.7%	13.4%

do you know what the "right" stock is? And who can predict the stock market cycles? Ah, the problems of not being omniscient. Therefore, investing in a diversified portfolio of stocks (a mutual fund) on a regular basis is a logical and effective way to start investing NOW, regardless of what the stock market is doing.

> If the choice is between starting now or not starting at all, then NOW is always a good time to invest!

CHAPTER 4

Jumping In

So, how does one actually start doing the investment thing? Several of the more common logistical issues and basic questions are addressed below, such as:

- What should I invest in, stocks or stock mutual funds?
- How do I actually invest?
- Who do I call?
- How much money is needed?
- What period of time does the investment require?
- Should I invest money all at once or smaller amounts each month?
- How long should I leave my money in the investments?

WHAT SHOULD I INVEST IN, STOCKS OR STOCK MUTUAL FUNDS?

The best answer is probably both. But a logical approach is to create an investment portfolio of several mutual funds and then, over time, add individual stocks. Mutual funds, being a diversified portfolio of stocks, provide balance and breadth. Individual stocks provide focus. This approach has been referred to as "Core and Explore." Mutual funds provide the *core,* while individual stocks or aggressive mutual funds represent ways to *explore.* The general idea is to build your investment base with mutual funds that include stocks of large U.S. companies, medium-sized U.S. companies, and small U.S. companies. It may require two or three mutual funds to accomplish those three objectives. Then, add a mutual fund or two that invest in companies outside the United States. Why? Simply put, the U.S. stock market is one of many in the world. The U.S. market happens to be the biggest, but there are many excellent companies outside the United States worth investing in, such as Sony, Toyota, Volvo, Elan, Vodafone Airtouch, British Petroleum Amoco, Honda, and many others. About 50 percent of all the world's stock exists outside the United States.

So, to build an investment portfolio that covers "the bases," you might need five or six thoughtfully selected mutual funds. Must you have exactly five or six funds? Certainly not. You can start with one fund and then add additional funds as your budget permits. If you can afford only one fund, don't worry, there are *global funds* that attempt to cover all the major bases for you.

HOW DO I ACTUALLY INVEST? WHO DO I CALL? HOW MUCH MONEY IS NEEDED?

For mutual funds there are several ways to actually invest. If your employer offers a tax-deferred annuity plan, such as a 401(k) or 403(b), you can invest via payroll deduction (ask at work for the details about this great way to save for retirement). Briefly, 401(k) and 403(b) retirement plans are employer-sponsored tax-sheltered annuities. An employee can put aside up to $10,000 each year (actually, the maximum amounts change periodically) in investment accounts. Mutual funds are a common choice for 401(k) and 403(b) accounts: 401(k) accounts are offered at for-profit organizations, such as corporations; 403(b) accounts are offered at not-for-profit organizations, such as universities. The employee's investment contribution is deducted from his or her paycheck and invested into a fund (or funds) of his or her choice.

The invested money grows tax-deferred, meaning that the employee pays no taxes on the investment, capital gains, or dividends until the money is withdrawn during retirement. This is advantageous inasmuch as many workers may be in a lower tax bracket during retirement. Another advantage is the fact that the monthly investment comes out of your paycheck before federal and state (if applicable) income taxes are calculated. This means that if you decide to invest $100 each month into a 401(k) account, your take-home pay may only be reduced by $85 (for example). Your withholding taxes go down because your monthly income has been reduced by the amount of your 401(k) investment. So, in other words, a $100 investment only costs you $85. The higher your tax bracket, the greater the tax savings each month.

You can also open mutual fund accounts without going through your employer. This type of account is referred to as a **regular account.** To do this, you simply need to call a mutual fund company and request a prospectus and fund application materials. If you want to set up accounts for children (or grandchildren, nieces, nephews, etc.), most mutual fund application forms include that as one of the account registration options. To be sure, tell the phone representative at the mutual fund company that you want to set up an account for a minor child; they'll make sure you get the needed materials. You can also request information for many different mutual funds from their web sites. (Web addresses for a number of mutual fund companies are listed in Appendixes H and I.)

For example, if you wanted to invest in the T. Rowe Price Equity Income Fund you would call T. Rowe Price at 1-800-638-5660 and request a prospectus and application for that particular fund. Alternatively, you could log onto the Internet and go to www.troweprice.com and download a prospectus for the Equity Income fund. If you choose to call T. Rowe Price, materials will arrive via U.S. mail in a couple of days. If you like what you read, you fill out the account application and send it in with a check for $2500.

Yikes, that's a lot of money. What's thrifty about that? Don't panic. If you don't like the sound of a $2500 initial investment requirement, T. Rowe Price (along with many other mutual fund companies) provide a much easier way to start an account. It's referred to by different names at different mutual fund companies, but the basic title is Automatic Investment Plan (AIP). Rather than send in $2500 to start an account, you can authorize T. Rowe Price to electronically withdraw money from your checking account each month and purchase shares of the mutual fund(s) you have selected. A common minimum monthly investment requirement for an AIP is $50 per month. At T. Rowe Price, a monthly investment of $50 automatically deducted from your checking or savings account opens an account with any of their mutual funds. *Most important, by choosing to invest through an AIP each month, the normal minimum initial investment is waived.* This represents a tremendous opportunity for investors who might find it challenging to come up with the needed initial investment to start a mutual fund account—commonly between $500 and $2500.

If you want to invest a lump sum, rather than a monthly investment, that's perfectly all right. Lump sum investing is very common, particularly when investing in individual stocks. The monthly plan (i.e., dollar-cost averaging) is very often used when investing in mutual funds. Monthly investing works best when the transaction costs of investing are low or zero, which is the case with no-load or low-load mutual funds.

Two stock mutual funds that qualify as *Super Thrifty* are Homestead Value and Homestead Small Company Stock. Not only are they pure no-load funds, they can also be started with as little as $1 per month using the AIP. Without an AIP, the Homestead Funds require at least $500 to open an account. However, just like the arrangement at T. Rowe Price, by choosing to participate in an automatic investment plan for as little as $1 per month, the $500 normal initial investment is waived. You can start your account by simply filling out an application, attaching a voided check (which provides the information needed by the mutual fund to establish the electronic withdrawal from your checking account), selecting the amount you wish to have withdrawn from your checking account, and then mailing the application to Homestead. Homestead can be reached at 1-800-258-3030.

The Thriftiest of Them All

Mutual Fund	Automatic Monthly Investment (aIP) Minimum	Normal Minimum Initial Investment to Open an Account Without AIP
Homestead Value Fund	$1	$500
Homestead Small Company Stock Fund	$1	$500

WHAT PERIOD OF TIME DOES THE INVESTMENT REQUIRE?

If you can leave invested money alone for at least four to six years, you should seriously consider investing in stock or stock mutual funds. Periods shorter than that get a little chancy because the stock market has been known to have a couple bad years in a row. However, since 1940 the stock market (as measured by the S&P 500) has never had a decade with more than three negative years, much less in a row. It's important to realize that when you make an investment in stock or stock mutual funds, you are committing yourself for at least four or five years. Ideally longer.

If you're interested in saving for retirement (age 65±) and you are less than 50 years old now, stocks/stock mutual funds would be a good choice. If you're saving for your children's college expenses and the kids are currently under the age of 13, you probably have sufficient time to consider a stock investment. If your child is currently 17 years old, it's a bit late to be investing in stock for their college savings account (unless you plan to only pay for their senior year of college!). You probably should consider certificates of deposit (CDs), money market accounts at a local bank or savings & loan, or money market mutual funds. Money market mutual funds are mutual funds that invest in short-term, nonstock assets. There is no stock market risk in a money market mutual fund.

If you are 62 years old and want to beef up your retirement account, you should probably consider some stock-based investments. Even though you are close to normal retirement age, you may live for 20 more years—so you actually have a fairly long investment horizon. At least, long enough to invest some portion in stocks or stock mutual funds.

SHOULD I INVEST MONEY ALL AT ONCE OR SMALLER AMOUNTS EACH MONTH?

This is the $20 question. If you're investing for a long period of time (say, 20 to 30 years or more) you are almost always better off investing your money as a lump sum. But that assumes you have a lump sum of money. A lot of people don't. So let's talk about investing smaller amounts on a regular basis.

As already mentioned, systematically investing money each month (or biweekly, quarterly, etc.) is the practice known as dollar-cost averaging, or DCA. Investing on a regular schedule takes the risk out of trying to time your lump sum investment at the perfect moment, a virtually impossible task. It reinforces several important elements of thrifty investing—discipline, endurance, and patience.

Investing on a regular schedule also reduces the inherent emotional risk. Emotions come into play during down markets, or those periods when the share price of a stock or mutual fund is declining. With a systematic investing schedule, one's perspective changes. During periods of falling prices, a monthly investment actually purchases more shares of a stock or a mutual fund than it would have if the market had gone up. So, down markets are actually advantageous to the monthly (or bimonthly, etc.) investor. DCA investors can actually benefit during down markets, something lump sum investors don't experience, inasmuch as they invested all their money at the beginning, unless they de-

posit another lump sum. But making repeated lump sum investments begins to look a lot like dollar-cost averaging! Eventually,
of course, the market needs to go up for the DCA (or lump sum)
investor to make a positive return.

Armed with this new "emotionally insulated" perspective,
regular folks become *thrifty investors* who can take dollar-cost averaging to the next level—**value-cost averaging.** Value-cost averaging requires that *additional* money be invested (if possible)
when prices have declined. In other words, we go shopping when
our investments are "on sale." Why? Because the goal of investing
is to purchase as many shares as possible (of a stock or mutual
fund) at the lowest possible price and then sell our shares at the
highest possible price in the future. Or, more succinctly, buy low
and sell high. It simply is not possible to know the exact moment
that the price of our stock or mutual fund has bottomed out or hit
its ultimate high. So, a practical alternative is to invest additional
funds in your investment accounts when their value has declined
a predetermined amount, say 10 percent. A unique web-based software tool that helps investors manage their mutual fund accounts
using a value-cost averaging technique is at www.fundbuilder.com.

Let's say the value of your mutual fund account is $600, and
two months later, after having invested another $100 (at $50 per
month), your account value has gone down to $615. You've invested
$700 and "lost" $85, which is more than a 10 percent decline in
value compared to what has been invested. (A loss of $70 in account
value would represent a 10 percent decline in an account in which
$700 has been invested.) At this point you might consider investing
some additional money, say an extra $50, into the mutual fund ac-
count. That's a simple example of how value-cost averaging works.

Putting into practice the "buy low" part of the "buy low, sell
high" mantra requires that investments be made when prices
have gone down. It sounds easy, but is surprisingly hard to do.
When prices are falling, many trigger-happy investors want to
bail out. They panic. Value-cost averaging forces the opposite be-
havior. Instead of selling low in a moment of panic, value-based
investors buy additional shares at lower prices. It's a simple approach that doesn't require much analysis, just a little attention
and courage. It's the stuff thrifty investors are made of.

Let's look at the results of monthly investing versus lump
sum investing over a 30-year period (Table 4.1). For simplicity,
I've selected six equity (or stock) mutual funds with long histo-

TABLE 4.1 Lump Sum vs. Dollar-Cost Averaging

30 Year Investment Period
1970 - 1999

LUMP SUM		DCA	
Stock Mutual Fund (ranked from high to low)	Average Annual Return	Stock Mutual Fund (ranked from high to low)	Average Annual Return
Century Shares	12.2%	Selected American Shares	14.6%
State Street Research Investors S	11.6%	Safeco Growth No-Load	14.4%
Dodge & Cox Balanced	11.4%	State Street Research Investors S	14.4%
Vanguard Wellington	11.3%	Century Shares	13.4%
Safeco Growth No-Load	11.3%	Vanguard Wellington	12.9%
Selected American Shares	10.7%	Dodge & Cox Balanced	12.9%

ries. It's very interesting to note that the mutual funds that were the best performers using a lump sum investment were the worst performers with monthly investing, and vice versa. These few examples don't prove that lump sum is better than DCA or that DCA is better than lump sum. Rather, they indicate that some investments (mutual funds and individual stocks) are better suited for lump sum investing, while others are better candidates for dollar-cost averaging.

The ominous question, "What should I invest in?" now expands to two questions: "What are my best investment options for a lump sum investment?" and "Which mutual funds or stocks are best suited for dollar-cost averaging?" Expanding the classic singular question into two equally relevant questions seems obvious, but is actually somewhat novel. Investment selection that takes into consideration how money will actually be invested (lump sum or periodically) is an important issue, yet has been virtually ignored in financial literature. Not anymore. This book addresses the issue of lump sum versus DCA in detail.

This issue of selecting mutual funds based upon *how* you will be investing applies to millions of employees who invest monthly or biweekly into a retirement account via payroll deduction. They are utilizing dollar-cost averaging whether they recognize it or not.

Therefore, the oft-asked question, "Which fund is best for my retirement account?" really should be, "Of the funds I can choose from, which are best suited for a dollar-cost averaging approach?"

HOW LONG SHOULD I LEAVE MY MONEY IN THE INVESTMENTS?

Generally, the longer the better. That advice, of course, assumes the investment is doing reasonably well. If you happen to choose a stock or fund that ends up being a clunker, you can hang on hoping it will revive or you can sell it and take a loss. However, for long-term, patient, well-diversified investors, the investing experience is generally a very positive one.

By investing sooner, rather than later, you create a longer investment horizon and thereby a higher probability of experiencing satisfying results. Figure 4.1 makes the "long-run" point quite clearly by showing the annual growth in the account value of $1000 invested in the S&P 500 for a 40-year period. Notice how rapidly the account grows in the last five years of the 40-year period. In fact, the account *doubled* in value during the last three years of the 40-year period. Granted, the stock market made tremendous gains during 1995–1999, but the more fundamental issue is the importance of compound growth over time, and particularly during the latter years of the investment.

FIGURE 4.1   Growth of $1000 Lump Sum Investment over 40-Year Period (1960–1999)

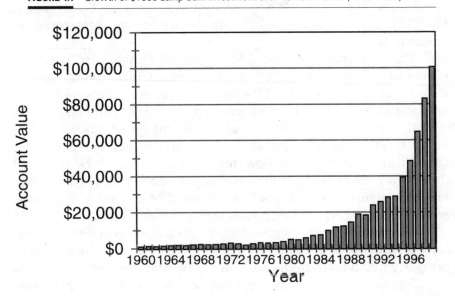

Compound growth simply means that interest earned, if reinvested into the account, earns interest along with the original investment. Hence the expression, *interest earning interest.* Compound growth (or compound interest) becomes more pronounced over longer periods of time. Think of compound interest as a snowball rolling down a mountain. As it rolls it gets bigger because it continues to pick up new snow. The key point being that it gets bigger at a faster and faster rate, just like an investment account during the latter stages of its growth.

Ironically, because of the great impact compound growth has in the later years of an investment, many retirees are hesitant to withdraw money from their retirement accounts because the annual growth in the account value can be so large—when the stock market is doing well!

CHAPTER **5**

Let's Get Specific

It's time to investigate the actual stocks and stock mutual funds that fit a thrifty investor's needs. Inasmuch as your investment base will most likely utilize mutual funds, let's look at them first.

One group of mutual funds that meet the requirements of a thrifty investor are those that can be started with an *automatic monthly investment of $50 or less*. Moreover, the monthly investment must waive the normal initial investment. Funds worthy of consideration need at least five years of performance history, and managers with a minimum of five years at the helm. They also must have a performance record in the upper 40 percent of their respective mutual fund category. Funds which charge front-end or back-end loads (i.e., sales commission when buying or selling mutual fund shares) are allowed if the commission is no higher than 3 percent. Finally, they need to invest primarily in stock, either in the United States or abroad.

Out of more than 6800 stock mutual funds, 40 made the cut. These 40 funds—*The Frugal Forty*—are listed in Table 5.1. Six of the 40 funds invest primarily in non-U.S. stocks and are highlighted in bold print in the Investment Category column. *Each fund can be started with an automatic monthly investment of at least $50.* This type of investment plan, as noted earlier, is generally referred to as AIP, or Automatic Investment Plan. Automated investments are electronic withdrawals from your checking account (known as EFT, or Electronic Funds Transfer). If you have a checking or savings account, your bank (or S&L or credit union) can most likely facilitate automatic transfers. There are a couple of favorable exceptions to the $50 rule.

TABLE 5.1   The Frugal Forty Mutual Funds

Fund Name (listed alphabetically)	Investment Category	Phone Number	Minimum Monthly AIP Investment
Alleghany/Montag & Caldwell Growth	Large Growth	800-992-8151	$50
Ariel Appreciation	Mid-Cap Blend	800-292-7435	$50
Columbia International Stock	**Foreign Stock (Large Growth)**	800-547-1707	$50
Columbia Real Estate Equity	Specialty-Real Estate (Mid Value)	800-547-1707	$50
Eclipse Small Cap Value	Small Value	800-872-2710	$50
Excelsior Value & Restructuring	Large Value	800-446-1012	$50
Fasciano	Small Growth	800-848-6050	$50
Fremont Global	Intl Hybrid (Large Blend)	800-548-4539	$50
Fremont U.S. Micro-Cap	Small Growth	800-548-4539	$50
Homestead Value	Mid-Cap Value	800-258-3030	$1
Invesco Dynamics	Mid-Cap Growth	800-525-8085	$50*
Invesco European	**Europe Stock (Large Growth)**	800-525-8085	$50*
Invesco Health Sciences	Specialty-Health (Large Growth)	800-525-8085	$50*
Invesco Total Return	Domestic Hybrid (Large Value)	800-525-8085	$50*
Legg Mason Spec Investment Prime	Mid-Cap Blend	800-577-8589	$50
Legg Mason Total Return Prime	Mid-Cap Value	800-577-8589	$50
Legg Mason Value Prime	Large Value	800-577-8589	$50
Preferred Asset Allocation	Domestic Hybrid (Large Value)	800-662-4769	$50
Preferred International	Foreign Stock (Large Value)	800-662-4769	$50
Preferred Value	Large Value	800-662-4769	$50
Safeco Equity No Load	Large Value	800-426-6730	$50**
Spectra	Large Growth	800-711-6141	$25
Strong American Utilities	Specialty-Utilities (Large Value)	800-368-1030	$50
Strong Asset Allocation	Domestic Hybrid (Large Value)	800-368-1030	$50
Strong Growth	Large-Cap Growth	800-368-1030	$50
Strong Opportunity	Mid-Cap Value	800-368-1030	$50
Strong Total Return	Large Growth	800-368-1030	$50
T. Rowe Price Blue Chip Growth	Large Blend	800-638-5660	$50
T. Rowe Price Equity Index 500	Large Blend	800-638-5660	$50
T. Rowe Price Equity Income	Large Value	800-638-5660	$50
T. Rowe Price European Stock	**Europe Stock (Large Growth)**	800-638-5660	$50
T. Rowe Price International	**Foreign Stock (Small Growth)**	800-638-5660	$50
T. Rowe Price International Stock	**Foreign Stock (Large Blend)**	800-638-5660	$50
T. Rowe Price Mid-Cap Growth	Mid-Cap Growth	800-638-5660	$50
T. Rowe Price Personal Strategy	Large Blend	800-638-5660	$50
T. Rowe Price Science & Technology	Specialty-Tech (Large Growth)	800-638-5660	$50
T. Rowe Price Small Cap Stock	Small Blend	800-638-5660	$50
T. Rowe Price Spectrum Growth	Large Blend	800-638-5660	$50
T. Rowe Price Value	Mid-Cap Value	800-638-5660	$50
USAA Growth & Income	Large Value	800-382-8722	$50

* $25 if IRA or UTMA accounts   ** Only for IRA and UTMA accounts, otherwise $100

- *Homestead Value,* as previously noted, can be started for as little as $1 per month.
- Investment accounts at *Invesco,* a mutual fund company headquartered in Denver, can be started for $25 per

month if it is a child's account (either as a UTMA account or an Education IRA). The funds from Invesco that made it into the Frugal Forty include the Dynamics Fund, European Fund, Health Sciences Fund, and Total Return Fund).

- The high-flying *Spectra* fund can be started for $25 per month.

The variety of funds in the Frugal Forty is extremely useful for investors. Assembling a personal portfolio of mutual funds with different objectives and performance characteristics is very wise. Consider, as a comparison, how an orchestra is created. Instruments of every kind are brought together. When skillfully combined, the diverse group of instruments produce beautiful music. The sounds of any separate subgroup, say percussion or strings, is beautiful, but certainly not equivalent to the rich sound produced by a full orchestra. In like manner, building a personal investment portfolio using nothing but comparable mutual funds and/or stocks will generally yield subpar performance *and* have higher risk compared to a well-diversified portfolio. Investments, like orchestras, benefit from diversity. Diversity is not a virtue in isolation. The benefits of diversity are achieved only through intelligent integration of *diverse* investments.

Table 5.2 groups the Frugal Forty by investment category into what looks like a tic-tac-toe box. Actually it's commonly referred to as an **equity style box.** Selecting mutual funds that are in different style boxes represents a common way to create diversity. For example, in attempting to create a portfolio of equity (i.e., stock) mutual funds that "intelligently integrates diverse investments," you might select a large-cap value fund, a mid-cap growth fund, a small-cap blend fund, and a fund that invests in non-U.S. stock.

The investment categories (or investment styles) in Table 5.2 are defined by Morningstar, which is an independent provider of financial information based in Chicago. They collect, analyze, and disseminate data pertaining to the performance and general characteristics of stocks and mutual funds. Their website address is www.morningstar.com. Knowing the investment category of each fund allows investors to create a well-diversified portfolio which utilizes funds from several of the nine different style boxes.

The three grid boxes in the upper-left-hand corner (Large-Cap Value, Large-Cap Blend, Mid-Cap Value) generally represent the least risky types of stock mutual funds. The three grid

TABLE 5.2   The Frugal Forty Mutual Funds—Grouped by Equity Style

(Equity Style as of January 2000)

White = Lower Risk   **Light Gray = Moderate Risk**   **Dark Gray = Higher Risk**

Large-Cap Value	**Large-Cap Blend**	**Large-Cap Growth**
Excelsior Value & Restructuring	Fremont Global	Alleghany/Montag & Caldwell
Invesco Total Return	T. Rowe Price Blue Chip Growth	Growth
Legg Mason Value Prime	T. Rowe Price Equity Index 500	Invesco Health Sciences
Preferred Asset Allocation	T. Rowe Price Personal	Spectra
Preferred Value	Strategy Growth	Strong Total Return
T. Rowe Price Equity-Income	T. Rowe Price Spectrum Growth	T. Rowe Price Science & Tech
Safeco Equity No-Load		Strong Growth
Strong American Utilities	***T. Rowe Price International***	
Strong Asset Allocation	***Stock***	***Columbia International Stock***
USAA Growth & Income		***Invesco European***
		T. Rowe Price European
Preferred International		***Stock***
Mid-Cap Value	**Mid-Cap Blend**	**Mid-Cap Growth**
Columbia Real Estate Equity	Ariel Appreciation	Invesco Dynamics
Homestead Value	Legg Mason Special	T. Rowe Price Mid-Cap Growth
Legg Mason Total Return Prime	Investment Prime	
Strong Opportunity		
T. Rowe Price Value		
Small-Cap Value	**Small-Cap Blend**	**Small-Cap Growth**
Eclipse Small Cap Value	T. Rowe Price Small Cap Stock	Fasciano
		Fremont U.S. Micro-Cap
		T. Rowe Price International
		Discovery

(Non-U.S. stock funds in **bold** *italicized* print)

Data Source: Morningstar Principia Pro Plus, January 2000

boxes shaded light-gray (Large-Cap Growth, Mid-Cap Blend, Small-Cap Value) represent categories of moderately risky stock mutual funds. The dark shaded grid boxes in the bottom-right-hand corner (Mid-Cap Growth, Small-Cap Blend, Small-Cap Growth) are typically the most aggressive mutual funds with the highest degree of volatility in their year-to-year returns.

It's important to realize that mutual funds will occasionally drift from one style box to another. Typically, the movement does not signal a cause for concern. For example, it wouldn't be unusual for a Large-Cap Blend fund to "drift" into the Large-Cap Growth category for a period of time and then drift back. As mutual fund managers change the holdings (i.e., stocks) of the fund, there is the chance for slight changes in how the fund is categorized within the style box rating system. Occasionally mutual funds might undergo radical paradigm shifts. The reasons are many but often relate to a change in fund manager, a dramatic shift in market conditions, or a fundamental reorientation of the investment purposes of the fund. In cases such as these, the fund's style drift may be significant, such as a Large-Cap Growth fund becoming a Small-Cap Blend fund. Style drift of this magnitude may necessitate a reconsideration of whether the "drifted" fund belongs in your personal investment portfolio. The funds in Table 5.1 have not historically tended to be drifters, but represent well-established investment philosophies.

As shown in Table 5.2, 34 of the Frugal Forty invest primarily in the stock of U.S. companies. Six funds (noted in italics) invest primarily in stocks of large, non-U.S. companies. Of the 34 funds that invest in U.S. stocks, 20 invest primarily in large U.S. companies. Of those 20, ten mutual funds focus on value stocks, five select growth stocks, and five funds choose a mixture (or blend) of value and growth stocks. Among funds that invest in medium-sized companies (i.e., mid-cap stocks), five target value stocks, two funds look for growth stocks, and three funds create a blend of value and growth. Four funds focus on small companies: one with a value orientation, two with an emphasis on growth, and one with a blend of value and growth stocks.

The term "cap" refers to market *cap*italization, which is calculated by multiplying the current share price of a company's stock by the number of outstanding shares of stock. Market cap determines whether a company is defined as a large, medium, or small stock. As the stock of a particular company increases in price, it will move from being classified as a small-cap stock to a mid-cap or a large-cap stock. As of January 2000, Morningstar categorized companies as large if their "market cap" exceeded $10 billion. Companies with market cap below $2 billion were treated as small-cap stocks, and companies in between were classified as mid-cap stocks.

The terms **value** and **growth** also need to be defined. *Value* indicates a bargain-hunter approach. More technically, it means that the price per share of a stock is not excessively high relative to the earnings per share of the company. Very simply, the price per share is reasonable.

The motto "Buy low, be patient, sell high" is the mantra of a value-minded fund manager. Sometimes companies have a couple of bad years. During such times, the price of their stock can plummet. Mutual fund managers with a value approach may buy a "depressed stock" because they believe it will rebound. If the stock price eventually rises, the potential gains are large. If the manager is wrong, the stock may end up being sold at an even lower price. In this type of situation, the value-minded fund manager is choosing stocks that are not only reasonably priced, but may be even cheap. Buying stock that is currently "out-of-favor" takes courage and farsightedness. Despite a stereotype of being a boring and cautious investment style, value investing can, at times, be a rather daring adventure. While the word *value* denotes a particular management paradigm, be assured that not all value funds are alike.

The term *growth* indicates that the price per share of a company in the mutual fund portfolio is quite high compared to earnings per share of the company. The management philosophy of *growth* mutual funds is typically more aggressive, whereas *value* funds are generally more conservative in nature. You probably also noticed that some of the mutual funds in Table 5.1 include in their name the term *value* or *growth*. The orientation toward either value or growth represents a very fundamental issue in mutual fund management. So, which investment style produces better results: value or growth? This is a much debated question. Over the past 15 years, growth funds have, on average, produced higher returns, as shown in Table 5.3. But, as is almost always the case, higher return brings with it higher risk. The annual returns of growth funds tend to be more volatile. Such has been the case over the past 15 years. Suffice it to say that both styles are important, and both should be included in a thrifty investor's overall portfolio. Think of it as an . . . orchestra thing.

As can be seen in Table 5.3, growth funds have had distinctly better performance (on average) than value funds among large-cap stocks during the 15-year period from 1985 to 1999. Growth funds slightly outperformed value funds in the mid-cap stock category during the same time period. Among small-cap stock, value edged out growth.

Let's look a little closer at the *T. Rowe Price Equity Income Fund*. As already noted, it's classified as a large-cap value fund.

TABLE 5.3   Historical Average Annual Returns by Equity Style, 15-Year Period: 1985–1999

Large-Cap Value	Large-Cap Growth
16.0%	21.4%
Mid-Cap Value	Mid-Cap Growth
15.1%	16.0%
Small-Cap Value	Small-Cap Growth
14.2%	13.8%

Wilshire Indexes (http://www.wilshire.com)

The manager of the fund, Brian Rogers, invests in the stock of large companies at what he believes to be reasonable share prices. In other words, stocks included in the Equity Income portfolio represent good "value." The T. Rowe Price Equity Income portfolio as of October 1999 included SBC Communications, Mellon Bank, ExxonMobil, GTE, Atlantic Richfield, General Mills, International Paper, American Home Products, BP Amoco, ALLTEL, 3M, as well as about 130 other companies. As a diversified open-end investment company (the technical term for "mutual fund"), the T. Rowe Price Equity Income Fund invests in a wide variety of stocks from many different sectors of the U.S. economy.

As a contrast to the Equity Income Fund, let's consider the *Strong American Utilities Fund*. While both are large-cap value funds, the Strong American Utilities Fund does not invest in a broad array of U.S. companies, but only those companies in the broadly defined utility sector, such as Enron, Ameren, Duke Energy, CMS Energy, and Wisconsin Energy. This fund also invests in energy-related companies (such as Texaco and Chevron), as well as communication companies such as AT&T, Ameritech, and Bell Atlantic. Utility companies are expanding into telecommunications, hence it is becoming more common for a mutual fund that invests in utility stocks to also purchase the stock of companies in the telecommunications business. As of year end 1999, the Strong American Utilities Fund had about 50 stocks in its portfolio.

Another term that has particular meaning in mutual fund parlance is the word *Income,* as used in the fund names T. Rowe Price Equity *Income,* and USAA Growth and *Income.* The word in an equity (i.e., stock) mutual fund title typically means that the fund pays out steady dividends because it purchases stocks that pay dividends. It's also common for mutual funds in the "Equity Income" and "Income" classifications to invest in bonds. Interest paid by bonds is comparable to dividends paid by companies to stockholders. Mutual funds that invest in utilities (such as Strong American Utilities Fund) often receive a substantial amount of dividends inasmuch as utility companies often pay dividends to the holders of their stock. Of course, when a mutual fund receives dividends from companies within its portfolio, the fund subsequently distributes those dividends to the investors in the mutual fund on a prorated basis.

Now, let's look at *growth* funds. The *Spectra Fund,* for example, invests in companies that are currently "hot," such as America Online, Microsoft, Yahoo, eBay, Sun Microsystems, Cisco Systems, Exodus Communications, Motorola, Home Depot, Dell Computer, and the like. The growth fund motto is, "Buy high, sell higher." Even though the manager is paying high prices for the stocks he or she is buying, there is a strong belief that the share prices will go even higher. The year-to-year performance of growth funds is typically more volatile than value funds. However, there are always exceptions because there are conservative growth funds and aggressive value funds.

The *T. Rowe Price Science & Technology Fund* is a large-cap growth fund. It invests in the stock of large companies within certain sectors of the economy, such as computer hardware and software, biotechnology, and other industries involved in "high" technology. (In addition to being categorized as a growth fund, it is also referred to as a "Sector" fund because it only invests in companies with certain market sectors.) Companies in its portfolio in late 1999 included Microsoft, Analog Devices, MCI World-

Com, Vodafone Airtouch, Oracle, Hewlett-Packard, Texas Instruments, EMC, and about 40 others.

The *Strong Growth Fund* is also a growth fund, but it focuses on large-cap and mid-cap stocks. It invests in companies like JDS Uniphase, Kohl's, Tyco International, Biogen, Veritas Software, Tandy, Sprint, and about 110 others. The *Fasciano Fund,* a low-risk, small-cap growth fund, seeks to invest in companies with market caps below $2 billion. The Fasciano Fund in late 1999 included International Speedway, Pulitzer, Gucci Group NY, Zebra Technologies, Keane, Tootsie Roll Industries, Central Newspapers, Midwest Express Holdings, and about 85 other companies.

Whether investing in large-, mid-, or small-cap funds, it is critical to remember that investing in stock presents risk. Risk is the possibility that the share price of the investment (in this case, the share price of the mutual fund) will fluctuate dramatically, causing large changes in the account value. This leads to the risk that the year-to-year return (i.e., percentage gain or loss) will fluctuate widely. Obviously, most investors wouldn't be too put out if the share price of the fund (and subsequently the total return of the fund) fluctuates in an upward direction. Investors must remember that volatility, whether large or small, is inherent in a stock investment. It's not a bad thing. It's just part of the investment deal.

Generally, as shown in Table 5.2, funds in the upper-left-hand section of the style grid (Large Value, Large Blend, Mid-Cap Value) offer the least amount of risk. Risk, in this context, is measured by **standard deviation of return,** which, whether based on monthly or annual returns, is a common measure of investment risk and represents the amount of variation surrounding an average. Funds considered to be "high risk" will have a higher standard deviation of return. The light-gray shaded sectors (Large Growth, Mid-Cap Blend, Small Value) offer somewhat higher risk, while funds in the bottom-right-hand section (Mid-Cap Growth, Small-Cap Blend, Small-Cap Growth) typically present the largest amount of risk.

Total return is the ultimate measure of a mutual fund's success. It is comprised of dividends and/or capital gains paid out by the mutual fund to the fund investor PLUS the change in share price of the fund over a one-year period. Calculating total return over a one-year period is important because many funds only pay out dividends and/or capital gains once per year. So, for example, if the share price of Mutual Fund A moves from $22 per share at the end of 2001 to $29.50 by the end of 2002, the capital return is 34.1 percent, as calculated by 29.5 minus 22 divided by 22. If the fund also paid out dividends and capital gains, those would be added into the year-ending price of $29.50. So, if 45 cents per share was paid out in dividends, and a $1.12 per share capital gain was distributed, the *total return* would be:

$$((29.5 + 1.12 + .45) - 22)/22 = .4123, \text{ or } 41.23\% \text{ annual total return}$$

Total return can be expressed as an annual figure for a one-year period or a multiyear period. The most pertinent total return figures are for multiyear periods, such as 3, 5, or 10 years. All the returns reported in this book, whether for mutual funds or individual stocks, are *total* returns.

Only over long time periods can the abilities of a mutual fund (i.e., mutual fund manager) accurately be assessed. Toward that end, Table 5.4 reports the total returns for the Frugal Forty Mutual Funds over the past 1-, 3-, 5-, 10-, and 15-year periods. Some of the funds have not been in existence for the 10- and 15-year periods, hence won't have return figures for those periods.

Table 5.5 reports the annual Lump Sum returns for the Frugal Forty over the five-year period from 1995 to 1999, the five-year average, and the five-year standard deviation of return. Table 5.6 reports the same performance results for monthly investing, or DCA. In both tables, funds are ranked by standard deviation of return from lowest to highest. A low standard deviation of return indicates that the year-to-year returns do not stray far from the average. Conversely, high standard deviation suggests that the investment (in this case, mutual funds) has year-to-year returns that are "all over the map."

Standard deviation of return is a surrogate measure for risk. What it really demonstrates is consistency of return from year to year. Consistency, however, is not necessarily a virtue. For example, an investment with *consistently* low returns is hardly anyone's goal. Obviously, people want an investment with consistently *high* returns. This is why average return and standard deviation of return must be evaluated as a pair.

As can be seen in both tables, funds with a low standard deviation of return have year-to-year returns that are more consistent. Moreover, funds with higher standard deviation of return sometimes have higher average return. That's the classic risk/

TABLE 5.4   Historical Returns for the Frugal Forty Funds

Fund Name	Total Percentage Return (as of December 31, 1999)				
	1 Year 1999	3 Year Avg. 1997-99	5 Year Avg. 1995-99	10 Year Avg. 1990-99	15 Year Avg. 1985-99
Alleghany/Montag&Caldwell Growth	22.5%	28.7%	31.4%	-	-
Ariel Appreciation	-3.8	16.6	19.5	13.6%	-
Columbia International Stock	57.9	25.7	19.5	-	-
Columbia Real Estate Equity	-2.5	2.2	11.5	-	-
Eclipse Small Cap Value	3.1	12.4	17.2	12.8	-
Excelsior Value & Restructuring	42.0	27.9	29.4	-	-
Fasciano	6.2	11.4	18.1	14.0	-
Fremont Global	22.4	14.0	15.0	11.0	-
Fremont U.S. Micro-Cap	129.5	36.2	42.1	-	-
Homestead Value	-3.2	9.9	16.0	-	-
Invesco Dynamics	71.8	38.1	33.1	24.1	20.1%
Invesco European	38.0	28.3	26.7	14.8	-
Invesco Health Sciences	0.6	19.6	24.8	19.5	22.1
Invesco Total Return	-1.4	11.9	15.3	12.4	-
Legg Mason Special Investment Prime	35.5	26.9	26.3	18.8	-
Legg Mason Total Return Prime	-6.6	8.6	17.0	12.0	-
Legg Mason Value Prime	26.7	37.0	38.0	21.6	19.4
Preferred Asset Allocation	1.3	15.9	18.9	-	-
Preferred International	32.9	16.2	15.1	-	-
Preferred Value	4.2	15.1	21.4	-	-
Safeco Equity No Load	9.4	19.3	21.6	17.2	17.9
Spectra	72.0	46.9	41.1	29.2	26.1
Strong American Utilities	0.6	15.6	18.0	-	-
Strong Asset Allocation	15.5	17.8	17.1	12.2	11.9
Strong Growth	75.1	38.3	34.9	-	-
Strong Opportunity	33.4	23.9	23.4	17.2	-
Strong Total Return	59.8	37.8	30.6	19.1	17.2
T. Rowe Price Blue Chip Growth	20.0	25.4	28.3	-	-
T. Rowe Price Equity Index 500	20.6	27.2	28.2	-	-
T. Rowe Price Equity Income	3.8	13.5	18.6	14.1	-
T. Rowe Price European Stock	19.7	20.8	22.0	-	-
T. Rowe Price International Discovery	155.0	36.7	22.7	13.0	-
T. Rowe Price International Stock	34.6	17.1	15.7	11.4	17.2
T. Rowe Price Mid-Cap Growth	23.8	21.4	25.8	-	-
T. Rowe Price Pers Strategy Growth	11.2	15.7	19.1	-	-
T. Rowe Price Science & Tech	101.0	42.8	38.9	30.2	-
T. Rowe Price Small Cap Stock	14.7	12.6	18.2	13.1	13.2
T. Rowe Price Spectrum Growth	21.2	17.4	20.4	-	-
T. Rowe Price Value	9.2	14.7	22.1	-	-
USAA Growth & Income	14.3	15.3	20.0	-	-

reward tradeoff. More risk often leads to greater reward. *But,* the risk/reward tradeoff is not consistent.

For example, the Alleghany/Montag & Caldwell Growth Fund has one of the highest five-year average returns *and* the fourth lowest standard deviation of return. This was true for lump sum investing and monthly investing. T. Rowe Price Blue

TABLE 5.5 The Frugal Forty: Five-Year Lump Sum Returns

ANNUAL TOTAL PERCENTAGE RETURNS WITH LUMP SUM INVESTING							
(Ranked by Standard Deviation of Return from Lowest to Highest)							
Fund Name	1995	1996	1997	1996	1999	5 Year Average Return	5 Year Standard Deviation
T. Rowe Price European Stock	21.9	25.9	17.0	25.8	19.7	22.0	3.5
Strong Asset Allocation	22.0	10.5	16.7	21.4	15.5	17.1	4.2
Fremont Global	19.3	14.0	9.9	10.0	22.4	15.0	5.0
Legg Mason Spec Invmnt Prime	22.5	28.7	22.1	23.3	35.5	26.3	5.1
Alleghany/Montag&Cald Gr N	38.7	32.7	31.9	31.9	22.5	31.4	5.2
T. Rowe Price Spectrum Growth	30.0	20.5	17.4	13.6	21.2	20.4	5.4
T. Rowe Price Blue Chip Growth	37.9	27.8	27.6	28.8	20.0	28.3	5.7
T. Rowe Price Equity Index 500	37.2	22.7	32.9	28.3	20.6	28.2	6.2
Safeco Equity No Load	25.3	25.0	24.2	24.9	9.4	21.6	6.2
Strong Opportunity	27.3	18.1	23.5	15.5	33.4	23.4	6.4
T. Rowe Price Pers Str Growth	31.4	17.7	20.6	15.7	11.2	19.1	6.8
Legg Mason Value Prime	40.8	38.4	37.1	48.0	26.7	38.0	6.9
T. Rowe Price Mid-Cap Growth	41.0	24.8	18.3	22.0	23.8	25.8	7.8
Invesco European	19.2	29.7	15.2	32.9	38.0	26.7	8.5
USAA Growth & Income	31.6	23.0	26.0	6.5	14.3	20.0	8.9
Preferred International	9.9	17.2	6.8	10.6	32.9	15.1	9.3
Fasciano	31.1	26.5	21.5	7.2	6.2	18.1	10.1
T. Rowe Price Intl Stock	11.4	16.0	2.7	16.1	34.6	15.7	10.4
Invesco Total Return	28.6	13.1	25.0	13.6	-1.4	15.3	10.6
Preferred Asset Allocation	32.8	15.1	21.0	27.1	1.3	18.9	10.8
T. Rowe Price Equity-Income	33.4	20.4	28.8	9.2	3.8	18.6	11.2
Excelsior Value & Restructuring	38.8	25.1	33.6	10.3	42.0	29.4	11.4
Preferred Value	37.8	25.3	28.0	14.4	4.2	21.4	11.6
T. Rowe Price Value	39.9	28.5	29.3	6.9	9.2	22.1	12.7
Eclipse Small Cap Value	19.7	29.9	33.3	3.4	3.1	17.2	12.8
T. Rowe Price Small Cap Stock	33.9	21.1	28.8	-3.5	14.7	18.2	13.0
Strong American Utilities	37.0	8.4	27.6	20.4	0.6	18.0	13.0
Homestead Value	33.8	17.9	26.7	8.3	-3.2	16.0	13.1
Ariel Appreciation	24.2	23.7	38.0	19.6	-3.8	19.5	13.6
Strong Total Return	27.0	14.1	24.2	32.1	59.8	30.6	15.3
Legg Mason Total Return Prime	30.4	31.1	37.5	-0.4	-6.6	17.0	18.1
Columbia Real Estate Equity	16.8	38.2	24.7	-12.3	-2.5	11.5	18.3
Spectra	47.7	19.4	24.6	48.0	72.0	41.1	18.9
Columbia International Stock	5.2	16.5	11.5	12.8	57.9	19.5	18.9
Invesco Dynamics	37.6	15.3	24.5	23.3	71.8	33.1	20.0
Strong Growth	41.0	19.5	19.1	27.0	75.1	34.9	20.9
Invesco Health Sciences	58.9	11.4	18.5	43.4	0.6	24.8	21.4
T. Rowe Price Science & Tech	55.5	14.2	1.7	42.4	101.0	38.9	34.8
Fremont U.S. Micro-Cap	54.0	48.7	7.0	2.9	129.5	42.1	45.6
T. Rowe Price Intl Discovery	-4.4	13.9	-5.7	6.1	155.0	22.7	61.4

Chip Growth is another example of a fund with consistently high return and low standard deviation of return.

Is there a way to evaluate mutual funds (or stocks) by taking into account historical return and standard deviation of return simultaneously? Because if there is, that would be really cool. Sure enough, while you were out mowing the front lawn, a smart

TABLE 5.6 The Frugal Forty: Five-Year DCA Returns

ANNUAL TOTAL PERCENTAGE RETURNS WITH MONTHLY INVESTING							
(Ranked by Standard Deviation of Return from Lowest to Highest)							
Fund Name	**1995**	**1996**	**1997**	**1996**	**1999**	**5 Year Average Return**	**5 Year Standard Deviation**
T. Rowe Price Blue Chip Growth	34.1	28.9	26.9	34.2	26.9	26.1	3.3
Alleghany/Montag&Cald Gr N	34.4	32.1	27.1	36.0	27.2	29.1	3.6
Strong Asset Allocation	22.7	14.5	17.1	24.6	19.3	17.3	3.7
T. Rowe Price Equity Index 500	34.2	25.0	29.0	32.1	24.5	26.5	3.8
T. Rowe Price Pers Str Growth	30.3	21.0	20.9	16.8	13.8	16.4	5.6
T. Rowe Price Spectrum Growth	30.5	21.1	17.0	15.6	29.7	18.5	6.3
T. Rowe Price Mid-Cap Growth	42.0	23.3	24.6	28.1	35.2	23.6	7.0
T. Rowe Price European Stock	21.2	27.8	17.9	17.9	37.4	21.6	7.4
Strong Opportunity	27.7	20.7	23.8	15.8	38.4	23.9	7.6
Safeco Equity No Load	25.1	27.9	20.6	27.5	7.0	19.6	7.8
USAA Growth & Income	30.8	26.1	22.3	8.0	11.5	16.4	8.6
Fremont Global	20.7	14.3	6.0	11.3	32.8	15.0	9.2
Legg Mason Spec Invmnt Prime	20.1	27.3	22.3	41.6	43.3	27.7	9.7
Fasciano	27.1	26.1	31.5	2.9	13.9	13.6	10.5
Invesco Total Return	26.6	15.6	24.1	14.2	-4.0	11.2	10.7
Preferred Value	32.8	26.3	24.5	12.4	2.3	15.8	10.9
Preferred Asset Allocation	30.5	18.6	20.3	32.9	0.2	15.6	11.6
Legg Mason Value Prime	39.7	45.0	27.6	57.1	22.9	37.0	12.2
T. Rowe Price Equity-Income	33.1	23.1	29.0	10.7	-1.2	13.9	12.6
T. Rowe Price Value	32.7	27.7	27.1	5.7	0.7	15.8	12.9
Eclipse Small Cap Value	21.0	35.0	33.4	2.1	9.0	13.5	13.0
T. Rowe Price Small Cap Stock	34.8	19.8	34.7	-0.4	29.1	14.5	13.2
Excelsior Value & Restructuring	38.4	27.9	30.0	11.2	54.9	28.6	14.3
Homestead Value	30.5	18.0	22.4	7.0	-11.5	9.7	14.5
Strong American Utilities	41.0	14.4	37.4	27.9	-0.8	15.0	15.5
Preferred International	10.8	18.0	-0.5	4.0	43.8	17.3	15.6
Ariel Appreciation	26.5	31.3	46.2	27.1	-7.1	16.3	17.4
T. Rowe Price Intl Stock	15.7	15.0	-2.7	13.5	55.5	18.7	19.3
Legg Mason Total Return Prime	28.4	35.2	39.2	2.0	-12.9	9.9	20.3
Invesco Health Sciences	65.8	7.8	15.9	42.3	8.7	19.2	22.6
Columbia Real Estate Equity	27.8	55.8	28.3	-10.7	-4.5	6.8	24.3
Invesco European	17.4	31.2	13.1	16.1	81.4	29.1	25.6
Strong Total Return	25.9	15.8	22.2	42.4	87.0	35.6	25.7
Invesco Dynamics	36.2	12.8	29.7	28.6	95.6	36.6	28.6
Columbia International Stock	15.3	15.8	3.7	14.2	89.6	26.5	31.3
Spectra	32.0	13.9	18.9	63.6	100.2	43.5	32.3
Strong Growth	41.1	14.3	17.7	39.8	117.6	38.5	37.4
T. Rowe Price Science & Tech	51.6	12.7	-0.9	64.7	126.8	43.0	44.9
Fremont U.S. Micro-Cap	55.0	42.9	5.5	22.3	173.8	44.3	59.4
T. Rowe Price Intl Discovery	1.9	6.7	-15.1	-2.9	205.2	37.3	83.3

fellow named William Sharpe came up with a simple idea that does exactly that. It's called (not surprisingly) the **Sharpe Ratio,** and it assesses the return of any given investment per unit of its own risk. In English that means it is a calculation that simultaneously evaluates both the *risk* AND *return* of an investment. Bottom line: *The higher the Sharpe Ratio, the better.*

Table 5.7 ranks, from high to low, the Frugal Forty by their five-year Sharpe Ratio. For a highly volatile mutual fund to have a high Sharpe Ratio (higher is better), it's going to have to produce really high returns. A conservative fund (i.e., low volatility of annual returns) will not need to have such high returns to have a favorable Sharpe Ratio. The logic of the Sharpe Ratio is

TABLE 5.7   The Frugal Forty and the Sharpe Ratio

Fund Name	5-Year Sharpe Ratio (1995-99) Higher Is Better
Preferred Asset Allocation	1.70
T. Rowe Price Equity Index 500	1.54
T. Rowe Price Blue Chip Growth	1.53
Legg Mason Value Prime	1.49
Alleghany/Montag&Caldwell Growth N	1.47
T. Rowe Price Personal Strategy Growth	1.43
T. Rowe Price European Stock	1.35
Spectra	1.28
Strong Total Return	1.27
Excelsior Value & Restructuring	1.26
Invesco Dynamics	1.26
Safeco Equity No Load	1.25
T. Rowe Price Equity-Income	1.25
Strong Asset Allocation	1.23
Invesco Total Return	1.22
Strong Opportunity	1.22
T. Rowe Price Value	1.21
Fremont U.S. Micro-Cap	1.19
Invesco Health Sciences	1.18
Strong American Utilities	1.18
T. Rowe Price Spectrum Growth	1.18
Invesco European	1.15
Strong Growth	1.13
T. Rowe Price Mid-Cap Growth	1.13
USAA Growth & Income	1.11
Ariel Appreciation	1.08
Preferred Value	1.08
Fremont Global	1.05
T. Rowe Price Science & Technology	1.02
Fasciano	0.99
Legg Mason Spec Investment Prime	0.97
Columbia International Stock	0.94
Homestead Value	0.90
Legg Mason Total Return Prime	0.90
T. Rowe Price Small Cap Stock	0.88
T. Rowe Price International Discovery	0.86
Eclipse Small Cap Value	0.81
Preferred International	0.79
T. Rowe Price International Stock	0.78
Columbia Real Estate Equity	0.57

the recognition that high volatility without high returns is typically unacceptable to most investors. Indeed, a fund with those characteristics will have a low Sharpe Ratio. The Sharpe Ratio is probably the best single measure of mutual fund performance because it takes into account both return and risk.

For investors with a long investment horizon (say, a three-year-old child's college savings account), it may not make sense to only consider those funds with the highest Sharpe Ratio score. With such a long investment period, risk (or volatility) during the next 10 to 12 years is not terrifically relevant. The most important issue for the long-term investor is return. For an investor who has a shorter investment horizon, or who may need to make withdrawals periodically from the account, or who simply can't stomach much volatility, choosing mutual funds with higher Sharpe Ratios makes a lot of sense.

The Sharpe Ratio, like all other measures of investment performance, is one piece of a decision-making process. It is most appropriately used when ranking mutual funds that share some basic commonalities, such as U.S. large-cap equity funds, U.S. small-cap funds, or non-U.S. funds. Using the Sharpe Ratio to simultaneously rank U.S. stock funds and U.S. bond funds would be inappropriate. It's helpful to remember that there is no one perfect analytical statistic for measuring investment suitability. And if there were, I doubt it would be shared in a book!

As can be seen in Table 5.7, funds with the highest average total return over the past five years do not always have the highest Sharpe Ratio. The Sharpe Ratio attempts to identify mutual funds that possess the best of both worlds—the highest return with the least amount of volatility. Some funds have a high Sharpe Ratio due to very high return (e.g., Spectra and Legg Mason Value Prime) despite also having high standard deviation of return. Other funds achieve a high Sharpe Ratio by having a more modest return and low standard deviation of return (e.g., Preferred Asset Allocation and Strong American Utilities). Occasionally a fund comes along that has a high Sharpe Ratio because of consistently high return, such as Alleghany/Montag & Caldwell Growth.

Aggressive investors who pay attention to the Sharpe Ratio will likely choose funds that generate high returns but also have fairly high volatility of return from year to year. Conservative investors will likely choose funds that behave more like Strong American Utilities or Invesco Total Return—modest returns with low volatility. Interestingly, the Sharpe Ratio can be similar for both types of funds. That's why it's important to look at the components of how the Sharpe Ratio is calculated, namely historical return and standard deviation of return (as reported in Tables 5.5 and 5.6).

Generally speaking, mutual funds with high Sharpe Ratios represent funds that: (1) have really high average returns and high standard deviation of return, or (2) have very minimal standard deviation of return and relatively low average returns. The funds that earn low Sharpe Ratios are those with a low average return coupled with high risk (i.e., high standard deviation of return)— precisely the ones that thrifty investors might want to be wary of. For U.S. stock mutual funds, Sharpe Ratios typically range from a minimum of –2 (worst) to a maximum of 2 (best). So, as you can see, the Frugal Forty all have very respectable Sharpe Ratios.

Table 5.8 is important. It shows which of the Frugal Forty had better performance using DCA compared to lump sum investing. Fund names in **bold** had comparable or higher return using DCA. In fact, 16 out of the 40 funds (40 percent) had, over the five-year period from 1995 to 1999, a higher five-year average return using a monthly investing approach compared to a lump sum investment. Twelve out of 40 funds (30 percent) had a comparable or lower standard deviation of annual return using a monthly investing approach rather than a onetime lump sum investment (noted by **bold** standard deviation data). This is quite impressive inasmuch as the five-year period from 1995–1999 was a very favorable period for lump sum investments. The information in Table 5.8 clearly demonstrates that dollar-cost averaging is an excellent investing technique, with the potential to produce returns that are comparable, and in some cases superior, to lump sum investing.

Tables 5.9 through 5.12 report the performance of the Frugal Forty over the past 1-, 3-, 5-, 10-, and 15-year periods. Each table ranks the funds by average annual total return in descending order.

Additional information (annual expense ratio, manager tenure, etc.) about the Frugal Forty funds is found in Table 5.13. Table 5.14 lists the Frugal Forty mutual funds in order of tax efficiency over the five-year period from 1995 to 1999. Tax efficiency is a measure of how much of the return generated by a mutual fund is exposed to taxation. Mutual funds that make large capital gain and dividend distributions to shareholders will be less tax-efficient. Many growth and income funds would fall

TABLE 5.8   The Frugal Forty—Lump Sum Returns Compared to Monthly Investing Returns, 1995–1999

Funds in **bold** had superior DCA performance compared to lump sum	LUMP SUM RETURNS		DCA RETURNS	
Fund Name	5-Year Average Return	5-Year Standard Deviation	5-Year Average Return	5-Year Standard Deviation
Alleghany/Montag&Caldwell Growth N	31.4	5.2	29.1	**3.6**
Ariel Appreciation	19.5	13.6	16.3	17.4
Columbia International Stock	19.5	18.9	**26.5**	31.3
Columbia Real Estate Equity	11.5	18.3	6.8	24.3
Eclipse Small Cap Value	17.2	12.8	13.5	**13.0**
Excelsior Value & Restructuring	29.4	11.4	28.6	14.3
Fasciano	18.1	10.1	13.6	10.5
Fremont Global	15.0	5.0	**15.0**	9.2
Fremont U.S. Micro-Cap	42.1	45.6	**44.3**	59.4
Homestead Value	16.0	13.1	9.7	14.5
Invesco Dynamics	33.1	20.0	**36.6**	28.6
Invesco European	26.7	8.5	**29.1**	25.6
Invesco Health Sciences	24.8	21.4	19.2	22.6
Invesco Total Return	15.3	10.6	11.2	**10.7**
Legg Mason Spec Investment Prime	26.3	5.1	**27.7**	9.7
Legg Mason Total Return Prime	17.0	18.2	9.9	20.3
Legg Mason Value Prime	38.0	6.9	37.0	12.2
Preferred Asset Allocation	18.9	10.8	15.6	11.6
Preferred International	15.1	9.3	**17.3**	15.6
Preferred Value	21.4	11.6	15.8	**10.9**
Safeco Equity No Load	21.6	6.2	19.6	7.8
Spectra	41.1	18.9	**43.5**	32.3
Strong American Utilities	18.0	13.0	15.0	15.5
Strong Asset Allocation	17.1	4.2	**17.3**	3.7
Strong Growth	34.9	20.9	**38.5**	37.4
Strong Opportunity	23.4	6.4	**23.9**	7.6
Strong Total Return	30.6	15.3	**35.6**	25.7
T. Rowe Price Blue Chip Growth	28.3	5.7	26.1	**3.3**
T. Rowe Price Equity Index 500	28.2	6.2	26.5	**3.8**
T. Rowe Price Equity-Income	18.6	11.2	13.9	12.6
T. Rowe Price European Stock	22.0	3.5	**21.6**	7.4
T. Rowe Price Intl Discovery	22.7	61.4	**37.3**	83.3
T. Rowe Price Intl Stock	15.7	10.4	**18.7**	19.3
T. Rowe Price Mid-Cap Growth	25.8	7.8	23.6	**7.0**
T. Rowe Price Pers Str Growth	19.1	6.8	16.4	**5.6**
T. Rowe Price Science & Tech	38.9	34.8	**43.0**	44.9
T. Rowe Price Small Cap Stk	18.2	13.0	14.5	**13.2**
T. Rowe Price Spectrum Growth	20.4	5.4	18.5	6.3
T. Rowe Price Value	22.1	12.7	15.8	**12.9**
USAA Growth & Income	20.0	8.9	16.4	**8.6**
Average	**23.6%**	**13.7%**	**22.7%**	**18.1%**

into that category. Bond funds (with the exception of nontaxable municipal bond funds) are typically less tax-efficient than stock funds. This is because bond funds make interest payments to shareholders, and those interest payments are taxable. Conversely, some stock mutual funds own companies that do not pay

TABLE 5.9 Top Performing Frugal Funds for 1999

Fund Name	1-Year % Return
T. Rowe Price International Discovery	155.0
Fremont U.S. Micro-Cap	129.5
T. Rowe Price Science & Technology	101.0
Strong Growth	75.1
Spectra	72.0
Invesco Dynamics	71.8
Strong Total Return	59.8
Columbia International Stock	57.9
Excelsior Value & Restructuring	42.0
Invesco European	38.0
Legg Mason Special Investment Prime	35.5
T. Rowe Price International Stock	34.6
Strong Opportunity	33.4
Preferred International	32.9
Legg Mason Value Prim	26.7
T. Rowe Price Mid-Cap Growth	23.8
Alleghany/Montag & Caldwell Growth	22.5
Fremont Global	22.4
T. Rowe Price Spectrum Growth	21.2
T. Rowe Price Equity Index 500	20.6
T. Rowe Price Blue Chip Growth	20.0
T. Rowe Price European Stock	19.7
Strong Asset Allocation	15.5
T. Rowe Price Small Cap Stock	14.7
USAA Growth & Income	14.3
T. Rowe Price Pers Str Growth	11.2
Safeco Equity No Load	9.4
T. Rowe Price Value	9.2
Fasciano	6.2
Preferred Value	4.2
T. Rowe Price Equity Income	3.8
Eclipse Small Cap Value	3.1
Preferred Asset Allocation	1.3
Invesco Health Sciences	0.6
Strong American Utilities	0.6
Invesco Total Return	-1.4
Columbia Real Estate Equity	-2.5
Homestead Value	-3.2
Ariel Appreciation	-3.8
Legg Mason Total Return Prime	-6.6

dividends, hence will not need to make any dividend payments to shareholders. This is common among small-cap funds. Moreover, if the turnover ratio of the stock fund is low, there may be little in the way of capital gain distributions to pay out to shareholders.

The bottom line: Use tax-efficient funds for regular, non-tax-deferred accounts, and less tax-efficient funds for tax-deferred accounts, such as 401(k), 403(b), and IRA.

Another important issue when creating mutual fund portfolios is the inclusion of funds that *invest in companies outside the*

TABLE 5.10 Top Performing Frugal Funds, 1997–1999

Fund Name	3-Year Average % Return
Spectra	46.9
T. Rowe Price Science & Technology	42.8
Strong Growth	38.3
Invesco Dynamics	38.1
Strong Total Return	37.8
Legg Mason Value Prime	37.0
T. Rowe Price International Discovery	36.7
Fremont U.S. Micro-Cap	36.2
Alleghany/Montag & Caldwell Growth	28.7
Invesco European	28.3
Excelsior Value & Restructuring	27.9
T. Rowe Price Equity Index 500	27.2
Legg Mason Special Investment Prime	26.9
Columbia International Stock	25.7
T. Rowe Price Blue Chip Growth	25.4
Strong Opportunity	23.9
T. Rowe Price Mid-Cap Growth	21.4
T. Rowe Price European Stock	20.8
Invesco Health Sciences	19.6
Safeco Equity No Load	19.3
Strong Asset Allocation	17.8
T. Rowe Price Spectrum Growth	17.4
T. Rowe Price International Stock	17.1
Ariel Appreciation	16.6
Preferred International	16.2
Preferred Asset Allocation	15.9
T. Rowe Price Personal Strategy Growth	15.7
Strong American Utilities	15.6
USAA Growth & Income	15.3
Preferred Value	15.1
T. Rowe Price Value	14.7
Fremont Global	14.0
T. Rowe Price Equity Income	13.5
T. Rowe Price Small Cap Stock	12.6
Eclipse Small Cap Value	12.4
Invesco Total Return	11.9
Fasciano	11.4
Homestead Value	9.9
Legg Mason Total Return Prime	8.6
Columbia Real Estate Equity	2.2

United States. Six of the Frugal Forty are international funds. Funds that invest "overseas" represent a very important part of an intelligently integrated mutual fund portfolio. You may remember from the data in Table 1.1 that non-U.S. stocks (based upon the aggregate MSCI EAFE Index) have not performed very well in recent years. This fact, combined with outstanding returns among large-cap U.S. stocks during most of the 1990s, has caused many investors to move away from non-U.S. stocks and focus more heav-

TABLE 5.11   Top Performing Frugal Funds, 1995–1999

Fund Name	5-Year Average %Return
Fremont U.S. Micro-Cap	42.1
Spectra	41.1
T. Rowe Price Science & Technology	38.9
Legg Mason Value Prime	38.0
Strong Growth	34.9
Invesco Dynamics	33.1
Alleghany/Montag & Caldwell Growth	31.4
Strong Total Return	30.6
Excelsior Value & Restructuring	29.4
T. Rowe Price Blue Chip Growth	28.3
T. Rowe Price Equity Index 500	28.2
Invesco European	26.7
Legg Mason Spec Investment Prime	26.3
T. Rowe Price Mid-Cap Growth	25.8
Invesco Health Sciences	24.8
Strong Opportunity	23.4
T. Rowe Price International Discovery	22.7
T. Rowe Price Value	22.1
T. Rowe Price European Stock	22.0
Safeco Equity No Load	21.6
Preferred Value	21.4
T. Rowe Price Spectrum Growth	20.4
USAA Growth & Income	20.0
Ariel Appreciation	19.5
Columbia International Stock	19.5
T. Rowe Price Personal Strategy Growth	19.1
Preferred Asset Allocation	18.9
T. Rowe Price Equity Income	18.6
T. Rowe Price Small Cap Stock	18.2
Fasciano	18.1
Strong American Utilities	18.0
Eclipse Small Cap Value	17.2
Strong Asset Allocation	17.1
Legg Mason Total Return Prime	17.0
Homestead Value	16.0
T. Rowe Price International Stock	15.7
Invesco Total Return	15.3
Preferred International	15.1
Fremont Global	15.0
Columbia Real Estate Equity	11.5

ily on U.S. stocks. This may be a serious mistake. Inasmuch as over half of the world's stock exists outside the United States, it is unwise for U.S.-based investors to ignore the rest of the world.

Investors who shun non-U.S. markets will be ignoring companies such as Nestlé, Sony, Canon, Nokia, Royal Dutch Petroleum, Bayer, Siemens, Makita, Volkswagen, Rolls-Royce, Honda, Toshiba, Cadbury Schweppes, BP Amoco, Swatch, Peugeot Citroën, Christian Dior, British Airways, Toyota Motor, and the list goes on.

TABLE 5.12   Top Performing Frugal Funds, 1990–1999 & 1985–1999

Fund Name	10-Year Average % Return
T. Rowe Price Science & Technology	30.2
Spectra	29.2
Invesco Dynamics	24.1
Legg Mason Value Prime	21.6
Invesco Health Sciences	19.5
Strong Total Return	19.1
Legg Mason Special Investment Prime	18.8
Strong Opportunity	17.2
Safeco Equity No Load	17.2
Invesco European	14.8
T. Rowe Price Equity Income	14.1
Fasciano	14.0
Ariel Appreciation	13.6
T. Rowe Price Small Cap Stock	13.1
T. Rowe Price International Discovery	13.0
Eclipse Small Cap Value	12.8
Invesco Total Return	12.4
Strong Asset Allocation	12.2
Legg Mason Total Return Prime	12.0
T. Rowe Price International Stock	11.4
Fremont Global	11.0

Fund Name	15-Year Average % Return
Spectra	26.1
Invesco Health Sciences	22.1
Invesco Dynamics	20.1
Legg Mason Value Prime	19.4
Safeco Equity No Load	17.9
Strong Total Return	17.2
T. Rowe Price International Stock	17.2
T. Rowe Price Small Cap Stock	13.2
Strong Asset Allocation	11.9

Remainder of funds have not been in existence for 10 or 15 years

Why is it important to include non-U.S. stocks in a portfolio? In a word, *balance*. All the world's stock markets do not rise and fall in unison. When the U.S. stock market is having a good year, other stock markets around the world may be having a bad year . . . and vice versa. It's the vice versa part that's important to remember. Not since 1974 have large U.S. stocks (as measured by the S&P 500) had a seriously bad year.

For investors focusing only on recent history, the superiority of large-cap U.S. stocks seems obvious. As shown in Table 5.15, during the five-year period from 1995 to 1999 the S&P 500 Index dramatically outperformed the small-cap stock index and the EAFE international stock index. The S&P 500 averaged 28.5 percent per year between 1995 and 1999, compared to 18.5 percent for small stocks and 13.1 percent for non-U.S. stocks. However, the benefits of intelligent investment integration (i.e., balanced investment portfolios) require a longer horizon. Only when considering longer-run performance data does it become evident that equities (large-cap or small-cap, U.S. or non-U.S.) tend to produce an "equity return" of around 12 to 13 percent annually.

Look at the 30-year averages in Table 5.15. U.S. large stocks produced an average return of 13.7 percent, U.S. small stocks 14.1 percent, and international stocks 13.2 percent. During shorter time periods disparities between the different equity groups are evident, as noted by the dominance of large-cap U.S. stocks during the past 5- and 10-year periods. Long-run data inform us that it is wise to be invested in the three major stock groups: large U.S. stocks, small U.S. stocks, and non-U.S. stocks. The bottom line:

> Long-run investment decisions should be guided by long-run performance data.

Accepting that (1) different types of stocks periodically outperform each other, and that (2) the timing of such periods of outperformance is unknowable in advance, suggests that exposure to each major group of stocks is a reasonable strategy for long-term investors.

Table 5.15 also presents long-term outcomes of two simple *balanced* portfolios. (Creating balanced portfolios is also often referred to as **Asset Allocation.**) The first "balanced portfolio" consists of equal weighting between large and small U.S. stocks. This implies that the portfolio is rebalanced at the start of each year so that large and small U.S. stocks each represent 50 percent of the total portfolio. The second "balanced portfolio" has one-third of its assets in large-cap U.S. stock, one-third in small-cap U.S. stock, and one-third in the EAFE Index at the start of each year. Notice that the 30-year annualized return of the blended portfolios (14.2 percent in both cases) is higher than any of the three separate asset classes (large U.S. stock, small U.S. stock, non-U.S. stock). Moreover, the 30-year standard deviation of return for the blended portfolios was lower than the standard deviation of return for the

TABLE 5.13 Frugal Forty Funds—Additional Information

Fund Name	Total Number of Holdings	1999 Annual Turnover Ratio (%)	1999 Annual Expense Ratio (%)	Fund Net Assets $ Million	Manager Tenure (Years)	Minimum Initial Lump Sum Purchase Regular Account	Minimum Initial Lump Sum Purchase IRA Account	Minimum Monthly Purchase Automatic Investment Plan
Alleghany/Montag&Caldwell Growth N	33	30	1.12	$1,736	6	$2,500	$500	$50
Ariel Appreciation	38	20	1.26	$325	11	$1,000	$250	$50
Columbia International Stock	114	74	1.54	$205	8	$1,000	$1,000	$50
Columbia Real Estate Equity	31	6	1.01	$211	6	$1,000	$1,000	$50
Eclipse Small Cap Value	321	73	1.14	$232	12	$1,000	$1,000	$50
Excelsior Value & Restructuring	73	43	0.93	$822	8	$500	$250	$50
Fasciano	87	20	1.20	$377	13	$1,000	$1,000	$50
Fremont Global	1057	75	0.85	$773	8	$2,000	$1,000	$50
Fremont U.S. Micro-Cap	74	170	1.94	$416	6	$2,000	$1,000	$50
Homestead Value	52	10	0.72	$425	10	$500	$200	$1
Invesco Dynamics	129	129	1.03	$3,725	5	$1,000	$250	$50*
Invesco European	113	102	1.34	$543	10	$1,000	$250	$50*
Invesco Health Sciences	51	92	1.12	$1,579	6	$1,000	$250	$50*
Invesco Total Return	182	20	0.83	$3,019	8	$1,000	$250	$50*
Legg Mason Spec Investment Prime	40	48	1.84	$2,423	9	$1,000	$1,000	$50
Legg Mason Total Return Prime	58	44	1.87	$492	8	$1,000	$1,000	$50
Legg Mason Value Prime	43	19	1.69	$12,158	18	$1,000	$1,000	$50
Preferred Asset Allocation	529	6	0.89	$227	8	$1,000	$250	$50
Preferred International	56	15	1.20	$334	8	$1,000	$250	$50
Preferred Value	38	23	0.84	$387	8	$1,000	$250	$50
Safeco Equity No Load	46	33	0.74	$2,048	5	$1,000	$250	$50**
Spectra	60	191	1.90	$629	14	$1,000	$250	$25
Strong American Utilities	51	69	1.00	$236	7	$2,500	$250	$50

TABLE 5.13 (Continued)

Fund Name	Total Number of Holdings	1999 Annual Turnover Ratio (%)	1999 Annual Expense Ratio (%)	Fund Net Assets $ Million	Manager Tenure (Years)	Minimum Initial Lump Sum Purchase Regular Account	Minimum Initial Lump Sum Purchase IRA Account	Minimum Monthly Purchase Automatic Investment Plan
Strong Asset Allocation	171	186	1.00	$348	5	$250	$250	$50
Strong Growth	119	249	1.30	$2,653	7	$2,500	$250	$50
Strong Opportunity	86	86	1.20	$2,371	9	$2,500	$250	$50
Strong Total Return	104	268	1.00	$1,339	7	$2,500	$250	$50
T. Rowe Price Blue Chip Growth	122	35	0.91	$6,325	7	$2,500	$1,000	$50
T. Rowe Price Equity Index 500	503	5	0.40	$4,760	10	$2,500	$1,000	$50
T. Rowe Price Equity-Income	132	23	0.77	$12,775	15	$2,500	$1,000	$50
T. Rowe Price European Stock	155	27	1.05	$1,438	8	$2,500	$1,000	$50
T. Rowe Price Intl Discovery	174	34	1.47	$512	7	$2,500	$1,000	$50
T. Rowe Price Intl Stock	251	12	0.85	$11,328	15	$2,500	$1,000	$50
T. Rowe Price Mid-Cap Growth	105	47	0.91	$4,714	8	$2,500	$1,000	$50
T. Rowe Price Personal Strategy Growth	698	36	1.10	$238	1	$2,500	$1,000	$50
T. Rowe Price Science & Tech	49	109	0.94	$10,021	9	$2,500	$1,000	$50
T. Rowe Price Small Cap Stock	220	26	1.01	$1,592	8	$2,500	$1,000	$50
T. Rowe Price Spectrum Growth	8	18	0.80	$2,836	1	$2,500	$1,000	$50
T. Rowe Price Value	89	72	0.98	$865	6	$2,500	$1,000	$50
USAA Growth & Income	79	25	0.89	$1,122	7	$3,000	$250	$50

* $25 for IRA and UTMA accounts   ** Only for IRA and UTMA accounts, otherwise $100

TABLE 5.14 Tax Efficiency Ratings of Frugal Forty Mutual Funds, 1995–1999

Fund Name	5-Year Tax Efficiency
Ranked from Highest to Lowest (100=Most Tax Efficient)	
T. Rowe Price Blue Chip Growth	98.4
Alleghany/Montag & Caldwell Growth N	98.3
Excelsior Value & Restructuring	97.2
T. Rowe Price Mid-Cap Growth	96.0
T. Rowe Price Equity Index 500	95.8
Legg Mason Value Prime	95.6
T. Rowe Price International Discovery	95.3
Fasciano	93.6
Preferred Value	92.1
USAA Growth & Income	92.0
Strong Growth	92.0
T. Rowe Price Personal Strategy Growth	91.8
T. Rowe Price Intl Stock	91.4
Legg Mason Spec Investment Prime	91.3
T. Rowe Price European Stock	91.2
Preferred International	90.7
Fremont U.S. Micro-Cap	90.7
Columbia International Stock	90.2
Homestead Value	89.8
T. Rowe Price Science & Tech	89.2
Invesco Total Return	88.1
T. Rowe Price Small Cap Stock	88.0
Ariel Appreciation	87.9
Spectra	87.5
Invesco European	87.3
Invesco Dynamics	87.1
Legg Mason Total Return Prime	86.8
T. Rowe Price Spectrum Growth	86.6
Strong American Utilities	85.6
Safeco Equity No Load	85.5
T. Rowe Price Equity Income	84.7
T. Rowe Price Value	84.5
Invesco Health Sciences	84.3
Strong Opportunity	83.9
Preferred Asset Allocation	83.6
Strong Total Return	83.2
Strong Asset Allocation	78.6
Columbia Real Estate Equity	77.8
Fremont Global	76.5
Eclipse Small Cap Value	76.3

100 percent small-cap and 100 percent EAFE portfolios and only slightly higher than that of the S&P 500 portfolio. You'll recall that standard deviation of return is one measure of risk, hence the smaller the standard deviation of return, the lower the risk.

Over shorter time horizons, such as the most recent 5 and 10 years, it was more profitable to invest in only large-cap U.S. stocks (i.e., the S&P 500). However, the blended portfolios were able to produce annualized returns second only to the S&P 500 portfolio over the past 5 and 10 years, and typically with comparable or lower risk (i.e., lower standard deviation of annualized return). Said differently, balanced portfolios generally achieve favorable risk/reward dynamics in which annualized return is comparable to or higher than any of the individual portfolio components, while at the same time reducing the overall volatility of the investor's portfolio.

A common error among new investors is chasing last year's hot investment asset, whether it be large caps, small caps, or international stock. When large-cap stocks have a really good year, money flows into large caps the following year. It's certainly possible that large-cap stocks (and large-cap mutual funds) may have a repeat performance, but maybe they won't. As it's not possible to know which of the three major asset classes (large U.S. stocks, small U.S. stocks, non-U.S. stocks) will be the "winner" each year, the more prudent approach is to balance investments between the three major investment groups. This balanced approach is illustrated by the last two columns in Table 5.15.

The variability of performance among the three major asset classes (U.S. large stock, U.S. small stock, non-U.S. stock) over short time periods is summarized in Table 5.16. Worth noting is the superiority of international stocks during the four-year period from 1985 through 1988. A $1000 investment in the EAFE Index at the start of 1985 was worth $4279 by the end of 1988, compared to an ending value of $1925 in the S&P 500 and $1486 in small-cap stocks. Over the four-year period ending in 1988, the EAFE Index averaged a 43.8 percent annual return, compared to 17.8 percent in the S&P 500 and 10.4 percent in small stocks. Clearly, at that time the EAFE Index enjoyed the same type of adoration that the S&P 500 Index enjoyed during the period from 1995 to 1999. How quickly we forget. Remember the fickle friend analogy? It strikes again.

Lest you think small stocks are always the whipping boy, consider the nine-year period beginning in 1975. A lump sum $1000 investment in small stocks became $15,195 by the end of 1983, for an annualized return of 35.3 percent (Table 5.16). Large U.S. stocks returned "only" 15.7 percent over the same nine-year period, and the EAFE Index averaged 15.6 percent. Small caps also dominated during the three-year period from 1991 to 1993. Only when taking a longer view does it become clear that three

TABLE 5.15 Total Annual Returns of Prominent Stock Indexes and Two Balanced Portfolios

Year	Large Stock S&P 500	Small Stock Ibbotson	Intl Stock EAFE	[– Balanced Portfolios –] 50% Lrg 50% Sml	33% Lrg 33% Sml 34% Intl
INDEX-->					
1970	4.0%	-17.4%	-10.5%	-6.7%	-8.0%
1971	14.3%	16.5%	31.2%	15.4%	20.8%
1972	19.0%	4.4%	37.6%	11.7%	20.5%
1973	-14.7%	-30.9%	-14.2%	-22.8%	-19.9%
1974	-26.5%	-20.0%	-22.2%	-23.2%	-22.9%
1975	37.2%	52.8%	37.1%	45.0%	42.3%
1976	23.8%	57.4%	3.7%	40.6%	28.1%
1977	-7.2%	25.4%	19.4%	9.1%	12.6%
1978	6.6%	23.5%	34.3%	15.0%	21.6%
1979	18.4%	43.5%	6.2%	31.0%	22.5%
1980	32.4%	39.9%	24.4%	36.2%	32.2%
1981	-4.9%	13.9%	-1.0%	4.5%	2.6%
1982	21.4%	28.0%	-.9%	24.7%	16.0%
1983	22.5%	39.7%	24.6%	31.1%	28.9%
1984	6.3%	-6.7%	7.9%	-0.2%	2.5%
1985	32.2%	24.7%	56.7%	28.4%	38.0%
1986	18.5%	6.9%	69.9%	12.7%	32.2%
1987	5.2%	-9.3%	24.9%	-2.0%	7.1%
1988	16.8%	22.9%	28.6%	19.9%	22.8%
1989	31.5%	10.2%	10.8%	20.8%	17.4%
1990	-3.2%	-21.6%	-23.2%	-12.4%	-16.1%
1991	30.5%	44.6%	12.5%	37.6%	29.0%
1992	7.7%	23.4%	-11.9%	15.6%	6.2%
1993	10.0%	21.0%	32.9%	15.5%	21.4%
1994	1.3%	3.1%	8.1%	2.2%	4.2%

TABLE 5.15 (Continued)

1995	37.4%	34.5%	11.6%	36.0%	27.7%
1996	23.1%	17.6%	6.4%	20.3%	15.6%
1997	33.4%	22.8%	2.1%	28.1%	19.2%
1998	28.6%	-7.3%	20.3%	10.6%	13.9%
1999	21.0%	29.8%	27.3%	25.4%	26.0%
Between 1970 and 1999 $1,000 grew to...	$47,355	$52,701	$41,265	$54,426	$54,578
30 YR AVE ANNUAL RETURN	13.7%	14.1%	13.2%	14.3%	14.3%
30 YR STD DEV	15.7%	22.4%	21.2%	17.4%	16.0%
Between 1990 and 1999 $1000 grew into...	$5,322	$4,078	$2,029	$4,779	$3,678
10 YR AVE RETURN	18.2%	15.1%	7.3%	16.9%	13.9%
10 YR STD DEV	13.3%	18.2%	15.3%	13.9%	12.4%
Between 1995 and 1999 $1000 grew into...	$3,509	$2,337	$1,854	$2,907	$2,526
5 YR AVE RETURN	28.5%	18.5%	13.1%	23.8%	20.4%
5 YR STD DEV	11.6%	14.6%	8.6%	11.2%	7.9%

TABLE 5.16 The Unpredictable Performance Spotlight

	S&P 500	Small U.S. Stock	International Stock
	Average Annualized Total Return (%)		
1975-1983 (9 years)	15.7	**35.3**	15.6
1985-1988 (4 years)	17.8	10.4	**43.8**
1991-1993 (3 years)	15.6	**29.2**	9.6
1995-1999 (5 years)	**28.5**	18.5	13.1

Annualized return figures assume a lump sum investment at the start of each period, no additional investments, reinvestment of all income and capital gains, no withdrawals during the period, and taxes paid out of pocket rather than out of the fund. Inflation ignored.

major groups—large-cap U.S. stocks, small-cap U.S. stocks, and international stocks—take turns basking in the spotlight.

To summarize, only when looking at long-run risk/return performance does the logic and safety of creating balanced portfolios become clear. The virtue of investment balance is best depicted graphically. Look at Figure 5.1. It is a risk/return graph. The ideal quadrant is the upper-left-hand corner, representing investments with higher return and lower risk (i.e., volatility of return). Mutual funds in the upper-left-hand quadrant typically have higher Sharpe Ratios as well—which is good!

Notice that both blended portfolios (from Table 5.15), as well as the S&P 500, reside in the desirable upper-left-hand quadrant. Small caps and international stock, by themselves, are in less desirable quadrants (primarily due to higher volatility as opposed to terribly low return). However, when blended together, international stock and small-cap stock actually benefit the large-cap U.S. stock portfolio (i.e., S&P 500). This enhancement represents true investment *synergy*. Achieving greater return at comparable (or even lower) levels of risk is *the* primary virtue of creating balanced portfolios.

So . . . creating a balanced portfolio of stock mutual funds and/or individual stocks involves two major issues: (1) balancing investments within the "equity style box," and (2) balancing investments between U.S. and non-U.S stocks. Using this paradigm

FIGURE 5.1   Risk and Return Quadrant Graph

For S&P 500, Small-Cap Stock, International Stock, and Two Blended Portfolios: 50% S&P, 50% Small Cap, and 33% S&P, 33% Small Cap, 34% International

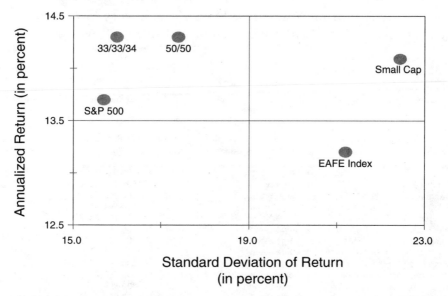

of balanced investing, let's now take a look at some example portfolios of mutual funds and individual stocks.

Before leaving this chapter there is one more group of "thrifty" mutual funds worth becoming familiar with. They are thrifty funds by a different measure, that being **annual expense ratio.** The annual expense ratio is a measure of how costly a fund is to the investor, and for U.S. stock mutual funds the average is 1.20 percent per year. For example, Fund X has an annual expense ratio of 1.20 percent and a total annual return of 20.0 percent. If Fund X did not have an expense ratio, the total annual return would have been 21.20 percent. But alas, all funds have expense ratios. However, they can differ significantly. And remember, the annual expense ratio takes a cut out of total percentage return each and every year. The longer you hold a mutual fund, the more impact the annual expense ratio has on your long-run return, so it's a cost worth paying attention to.

Two general observations about mutual funds and expense ratios:

- Expensive funds are generally small funds (in terms of net assets).

- Equity funds with large net assets enjoy economies of scale not generally evident in small funds. Large funds *generally* have lower expense ratios.

The stock mutual funds in Table 5.17 have very low annual expense ratios. The cutoff for inclusion in Table 5.17 was an ex-

TABLE 5.17   Thrifty Stock Funds with Low Expense Ratios (.50% and Lower)

Fund Name	Morningstar Category	1999 Annual Expense Ratio	Phone Number
SSgA S&P 500 Index	Large Blend	0.17	800-647-7327
Orbitex Focus 30 Dow	Large Blend	0.18	800-445-2763
Vanguard 500 Index	Large Blend	0.18	800-662-7447
Fidelity Spartan Market Index	Large Blend	0.19	800-544-8888
Vanguard Tax-Mgd Balanced	Domestic Hybrid	0.19	800-662-7447
Vanguard Tax-Mgd Cap App	Large Growth	0.19	800-662-7447
Vanguard Tax-Mgd Gr&Inc	Large Blend	0.19	800-662-7447
California Invmt S&P 500 Index	Large Blend	0.20	800-225-8778
Vanguard Tot Stk Market Index	Large Blend	0.20	800-662-7447
Vanguard Balanced Index	Domestic Hybrid	0.21	800-662-7447
Vanguard Growth Index	Large Growth	0.22	800-662-7447
Vanguard Value Index	Large Value	0.22	800-662-7447
Vanguard Extend Mkt Index	Mid-Cap Blend	0.23	800-662-7447
Vanguard Small Cap Index	Small Blend	0.24	800-662-7447
Montgomery Balanced R	Domestic Hybrid	0.25	800-572-3863
Vanguard Windsor	Large Value	0.27	800-662-7447
Vanguard LifeStrat Income	Domestic Hybrid	0.28	800-662-7447
Vanguard LifeStrat Cons Growth	Domestic Hybrid	0.29	800-662-7447
Vanguard LifeStrat Growth	Large Blend	0.29	800-662-7447
Vanguard LifeStrat Mod Growth	Domestic Hybrid	0.29	800-662-7447
Vanguard Wellesley Income	Domestic Hybrid	0.31	800-662-7447
Vanguard Wellington	Domestic Hybrid	0.31	800-662-7447
Vanguard Growth & Income	Large Value	0.36	800-662-7447
Vanguard Health Care	Specialty-Health	0.36	800-662-7447
Vanguard STAR	Domestic Hybrid	0.37	800-662-7447
Vanguard Energy	Specialty-Natural Res	0.38	800-662-7447
Vanguard Utilities Income	Specialty-Utilities	0.38	800-662-7447
Vanguard Equity-Income	Large Value	0.39	800-662-7447
California Invmt S&P MidCap	Mid-Cap Blend	0.40	800-225-8778
Galaxy II Small Co Index Ret	Small Blend	0.40	800-628-0414
Galaxy II Utility Index Ret	Specialty-Utilities	0.40	800-628-0414
T. Rowe Price Equity Index 500	Large Blend	0.40	800-638-5660
Vanguard U.S. Growth	Large Growth	0.41	800-662-7447
Vanguard Windsor II	Large Value	0.41	800-662-7447
Vanguard Morgan Growth	Large Blend	0.44	800-662-7447
Schwab 1000 Inv	Large Blend	0.46	800-435-4000
Galaxy II Large Co Index Return	Large Blend	0.47	800-628-0414
Schwab Small Cap Index Inv	Small Blend	0.49	800-435-4000
Vanguard Asset Allocation	Domestic Hybrid	0.49	800-662-7447
Dreyfus MidCap Index	Mid-Cap Blend	0.50	800-373-9387
Dreyfus S&P 500 Index	Large Blend	0.50	800-373-9387

pense ratio of .50 percent or less. A .50 percent annual expense ratio means that the mutual fund charges each investor 50 cents per $100 of account value each year to pay the expenses incurred by the fund. Therefore, an investor with $2000 in a mutual fund account would be "charged" $10 by the fund over the course of the year. Inasmuch as annual expense ratios occur every year, it behooves the thrifty investor to consider choosing mutual funds with low expense ratios.

Many of the funds in Table 5.17 belong to The Vanguard Group. Vanguard mutual funds are well-known for having the lowest expense ratios in the mutual fund universe. However, a few funds from other fund families made it into the "Thrifty Group." Many of them are index funds, meaning that they track (or mimic) a preselected market index. The most common index to mimic is overwhelmingly the Standard & Poor's 500 Index. Growth in both the number of index funds and the assets invested in index funds (particularly those based upon the S&P 500) may represent a recognition of the merits of indexing: low turnover ratios, superior tax efficiency, and lower than average expense ratios. However, the unusually robust performance of the S&P 500 Index in recent years is more likely the reason for burgeoning index fund assets. As such, newcomers to investing (particularly index fund investing) may be disappointed were the broad-based, large-cap market to experience a period similar to 1992–1994 (refer back to Table 5.15). During that three-year period the S&P 500 averaged only 6.3 percent per year.

Moreover, the S&P 500 Index does not offer any diversification in non-U.S. equities, small-cap U.S. equities, bonds, or cash. Understandably, this focus has led to its stunning returns in recent years. Nevertheless, if large-cap U.S. equities stumble, managers of funds that mirror the S&P 500 have no place to hide—they must stay the course in large-cap U.S. equities. In the long run this is a very defensible investment position. In the shorter run it may be difficult to defend, particularly to investors who have developed unreasonable performance expectations based upon only the most recent past. Thrifty investors focus also on the "nonperformance" related virtues of indexing, such as superior tax efficiency. This may encourage thoughtful placement of investment assets, such as *choosing index funds for*

TABLE 5.18 Performance Data for Thrifty Stock Funds with Low Expense Ratios

Fund Name (Ranked by Expense Ratio from Lowest to Highest)	3 Year Average Return 1997-99	5 Year Average Return 1997-99	10 Year Average Return 1997-99	5 Year Tax Efficiency (100=best)	Net Assets ($ Million)	Manager Tenure (Years)	Minimum Initial Purchase	Minimum IRA Purchase	Minimum AIP Purchase
SSgA S&P 500 Index	27.4	28.3	-	89.6	2,930	5	$10,000	$250	$1,000
Orbitex Focus 30 Dow	22.9	24.5	-	91.8	20	9	$1,000	$500	$1,000
Vanguard 500 Index	27.5	28.5	18.1	96.5	98,196	13	$3,000	$1,000	$3,000
Fidelity Spartan Market Index	27.3	28.2	-	95.4	9,813	3	$10,000	$500	$10,000
Vanguard Tax-Mgd Balanced	16.3	17.1	-	96.7	308	5	$10,000	-	$10,000
Vanguard Tax-Mgd Cap App	29.6	28.7	-	99.0	2,113	6	$10,000	-	$10,000
Vanguard Tax-Mgd Gr&Inc	27.6	28.6	-	97.3	2,073	6	$10,000	-	$10,000
California Invmt S&P 500 Index	27.5	28.4	-	93.4	146	8	$5,000	$0	$5,000
Vanguard Tot Stk Mkt Index	26.0	26.8	-	96.0	16,312	8	$3,000	$1,000	$3,000
Vanguard Balanced Index	17.9	19.1	-	90.2	2,903	6	$3,000	$1,000	$3,000
Vanguard Growth Index	35.7	33.7	-	97.2	13,610	8	$3,000	$1,000	$3,000
Vanguard Value Index	18.8	22.8	-	89.0	3,272	8	$3,000	$1,000	$3,000
Vanguard Extend Mkt Index	23.2	24.1	16.3	88.8	740	13	$3,000	$1,000	$3,000
Vanguard Small Cap Index	14.3	17.8	14.2	87.2	3,179	11	$3,000	$1,000	$3,000
Montgomery Balanced R	12.6	16.4	-	75.7	69	1	$1,000	$1,000	$1,000
Vanguard Windsor	11.1	17.7	13.0	77.2	16,867	2	$3,000	$1,000	$3,000
Vanguard LifeStrat Income	10.0	12.0	-	78.5	560	6	$3,000	$1,000	$3,000
Vanguard LifeStrat Cons Growth	13.4	14.9	-	84.4	1,714	6	$3,000	$1,000	$3,000
Vanguard LifeStrat Growth	20.3	21.0	-	92.3	2,938	6	$3,000	$1,000	$3,000
Vanguard LifeStrat Mod Growth	16.9	18.2	-	89.4	3,300	6	$3,000	$1,000	$3,000
Vanguard Wellesley Income	8.8	12.7	10.6	70.9	7,314	16	$3,000	$1,000	$3,000
Vanguard Wellington	13.0	17.4	12.6	82.3	25,846	6	$3,000	$1,000	$3,000
Vanguard Growth & Income	28.4	28.8	18.5	87.7	8,022	8	$3,000	$1,000	$3,000
Vanguard Health Care	24.7	27.8	21.5	93.0	10,634	16	$10,000	$1,000	$3,000
Vanguard STAR	13.4	16.9	12.3	81.8	8,057	15	$1,000	$1,000	$1,000
Vanguard Energy	3.4	13.2	9.3	88.8	1,019	16	$3,000	$1,000	$3,000
Vanguard Utilities Income	13.9	15.9	-	82.9	880	4	$3,000	$1,000	$3,000
Vanguard Equity-Income	15.4	19.9	12.9	87.6	3,023	5	$3,000	$1,000	$3,000

TABLE 5.18 (Continued)

Fund Name (Ranked by Expense Ratio from Lowest to Highest)	3 Year Average Return 1997-99	5 Year Average Return 1997-99	10 Year Average Return 1997-99	5 Year Tax Efficiency (100=best)	Net Assets ($ Million)	Manager Tenure (Years)	Minimum Initial Purchase	Minimum IRA Purchase	Minimum AIP Purchase
California Invmt S&P MidCap	21.5	22.7	-	84.7	49	8	$5,000	$0	$5,000
Galaxy II Small Co Index Ret	10.7	16.6	-	77.1	273	2	$2,500	$500	$0
Galaxy II Utility Index Ret	10.1	13.6	-	79.5	50	2	$2,500	$500	$0
T. Rowe Price Equity Index 500	27.2	28.2	-	95.8	4,760	10	$2,500	$1,000	$1,000
Vanguard U.S. Growth	29.2	30.3	19.8	93.6	17,801	9	$3,000	$1,000	$3,000
Vanguard Windsor II	13.2	20.1	13.8	84.6	29,034	10	$3,000	$1,000	$3,000
Vanguard Morgan Growth	29.0	29.2	18.1	84.9	4,541	8	$3,000	$1,000	$3,000
Schwab 1000 Inv	26.6	27.5	-	98.2	4,900	5	$1,000	$500	$1,000
Galaxy II Large Co Index Ret	27.0	28.1	-	94.9	1,047	2	$2,500	$500	$0
Schwab Small Cap Index Inv	14.6	17.3	-	97.6	495	5	$1,000	$500	$1,000
Vanguard Asset Allocation	18.9	21.4	14.8	84.5	8,589	12	$3,000	$1,000	$3,000
Dreyfus MidCap Index	21.1	22.4	-	83.2	323	3	$2,500	$750	$100
Dreyfus S&P 500 Index	26.9	27.9	17.5	96.1	3,057	4	$2,500	$750	$100

regular (i.e., non-tax-deferred) accounts due to their superior tax efficiency.

Finally, Table 5.18 provides additional information (historical performance data, minimum investment requirements, etc.) about the 41 stock mutual funds with low expense ratios.

CHAPTER 6

Mutual Fund Portfolios

First off, there is no perfect portfolio of mutual funds. "Model portfolios" only attempt to illustrate the importance of balancing your investment dollars among different equity styles and between U.S. and non-U.S. stocks. For example, a lump sum commitment of $4500 could create the three-fund mutual fund portfolio shown in Table 6.1. The minimum initial investment requirement for both the Fasciano and the Columbia International Stock funds is $1000. Strong American Utilities requires a $2500 lump sum to open an account.

The "model" three-fund portfolio demonstrates several key issues. First, the average return over the five-year period was higher than the average return of two out of the three funds that comprise the portfolio. Second, the standard deviation of return over the five-year period was dramatically lower for the three-fund portfolio. Indeed, the objective of a balanced portfolio is to provide return that equals or exceeds any of the portfolio's individual components *while at the same time* reducing the standard deviation of return over time (e.g., risk). Equal or better return at lower risk. That's what investment balance attempts to achieve.

What about monthly investing, or what's been referred to as dollar-cost averaging? Problem: Some investors may not have $4500 available at one time to invest. Solution: The same portfolio of three funds can be started with a commitment of $150 per month. An account in each separate fund can be started with an automatic monthly investment of at least $50. The thrifty investor's dream! As seen in Table 6.2, the benefits of portfolio balance also apply to DCA.

TABLE 6.1   Performance Figures for Lump Sum Investment

							Total Annual Percentage Return	
Equity Style Category	Mutual Fund	1995	1996	1997	1998	1999	5 Year Average Return	5 Year Standard Deviation
Large Cap	Strong American Utilities	37.0	8.4	27.6	20.4	0.6	18.0	13.0
Small Cap	Fasciano	31.1	26.5	21.5	7.2	6.2	18.1	10.1
Non-U.S. Stock	Columbia International Stock	5.2	16.5	11.5	12.8	57.9	19.5	18.9
Mutual Fund Portfolio	All Three Funds Combined	24.4	17.2	20.1	13.4	21.6	18.5	3.8

The five-year average return for the three-fund mutual fund portfolio was second only to the average return of the Columbia International Stock fund, but had the lowest standard deviation of return. In fact, the risk level of the three-fund portfolio was one-fifth that of the Columbia International Stock fund. Whether by lump sum investing or monthly investing, the benefit of investment balance generally applies; namely, less volatile year-to-year returns. Moreover, the average return of a balanced portfolio

TABLE 6.2   Performance Figures for Monthly Investing (DCA)

							Total Annual Percentage Return	
Equity Style Category	Mutual Fund	1995	1996	1997	1998	1999	5 Year Average Return	5 Year Standard Deviation
Large Cap	Strong American Utilities	41.0	14.4	37.4	27.9	-0.8	15.0	15.5
Small Cap	Fasciano	27.1	26.1	31.5	2.9	13.9	13.6	10.5
Non-U.S. Stock	Columbia International Stock	15.3	15.8	3.7	14.2	89.6	26.5	31.3
Mutual Fund Portfolio	All Three Funds Combined	27.7	18.7	23.9	14.9	32.6	18.7	6.3

is often higher than some (or all) of the funds that make up the portfolio.

> The key to creating a balanced mutual fund portfolio is combining funds that behave differently over time. Typically, funds that focus on large-cap stocks behave differently than funds that invest in small stocks. Funds that invest primarily in U.S. stock generally have year-to-year returns that are different from non-U.S. stock funds.

The unpredictable performance spotlight is evident in the variability of year-to-year performance for each individual mutual fund (see Tables 6.1 and 6.2). In any given year at least one fund had a very good year, sometimes two funds did well. Not very often do all three funds have banner years at the same time. By combining funds that perform countercyclically (i.e., have good performance at different times), the portfolio effect is created—and it is good.

> Achieving investment balance requires the intelligent integration of *diverse* investments.

On the following pages are examples of specific mutual fund portfolios. Each portfolio is designed around two rules:

1. diversify within the equity style box
2. diversify between U.S. and non-U.S. stocks

Following these two simple rules creates balanced investment portfolios. *No attempt will be made to include every one of the funds in the Frugal Forty* in these example portfolios. Rather, these represent "portfolio prototypes." They are templates that can guide your efforts to create a balanced portfolio. Yes, the actual funds plugged into any given portfolio are important, but the main point is, *to achieve investment balance, the two rules noted above need to be followed.*

The example portfolios include the following:

- Ultra Affordable Portfolio
- Low-Risk Portfolio

- Below-Average-Risk Portfolio
- Average-Risk Portfolio
- Above-Average-Risk Portfolio
- High-Risk Portfolio

In addition to the five multifund portfolios noted above, several individual mutual funds among the Frugal Forty are balanced by their very design. These funds will be referred to as:

"Single Fund Portfolios"

These somewhat unique "Single Fund Portfolios" will be discussed separately. First, an overview of each balanced portfolio. Then each one will be examined in detail. Table 6.3 is provided to refresh your memory regarding the location of each Frugal Forty mutual fund within the equity style box.

Table 6.4 presents an overview of the five example portfolios. In an attempt to keep the monthly investment requirement to a minimum (a thrifty thing), each portfolio was limited to three funds. If your finances allow for a portfolio of four or five funds—have at it.

Table 6.5 reports the average return (either as a lump sum investment or a monthly DCA approach) for each portfolio over the five-year period from 1995 to 1999. Historical performance figures for a period longer than five years would be desirable. However, many mutual funds have not been around for 10 years, making long-term analysis using actual mutual funds a bit challenging. The 30-year performance data reported in Table 5.15 resolves this dilemma. It clearly illustrates the benefits of balancing investments between large stocks, small/medium stocks, and non-U.S. stocks. The benefits—enhanced return and reduced risk—are experienced over the long run.

As is often the case in investing, you will notice in Table 6.5 that at higher risk levels the returns are usually higher. While not always true, this axiom of investing seems to generally apply in these examples of balanced mutual fund portfolios. It's also worth noting in the same table that the annualized returns from monthly investing (or DCA) are superior to those achieved by lump sum investing in four out of six portfolios.

Remember . . .

All the funds in the Frugal Forty can be started with an automated monthly investment of at least $50.

Let's now look more closely at the first portfolio, which has
the Ultra Thrifty Investor in mind. The funds that comprise this
portfolio each have very low monthly investment requirements.
As shown in Tables 6.6a and 6.6b, the Ultra Affordable Portfolio is
made up of three funds: *Homestead Value, Invesco European,* and

TABLE 6.3   The Frugal Forty Mutual Funds—Grouped by Equity Style

White = Lower Risk   **Light Gray = Moderate Risk**   **Dark Gray = Higher Risk**

Large-Cap Value	Large-Cap Blend	Large-Cap Growth

Excelsior Value & Restructuring
Invesco Total Return
Legg Mason Value Prime
Preferred Asset Allocation
Preferred Value
T. Rowe Price Equity-Income
Safeco Equity No-Load
Strong American Utilities
Strong Asset Allocation
USAA Growth & Income
 	
Preferred International
	Fremont Global
	T. Rowe Price Blue Chip Growth
	T. Rowe Price Equity Index 500
	T. Rowe Price Personal
	   Strategy Growth
	T. Rowe Price Spectrum Growth
	
	***T. Rowe Price International
	Stock***
		Alleghany/Montag & Caldwell
		   Growth
		Invesco Health Sciences
		Spectra
		Strong Total Return
		T. Rowe Price Science & Tech
		Strong Growth
		
		***Columbia International Stock
		Invesco European
		T. Rowe Price European
		Stock***

Mid-Cap Value	Mid-Cap Blend	Mid-Cap Growth
Columbia Real Estate Equity Homestead Value Legg Mason Total Return Prime Strong Opportunity T. Rowe Price Value	Ariel Appreciation Legg Mason Special Investment Prime	Invesco Dynamics T. Rowe Price Mid-Cap Growth
Small-Cap Value	Small-Cap Blend	Small-Cap Growth
Eclipse Small Cap Value	T. Rowe Price Small Cap Stock	Fasciano Fremont U.S. Micro-Cap ***T. Rowe Price International Discovery***

(Non-U.S. stock funds in **bold** *italicized* print)

Data Source: Morningstar Principia Pro Plus, January 2000

TABLE 6.4   Balanced Portfolios of Mutual Funds

Portfolio	Mutual Funds in Portfolio	Investment Style	Monthly Investment Requirement
Ultra Affordable Portfolio	Spectra	Large Growth	$25
	Homestead Value	Mid-Cap Value	$1
	Invesco European	Large Non-U.S.	$50
Low Risk Portfolio	T. Rowe Price Equity Income	Large Value	$50
	Fasciano	Small Blend	$50
	Columbia International Stock	Large Non-U.S.	$50
Below Average Risk Portfolio	T. Rowe Price Equity Index 500	Large Blend	$50
	Strong Opportunity	Mid-Cap Value	$50
	T. Rowe Price European	Large Non-U.S.	$50
Average Risk Portfolio	Legg Mason Value Prime	Large Value	$50
	Invesco Dynamics	Mid-Cap Growth	$50
	T. Rowe Price International Stock	Large Non-U.S.	$50
Above Average Risk Portfolio	Alleghany/Montag & Caldwell Growth N	Large Growth	$50
	Legg Mason Special Invest Prime	Mid Cap Blend	$50
	Preferred International	Large Non-U.S.	$50
High Risk Portfolio	T. Rowe Price Science & Tech	Large Growth	$50
	Fremont U.S. Micro Cap	Small Growth	$50
	T. Rowe Price Intl Discovery	Small Non-U.S.	$50

Spectra. The Homestead Value fund can be started with an automatic monthly investment of as little as $1. Spectra requires at least $25 to open an account. Invesco European is the "expensive" one of the group with a monthly requirement of at least $50. However, Invesco allows UTMA (Uniform Transfers to Minor's Act) ac-

TABLE 6.5 Historical Performance of Balanced Portfolios of Mutual Funds, 1995–1999

Portfolio	LUMP SUM 5 Year Average % Return	DCA 5 Year Average % Return
Ultra Affordable Portfolio	29.3	29.4
Low Risk Portfolio	18.7	18.4
Below Average Risk Portfolio	24.5	24.0
Average Risk Portfolio	30.1	31.5
Above Average Risk Portfolio	24.9	25.0
High Risk Portfolio	35.2	41.6

counts to be started with an automated monthly investment of at least $25. (See Chapter 3 for information about UTMA accounts.)

The Ultra Affordable Portfolio can (in theory) be started for as little as $76 per month ($50 for Invesco European, $25 for Spectra, and $1 for Homestead Value). A more logical allocation might be $100 per month, with $25 going to Spectra and Homestead Value and $50 to Invesco European. Even still, $100 per month might be too much for some people. In that case, one option is to choose only Homestead Value and invest whatever you can each month. Later, as finances permit, add Spectra and/or Invesco European (or any other Frugal Forty fund) to your portfolio. *The important thing here is to get started.* If you can't afford to create the whole portfolio, don't sell the farm. *Do what you can with your current resources.* You may find that with careful planning, you can squeeze a few more dollars out of your monthly budget, allowing you to start all three funds.

Table 6.6c summarizes the performance of the Ultra Affordable Portfolio over the five-year period from 1995 to 1999. In this particular portfolio (and over this particular five-year period) monthly investing actually generated a slightly higher average annual return than did a lump sum investment.

Now, we move on to five portfolios ranging from low risk to high risk. Over the five-year period from 1995 to 1999 each portfolio provided impressive returns. The average annual return of

TABLE 6.6a   Ultra Affordable Mutual Fund Portfolio

Mutual Fund	Minimum Automatic Monthly Investment Requirement	5 Year Average Returns (1995-99)	
		LUMP SUM	**DCA**
Homestead Value	$1	16.0%	9.7%
Invesco European	$50	26.7	29.1
Spectra	$25	41.1	43.5
3 Fund Portfolio	**$100[a]**	**29.3[b]**	**29.4[b]**

Funds and Phone Numbers:

Homestead	1-800-258-3030
Invesco	1-800-525-8085
Spectra	1-800-711-6141

[a] $50 per month into Invesco European, $25 per month into both Homestead Value and Spectra.

[b] Performance figures assume equal investments into each fund.

the High-Risk Portfolio was almost twice that of the Low-Risk Portfolio. But it also had a standard deviation of return 2.3 times greater than the Low-Risk Portfolio. Higher return at higher risk. A common theme.

Tables 6.7 through 6.11 summarize the five-year performance of (in order) the following balanced mutual fund portfolios:

- Low Risk
- Below Average Risk
- Average Risk
- Above Average Risk
- High Risk

TABLE 6.6b   Style Box Location of Funds in Ultra Affordable Mutual Fund Portfolio

Large-Cap Value	Large-Cap Blend	Large-Cap Growth *Spectra Invesco European*
Mid-Cap Value *Homestead Value*	Mid-Cap Blend	Mid-Cap Growth
Small-Cap Value	Small-Cap Blend	Small-Cap Growth

Fund Descriptions:

Homestead Value: Mid-cap value fund. Seeks out undervalued or overlooked stocks. May invest up to 10% of assets in non-U.S. stock.

Invesco European: Large-cap growth fund. Invests in companies in England, France, Germany, Belgium, Italy, the Netherlands, Switzerland, Denmark, Sweden, Norway, Finland, and Spain.

Spectra: Large-cap growth fund. Invests in companies experiencing change. May invest up to 20% of assets in non-U.S. stock. Part of the Alger family of mutual funds.

Let's take a quick break and review what we now know about balanced mutual fund portfolios.

> Compared to investing in just one mutual fund, a balanced portfolio of three funds can substantially reduce risk (i.e., standard deviation of return) without sacrificing overall return.

This was particularly noticeable in the Ultra Affordable and Low-Risk Portfolios. The standard deviation of return over the five-year period from 1995 to 1999 for the Ultra Affordable Port-

TABLE 6.6c   Ultra Affordable Mutual Fund Portfolio Performance History

5 Year Performance History

Mutual Fund	Total % Return					5 Year Average Return (%)	Standard Dev. of Return
	1995	1996	1997	1998	1999		
LUMP SUM INVESTMENT ANNUAL RETURNS							
Spectra	47.7	19.4	24.6	48.0	72.0	41.1	18.9
Homestead Value	33.8	17.9	26.7	8.3	-3.2	16.0	13.1
Invesco European	19.2	29.7	15.2	32.9	38.0	26.7	8.5
3 Fund Portfolio	**33.1**	**22.2**	**22.0**	**29.5**	**35.3**	**29.3**	**5.5**
MONTHLY INVESTING ANNUAL RETURNS							
Spectra	32.0	13.9	18.9	63.6	100.2	43.5	32.3
Homestead Value	30.5	18.0	22.4	7.0	-11.5	9.7	14.5
Invesco European	17.4	31.2	13.1	16.1	81.4	29.1	25.6
3 Fund Portfolio	**26.6**	**21.0**	**18.1**	**28.3**	**54.2**	**29.4**	**12.8**

Underlined return figures represent DCA returns equal to or greater than LUMP SUM returns.

folio was 5.5 percent (lump sum). The standard deviations of return for the individual funds comprising the portfolio were 18.9, 13.1, and 8.5 percent. For monthly investing, the portfolio standard deviation was 12.8 percent, compared to 32.3, 14.5, and 25.6 percent for each separate fund. It's clear that combining dissimilar funds significantly reduces the volatility in year-to-year returns—the portfolio effect.

TABLE 6.7a   Low-Risk Mutual Fund Portfolio

Mutual Fund	Minimum Automatic Monthly Investment Requirement	5 Year Average Returns (1995-99)	
		LUMP SUM	**DCA**
T. Rowe Price Equity Income	$50	18.6%	13.9%
Fasciano	$50	18.1	13.6
Columbia International Stock	$50	19.5	26.5
3 Fund Portfolio	**$150**	**18.7%**	**18.4%**

Funds and Phone Numbers:

T. Rowe Price	1-800-638-5660
Fasciano	1-800-848-6050
Columbia	1-800-547-1707

Using *lump sum* results we observe that the Ultra Affordable Portfolio had:

  71 percent less risk and 29 percent less return than Spectra
  58 percent less risk and 83 percent *more* return than Homestead Value
  35 percent less risk and 10 percent *more* return than Invesco European

Using *monthly investing* results the Ultra Affordable Portfolio had:

  60 percent less risk and 32 percent less return than Spectra
  12 percent less risk and 203 percent *more* return than Homestead Value
  50 percent less risk and 1 percent *more* return than Invesco European

TABLE 6.7b   Style Box Location of Funds in Low-Risk Mutual Fund Portfolio

Large-Cap Value	Large-Cap Blend	Large-Cap Growth
T. Rowe Price Equity Income		*Columbia International Stock*
Mid-Cap Value	Mid-Cap Blend	Mid-Cap Growth
Small-Cap Value	Small-Cap Blend	Small-Cap Growth *Fasciano*

Fund Descriptions:

T. Rowe Price Equity Income: Large-cap value fund. Invests at least 65% of assets in stocks that pay dividends. The fund also can invest in bonds and up to 25% of assets in non-U.S. stocks.

Fasciano: Small-cap growth fund. Invests in conservatively managed companies with market capitalizations of $1 billion or less.

Columbia International Stock: Large-cap growth fund. Normally invests 65% of assets in established companies in at least three countries outside the U.S. May invest in companies anywhere in the world, and can invest up to 35% of assets in U.S. stock.

For each of the three funds, the "portfolio effect" *reduced* year-to-year volatility of return (i.e., risk) and for two out of three funds *enhanced* the five-year average return. Results of a similar magnitude were observed in the Low-Risk Portfolio as well. In fact, a portfolio effect is noticeable in all the portfolios, though not as profound as in the Ultra Affordable and Low-Risk Portfolios. Interestingly, the High-Risk Portfolio was least benefited by the "portfolio effect" among the six portfolios being considered. However, as shown in Table 6.2, monthly investing (DCA) produced higher five-year average returns among each of the funds in the High-Risk Portfolio (and the portfolio itself).

TABLE 6.7c   Low-Risk Mutual Fund Portfolio Performance History

5 Year Performance History

Mutual Fund	Total % Return					5 Year Average Return (%)	Standard Dev. of Return
	1995	1996	1997	1998	1999		
LUMP SUM INVESTMENT ANNUAL RETURNS							
T. Rowe Price Equity Income	33.4	20.4	28.8	9.2	3.8	18.6	11.2
Fasciano	31.1	26.5	21.5	7.2	6.2	18.1	10.1
Columbia International Stock	5.2	16.5	11.5	12.8	57.9	19.5	18.9
3 Fund Portfolio	**23.2**	**21.2**	**20.6**	**9.7**	**22.6**	**18.7**	**5.0**
MONTHLY INVESTING ANNUAL RETURNS							
T. Rowe Price Equity-Income	33.1	23.1	29.0	10.7	-1.2	13.9	12.6
Fasciano	27.1	26.1	31.5	2.9	13.9	13.6	10.5
Columbia International Stock	15.3	15.8	3.7	14.2	89.6	26.5	31.3
3 Fund Portfolio	**25.1**	**21.6**	**21.2**	**9.2**	**32.5**	**18.4**	**7.5**

Underlined return figures represent DCA returns equal to or greater than LUMP SUM returns.

A "portfolio effect" of reduced risk and enhanced return occurs through intelligent integration of diverse investments, or in these examples, different mutual funds. Among highly volatile (i.e., high-risk) mutual funds, monthly investing may serve to enhance average returns, though may not reduce volatility of year-to-year returns.

Now, on to the *single fund portfolios*. Some mutual funds are designed with the concept of balance in mind. In fact, such mu-

TABLE 6.8a Below-Average Risk Mutual Fund Portfolio

Mutual Fund	Minimum Automatic Monthly Investment Requirement	5 Year Average Returns (1995–99)	
		LUMP SUM	DCA
T. Rowe Price Equity Index 500	$50	28.2%	26.5%
Strong Opportunity	$50	23.4%	23.9%
T. Rowe Price European	$50	22.0%	21.6%
3 Fund Portfolio	**$150**	**24.5%**	**24.0%**

Funds and Phone Numbers:

T. Rowe Price   1-800-638-5660

Strong   1-800-368-1030

tual funds are often referred to as "balanced funds." Balanced funds typically divide their portfolio holdings between U.S. stock, non-U.S. stock, and bonds.

This book hasn't (and won't) talk too much about bonds. Suffice it to say that bonds are corporate and government forms of debt. A person who purchases a bond is lending money to the issuer of the bond. For example, if you buy a bond issued by Kodak you are lending money to Kodak. In turn, Kodak promises (1) they will pay you interest each year, and (2) after the bond expires, you will receive the face value of the bond—which is $1000. No matter what price you may have purchased the bond at, you will receive $1000 if you own the bond when it matures (i.e., expires). Long-term bonds are generally 30 years in length, but shorter length bonds also exist.

TABLE 6.8b   Style Box Location of Funds in Below-Average Risk Mutual Fund Portfolio

Large-Cap Value	Large-Cap Blend	Large-Cap Growth
	T. Rowe Price Equity Index 500	*T. Rowe Price European Stock*
Mid-Cap Value	Mid-Cap Blend	Mid-Cap Growth
Strong Opportunity		
Small-Cap Value	Small-Cap Blend	Small-Cap Growth

Fund Descriptions:

T. Rowe Price Equity Index: Large-cap blend fund. Replicates the holdings and performance of the Standard & Poor's 500 Index.

Strong Opportunity: Mid-cap value fund. Invests at least 70% of assets in U.S. stock. May invest up to 30% of assets in U.S. bonds and 25% of assets in non-U.S. stock.

T. Rowe Price European Stock: Large-cap growth fund.   Invests at least 65% of assets in stocks from at least five European countries. .

Corporate bonds, and government bonds, have a fixed rate of interest. The riskier the company, the higher the rate of interest they will have to pay due to greater business risk. Bonds issued by companies in financial difficulty often offer very high interest rates (due to the greater risk accepted by the buyer of the bond). Such bonds are referred to as "high yield" bonds, or "junk" bonds.

Why commingle stock and bonds in a mutual fund or portfolio of funds? The short answer is *balance*. The annual returns of the bond market do not generally move in sync with the stock market, so an investment in both markets may smooth out the overall return of an investor's portfolio. (Bonds do not refer to

TABLE 6.8c   Below-Average Risk Mutual Fund Portfolio Performance History

5 Year Performance History

Mutual Fund	Total % Return 1995	1996	1997	1998	1999	5 Year Average Return (%)	Standard Dev. of Return
LUMP SUM INVESTMENT ANNUAL RETURNS							
T. Rowe Price Equity Index 500	37.2	22.7	32.9	28.3	20.6	28.2	6.2
Strong Opportunity	27.3	18.1	23.5	15.5	33.4	23.4	6.4
T. Rowe Price European	21.9	25.9	17.0	25.8	19.7	22.0	3.5
3 Fund Portfolio	**28.8**	**22.2**	**24.4**	**23.0**	**24.3**	**24.5**	**2.3**
MONTHLY INVESTING ANNUAL RETURNS							
T. Rowe Price Equity Index 500	34.2	_25.0_	29.0	_32.1_	_24.5_	26.5	3.8
Strong Opportunity	_27.7_	_20.7_	_23.8_	15.8	_38.4_	_23.9_	7.6
T. Rowe Price European	21.2	_27.8_	_17.9_	17.9	_37.4_	21.6	7.4
3 Fund Portfolio	**27.7**	**_24.5_**	**23.6**	**21.9**	**_33.4_**	**24.0**	**4.1**

Underlined return figures represent DCA returns equal to or greater than LUMP SUM returns.

U.S. savings bonds, but rather long-term U.S. government and corporate bonds.)

The correlation between the year-to-year returns of large U.S. stocks and bonds is about 40 percent. For small U.S. stock, the correlation with U.S. bonds is about 20 percent. Both of those correlations are fairly low. For comparison, the correlation between the year-to-year returns of large U.S. stock and small U.S. stock is about 80 percent. In other words, stock returns (large and small) behave with similarity about 80 percent of the time.

TABLE 6.9a   Average-Risk Mutual Fund Portfolio

Mutual Fund	Minimum Automatic Monthly Investment Requirement	5 Year Average Returns (1995-99)	
		LUMP SUM	**DCA**
Legg Mason Value Prime	$50	38.0%	37.0%
Invesco Dynamics	$50	33.1	36.6
T. Rowe Price International Stock	$50	15.7	18.7
3 Fund Portfolio	**$150**	**30.1**	**31.5**

Funds and Phone Numbers:

Legg Mason	1-800-577-8589
Invesco	1-800-525-8085
T. Rowe Price	1-800-638-5660

Clearly, bonds march to a drummer different than the drummer for stocks. Such differences are very useful if portfolio balance is the goal. Therefore, combining stocks and bonds is one common approach in creating portfolio balance.

One drawback of bonds is their relatively poor performance relative to stocks, as shown in Table 6.12. In recent years, U.S. stocks (both large and small) have dramatically outperformed U.S. bonds. Notice also that bonds have years with negative return. In fact, during the nineties bonds experienced two years with a negative return compared to only one year for large stocks (at least as measured by the S&P 500). The year-to-year returns are more volatile than many people realize, and the returns are significantly lower. So, a small dose of bonds in a portfolio goes a long way!

Now, if the stock market were to suffer several bad years in a row, a bond return of 7 or 8 percent per year would look pretty attractive. You have to make your own call here. If you are a

TABLE 6.9b   Style Box Location of Funds in Average-Risk Mutual Fund Portfolio

Large-Cap Value *Legg Mason Value Prime*	Large-Cap Blend *T. Rowe Price International Stock*	Large-Cap Growth
Mid-Cap Value	Mid-Cap Blend	Mid-Cap Growth *Invesco Dynamics*
Small-Cap Value	Small-Cap Blend	Small-Cap Growth

Fund Descriptions:

Legg Mason Value Prime: Large-cap value fund. Invests primarily in U.S. stocks that are undervalued. May invest up to 25% of assets in non-U.S. stocks and 25% in bonds.

Invesco Dynamics: Invests in the stock of U.S. companies. Short-term factors are emphasized in the stock selection. May invest up to 25% of assets in non-U.S. stock.

T. Rowe Price International Stock: Large-cap blend fund. Normally invests at least 65% of assets in non-U.S. stock with the balance invested in non-U.S. preferred stock or bonds. Invests in both industrialized and developing nations.

really conservative person with a relatively short investment horizon (less than five years), you'll probably want some bonds in your investment portfolio. If you're an aggressive, fairly young (whatever "young" is?) investor with a long-term investment horizon, you probably won't need to consider bonds, or if you do, only in small doses.

For those who may want (or need) to consider adding a bond fund to their investment portfolio, Table 6.13 lists five bond funds that can be started for a $50 monthly investment. They are aptly named *The Frugal Five Bond Funds*. They are offered by mutual fund families you are already familiar with.

Tables 6.14a, 6.14b, and 6.14c provide information regarding Single Fund "Balanced Portfolios." The words *balanced portfolios* are in quotes because a balanced portfolio typically suggests a heterogenous group of items (e.g., various pictures, different rocks, collection of stamps, variety of stocks, different

TABLE 6.9c Average-Risk Mutual Fund Portfolio Performance History

5 Year Performance History

Mutual Fund	Total % Return					5 Year Average Return (%)	Standard Dev. of Return
	1995	1996	1997	1998	1999		
LUMP SUM INVESTMENT ANNUAL RETURNS							
Legg Mason Value Prime	40.8	38.4	37.1	48.0	26.7	38.0	6.9
Invesco Dynamics	37.6	15.3	24.5	23.3	71.8	33.1	20.0
T. Rowe Price Intl Stock	11.4	16.0	2.7	16.1	34.6	15.7	10.4
3 Fund Portfolio	**29.9**	**23.2**	**21.1**	**28.6**	**44.1**	**30.1**	**8.1**
MONTHLY INVESTING ANNUAL RETURNS							
Legg Mason Value Prime	39.7	45.0	27.6	57.1	22.9	37.0	12.2
Invesco Dynamics	36.2	12.8	29.7	28.6	95.6	36.6	28.6
T. Rowe Price Intl Stock	15.7	15.0	-2.7	13.5	55.5	18.7	19.3
3 Fund Portfolio	**30.4**	**24.0**	**17.9**	**32.7**	**57.2**	**31.5**	**13.4**

Underlined return figures represent DCA returns equal to or greater than LUMP SUM returns.

types of bonds, dissimilar mutual funds, etc.). Hence, to refer to a single mutual fund as a balanced portfolio is somewhat odd, because most mutual funds typically focus on a certain type of investment asset, such as large U.S. stocks, small U.S. stocks, non-U.S. stocks, and so on.

Nevertheless, because of their design, balanced mutual funds can accurately be thought of as a *balanced portfolio* because they integrate into one fund the various investment assets that create balance, namely U.S. stock, non-U.S. stock, and bonds. Where balanced funds may fall short of "true" balance is in the area of small and medium stocks. Occasionally, balanced funds are also underweighted in the area of non-U.S. stocks.

TABLE 6.10a   Above-Average Risk Mutual Fund Portfolio

Mutual Fund	Minimum Automatic Monthly Investment Requirement	5 Year Average Returns (1995-99)	
		LUMP SUM	**DCA**
Alleghany/Montage & Caldwell Growth N	$50	31.4%	29.1%
Legg Mason Special Investment Prime	$50	26.3	27.7
Preferred International	$50	15.1	17.3
3 Fund Portfolio	**$150**	**24.9**	**25.0**

Funds and Phone Numbers:

Alleghany/Montag & Caldwell   1-800-992-8151

Legg Mason   1-800-577-8589

Preferred   1-800-662-4769

As might be expected, the year-to-year performance of "balanced" funds is fairly consistent, resulting in relatively low standard deviations of return. Individual mutual funds with a balanced approach seek to create a risk/return level of performance that simulates a balanced portfolio of three or more mutual funds.

For thrifty investors who would rather invest in a fund that does "the balance thing" for them, the Single Fund Portfolios will probably do the job. Basically, if you are able to choose only one fund (for whatever reason) you might consider one of the funds in Table 6.14a. They represent the one-size-fits-all mutual fund. Conservative, yes. Balanced, yes. Will they crank out an 85 percent return in any one year? Nope. But they won't likely experience a meltdown either.

TABLE 6.10b   Style Box Location of Funds in Above-Average Risk Mutual Fund Portfolio

Large-Cap Value	Large-Cap Blend	Large-Cap Growth
Preferred International		*Alleghany/Montag & Caldwell Growth N*
Mid-Cap Value	**Mid-Cap Blend** *Legg Mason Special Investment Prime*	**Mid-Cap Growth**
Small-Cap Value	**Small-Cap Blend**	**Small-Cap Growth**

Fund Descriptions:

Alleghany/Montag & Caldwell Growth N: Large-cap growth fund. Normally invests in common stock and convertible bonds. Purchases companies with established records and newer companies. May invest up to 30% of assets in non-U.S. stock.

Legg Mason Special Investment Prime: Mid-cap blend fund. Invests in medium to small companies that appear to be undervalued. May invest up to 20% of assets in companies involved in reorganization or restructuring.

Preferred International: Large-cap value fund. Invests at least 65% of assets in undervalued stocks in three or more non-U.S. countries. The fund may also invest in bonds.

TABLE 6.10c   Above-Average Risk Mutual Fund Portfolio Performance History

5-Year Performance History

Mutual Fund	Total % Return					5-Year Average Return (%)	Standard Dev. of Return
	1995	1996	1997	1998	1999		
LUMP SUM INVESTMENT ANNUAL RETURNS							
Alleghany/Montag & Caldwell Growth N	38.7	32.7	31.9	31.9	22.5	31.4	5.2
Legg Mason Special Investment Prime	22.5	28.7	22.1	23.3	35.5	26.3	5.1
Preferred International	9.9	17.2	6.8	10.6	32.9	15.1	9.3
3 Fund Portfolio	**23.7**	**26.1**	**20.2**	**21.7**	**30.0**	**24.9**	**3.5**
MONTHLY INVESTING ANNUAL RETURNS							
Alleghany/Montag & Caldwell Growth N	34.4	32.1	27.1	<u>36.0</u>	<u>27.2</u>	29.1	3.6
Legg Mason Special Investment Prime	20.1	27.3	<u>22.3</u>	<u>41.6</u>	<u>43.3</u>	<u>27.7</u>	9.7
Preferred International	<u>10.8</u>	<u>18.0</u>	-0.5	4.0	<u>43.8</u>	<u>17.3</u>	15.6
3 Fund Portfolio	**21.6**	**25.7**	**16.1**	**<u>26.9</u>**	**<u>38.0</u>**	**<u>25.0</u>**	**7.2**

<u>Underlined return figures</u> represent DCA returns equal to or greater than LUMP SUM returns.

TABLE 6.11a High-Risk Mutual Fund Portfolio

Mutual Fund	Minimum Automatic Monthly Investment Requirement	5 Year Average Returns (1995-99)	
		LUMP SUM	DCA
T. Rowe Price Science & Technology	$50	38.9	43.0
Fremont U.S. Micro Cap	$50	42.1	44.3
T. Rowe Price International Discovery	$50	22.7	37.3
3 Fund Portfolio	**$150**	**35.2**	**41.6**

Funds and Phone Numbers:

T. Rowe Price Science & Technology Intl Discovery	1-800-638-5660
Fremont U.S. Micro Cap	1-800-548-4539

TABLE 6.11b   Style Box Location of Funds in High-Risk Mutual Fund Portfolio

Large-Cap Value	Large-Cap Blend	Large-Cap Growth
		T. Rowe Price Science & Technology
Mid-Cap Value	Mid-Cap Blend	Mid-Cap Growth
Small-Cap Value	Small-Cap Blend	Small-Cap Growth
		Fremont U.S. Micro Cap
		T. Rowe Price International Discovery

Fund Descriptions:

T. Rowe Price Science & Technology: Large-cap growth fund. Normally invests at least 65% of its portfolio assets in companies, U.S. and non-U.S., that develop or use scientific and technological advances. Industries include computers, software, electronics, pharmaceuticals, medical devices, telecommunications, biotechnology, waste management, chemicals, synthetic materials, defense, aerospace.

Fremont U.S. Micro Cap: Small-cap growth fund. Normally invests at least 65% of assets in U.S. companies in the smallest decile (10%). Seeks to invest in new companies that have potential for significant growth. Can invest up to 25% of assets in small, non-U.S. companies.

T. Rowe Price International Discovery: Small-cap international stock funds. Normally invests in the stock of small to medium sized companies outside the U.S. This fund seeks out companies that are rapidly growing and may invest in any type of security, whether in developed countries or not. The fund usually owns stock in at least 100 different companies in at least 10 different non-U.S. countries.

TABLE 6.11c High-Risk Mutual Fund Portfolio Performance History

5 Year Performance History

Mutual Fund	Total % Return					5 Year Average Return (%)	Standard Dev. of Return
	1995	1996	1997	1998	1999		
LUMP SUM INVESTMENT ANNUAL RETURNS							
T. Rowe Price Science & Technology	55.5	14.2	1.7	42.4	101.0	38.9	34.8
Fremont U.S. Micro Cap	54.0	48.7	7.0	2.9	129.5	42.1	45.6
T. Rowe Price International Discovery	−4.4	13.9	−5.7	6.1	155.0	22.7	61.4
3 Fund Portfolio	**35.1**	**25.6**	**0.9**	**16.9**	**126.0**	**35.2**	**44.0**
MONTHLY INVESTING ANNUAL RETURNS							
T. Rowe Price Science & Technology	51.6	12.7	−0.9	<u>64.7</u>	<u>126.8</u>	<u>43.0</u>	44.9
Fremont U.S. Micro Cap	<u>55.0</u>	42.9	5.5	<u>22.3</u>	<u>173.8</u>	<u>44.3</u>	59.4
T. Rowe Price International Discovery	<u>1.9</u>	6.7	−15.1	−2.9	<u>205.2</u>	<u>37.3</u>	83.3
3 Fund Portfolio	**<u>35.5</u>**	**20.5**	**-3.6**	**<u>27.2</u>**	**<u>168.1</u>**	**<u>41.6</u>**	**60.7**

<u>Underlined return figures</u> represent DCA returns equal to or greater than LUMP SUM returns.

TABLE 6.12 Annual Returns for U.S. Bonds and Stocks, 1990–1999

Index	1990	1991	1992	1993	1994	1995	1996	1997	1998	1999	10 Year Ave Return	10 Year Standard Deviation of Return
Government Bonds	8.7	15.3	7.2	10.7	-3.4	18.3	2.8	9.6	9.9	-2.3	7.5	6.6
Corporate Bonds	7.2	18.5	8.7	12.2	-3.9	22.2	3.3	10.2	8.5	-1.9	8.2	7.7
Standard & Poor's 500 Stock Index	-3.1	30.5	7.6	10.1	1.3	37.5	23.0	33.4	28.6	21.0	18.2	13.4
Russell 2000 Small Co. Stock Index	-19.5	46.1	18.4	18.9	-1.8	28.4	16.5	22.4	-2.6	21.3	13.4	17.5

Bond Data: Lehman Brothers Indexes

TABLE 6.13   The Frugal Five Bond Funds

Each fund can be started with $50 monthly Automatic Investment Plan (AIP)

Bond Funds	3 Yr Ave Return 1997-99	5 Yr Ave Return 1995-99	5 Yr Tax Efficiency (%)	Annual Expense Ratio (%)	Net Assets $ Million	Manager Tenure (Yrs)
Columbia High-Yield	9.1%	11.1%	62.2	0.95	77	7
Legg Mason High-Yield Prime	7.5	11.0	67.3	1.30	382	6
Strong Govt Securities Fund	5.3	7.5	64.8	0.80	1,315	6
Strong Short-Term Global Bond	5.5	7.4	60.2	0.90	45	1
T. Rowe Price Spectrum Income	6.2	9.0	66.9	0.75	2,589	2

TABLE 6.14a   Single-Fund Portfolios ("Balance" in One Fund)

Mutual Fund	Minimum Automatic Monthly Investment Requirement	5 Year Average Returns (1995–99)	
		LUMP SUM	**DCA**
Fremont Global	50	15.0%	15.0%
Invesco Total Return	50	15.3	11.2
Preferred Asset Allocation	50	18.9	15.6
Strong Asset Allocation	50	17.1	17.3
T. Rowe Price Personal Strategy Growth	50	19.1	16.4

Funds and Phone Numbers:

Fremont	1-800-548-4539
Invesco	1-800-525-8085
Preferred	1-800-662-4769
Strong	1-800-368-1030
T. Rowe Price	1-800-638-5660

TABLE 6.14b   Style Box Location of Single Fund Portfolios

Large-Cap Value	Large-Cap Blend	Large-Cap Growth
Invesco Total Return *Preferred Asset Allocation* *Strong Asset Allocation*	*Fremont Global* *T. Rowe Price Personal* *Strategy Growth*	
Mid-Cap Value	Mid-Cap Blend	Mid-Cap Growth
Small-Cap Value	Small-Cap Blend	Small-Cap Growth

Fund Descriptions:

Fremont Global: International hybrid, large-cap blend fund. Allocates fund assets among U.S. and non-U.S. stocks and bonds, real estate securities, precious metals, and cash.

Invesco Total Return: Large-cap value fund. Invests at least 30% of assets in stock and 30% in bonds. May also invest up to 25% of assets in non-U.S. stock.

Preferred Asset Allocation: Domestic hybrid, large-cap blend fund. Invests in stocks, bonds, and cash. Stocks included in the fund are generally found in the S&P 500 Index. May invest up to 10% of assets in non-U.S. stocks.

Strong Asset Allocation: Large-cap value fund. Normally invests 60% of assets in stock, 35% in bonds and 5% in cash. Up to 25% of fund assets can be invested in stock outside the U.S.

T. Rowe Price Personal Strategy Growth: Large-cap blend fund. Typically invests 80% of assets in stock and 20% in bonds or cash. May invest up to 35% of assets in non-U.S. stock.

TABLE 6.14c   Single Fund Portfolios Performance History

5 Year Performance History

Mutual Fund	Total % Return					5 Year Average Return (%)	Standard Dev. of Return
	1995	1996	1997	1998	1999		
LUMP SUM INVESTMENT ANNUAL RETURNS							
Fremont Global	19.3	14.0	9.9	10.0	22.4	15.0	5.0
Invesco Total Return	28.6	13.1	25.0	13.6	-1.4	15.3	10.6
Preferred Asset Alloc.	32.8	15.1	21.0	27.1	1.3	18.9	10.8
Strong Asset Allocation	22.0	10.5	16.7	21.4	15.5	17.1	4.2
T. Rowe Price Personal Strategy Growth	31.4	17.7	20.6	15.7	11.2	19.1	6.8
MONTHLY INVESTING ANNUAL RETURNS							
Fremont Global	20.7	14.3	6.0	11.3	32.8	15.0	9.2
Invesco Total Return	26.6	15.6	24.1	14.2	-4.0	11.2	10.7
Preferred Asset Allocation	30.5	18.6	20.3	32.9	0.2	15.6	11.6
Strong Asset Allocation	22.7	14.5	17.1	24.6	19.3	17.3	3.7
T. Rowe Price Personal Strategy Growth	30.3	21.0	20.9	16.8	13.8	16.4	5.6

Underlined return figures represent DCA returns equal to or greater than LUMP SUM returns.

CHAPTER 7

Buying Stocks Direct

Now let's look at investing in individual stocks. Mutual funds, for many investors, represent the *core* of their investment plan. Individual stocks represent an opportunity to *explore.* Just as there are differences among mutual funds (e.g., large-cap versus small-cap, value versus growth), there are important differences between stocks. There are large company stocks and small company stocks . . . and medium-sized company stocks. There are growth stocks and there are value stocks. So, the same type of criteria used to evaluate mutual funds can obviously apply to individual stocks. In fact, it's probably more accurate to think of the reverse being true—mutual fund characteristics are the *result of* the characteristics of the stocks they invest in. But because mutual funds often represent the investment core, they were discussed first in this book.

This chapter will help you identify direct stock purchase plans that can be started for $50 per month or less. The two techniques discussed here include:

Option A Purchase stock directly from the company itself. A comprehensive web site for information about Direct Stock Purchase Plans is at www.netstockdirect.com

Option B Purchase stock through an Internet service known as ShareBuilder.com. Their site is at www.sharebuilder.com

Let's discuss direct stock purchase plans first, and specifically Option A, which involves purchasing stock directly from a company. But first, a bit of background regarding how stock is typically purchased.

Investing in stock typically requires working through a broker, whether it be a full-service broker (Merrill-Lynch, A.G. Edwards, etc.), a discount broker (Charles Schwab), or an on-line broker (e.g., E-Trade, Suretrade, etc.). Through the broker, you place an order to purchase shares of a company. You pay a commission to the broker. The full-service broker typically charges the most, but they also provide account management and advice. Advice from a prudent broker is probably money well spent, particularly if an investor isn't willing to do their own research prior to investing. The commission to purchase stock will generally be highest at a full-service broker and lowest using an on-line brokerage service. The lowest Internet-based commission is somewhere in the range of $6 to $8 per trade.

Here's the scenario: You want to purchase stock in a particular company, say Wal-Mart. But, not having a big chunk of money right now, you would like to invest smaller amounts each month, say $25. A very reasonable plan. One problem. A commission of $7 represents 28 percent of your $25 monthly investment. For comparison, the average purchase commission for stock mutual funds that charge a commission is under 2 percent. A commission of 28 percent just won't work because you are losing 28 percent of your investment dollar at the start. Your investment would have to gain 28 percent just to break even (actually more than 28 percent due to the impact of taxes and inflation). So, despite a $7 purchase commission being very low, it only becomes cost-effective to purchase stock through a broker (of any kind) when you have a larger lump sum of money. Attempting to purchase stock through a broker by investing smaller amounts of money simply is not efficient (i.e., not thrifty) because of the brokerage commission.

Solution: purchasing stock through a direct investment plan. Direct investing involves purchasing stock directly from companies, whether it be Wal-Mart, Goodyear, IBM, Campbell Soup, etc., without going through a broker. Direct investing may not always eliminate commissions, but typically lowers them significantly. As already mentioned, the most comprehensive web site for information about direct stock purchase plans (DSPPs) and dividend reinvestment plans (DRIPs) is at www.netstockdirect.com. I won't talk much about DRIPs in this book because to participate you already need to own at least one share of stock.

Direct stock purchase plans have all the advantages of DRIPs, but usually do not require the investor to already own stock.

For example, IBM offers a direct stock purchase plan. There is no purchase commission to buy shares of IBM stock through their DSPP other than a $1 fee per transaction. When you choose to sell your IBM stock, there is a $15 sale fee plus a 10 cents per share commission. There is also a onetime $15 setup fee in IBM's plan. Therefore, if a person decided to invest $50 in IBM stock each month via IBM's automated direct stock purchase plan, it would cost $51 ($50 investment plus a $1 transaction fee). A $1 fee represents a 2 percent commission—which is a whole lot more acceptable than 28 percent.

Many direct stock purchase plans charge no setup fee. For those that do charge a onetime setup fee, the range is typically from $5 to $20. In addition, most of these plans charge a sales commission when you sell your shares, commonly between $10 to $15 plus 10 to 12 cents per share. There are a handful of companies that don't even charge sales commissions, meaning that they absorb all the investor's costs associated with the buying and selling of their stock. At this point, some companies are essentially offering no-load stock investing (comparable to no-load mutual funds). There is one key difference however. Mutual funds have annual expense ratios, most direct stock purchase plans don't. But mutual funds represent (in most cases) a *diversified* portfolio, whereas purchasing a single stock is a very *focused* investment. Focus is not bad, it's just a bit more risky.

Table 7.1 lists ten companies that allow investors to start a direct stock purchase plan with a monthly investment of at least $25. *There is no initial investment requirement—just the $25 monthly commitment.* Six of the ten companies are S&P 500 companies. Recall that the S&P 500 represents the most commonly cited index of U.S. large-cap stock performance. Wal-Mart (symbol WMT) is also one of the 30 Dow Jones Industrial Average stocks.

Table 7.2 reports on the annual performance of the ten stocks available for $25 per month. It's worth noting that three of the ten produced a higher five-year average return if purchased via a monthly investment plan versus a single lump sum investment (as noted by underlining). The three companies were CMP Group, C R Bard, and Wal-Mart. Obviously, there is no guarantee that they will always perform better under a monthly investing approach (i.e., dollar-cost averaging).

Table 7.3 shows the style box location (according to Morn-

TABLE 7.1 Direct Stock Purchase Plans for $25 Per Month

Company (Listed alphabetically)	Ticker Symbol	DJIA Stock	S&P 500 Stock	Industry	Automatic Monthly Investment Fee	Phone Number for Information
American Electric Power	AEP		✓	Utility	$0	800-955-4740
CMP Group	CTP			Utility	$0	800-736-3001
C R Bard	BCR		✓	Health	$1	800-828-1639
Energen	EGN			Utility	$0	800-946-4316
Fannie Mae	FNM		✓	Financial	$2	888-289-3266
Goodyear Tire & Rubber	GT		✓	Consumer Durables	$0	800-453-2440
MCN Energy Group	MCN			Utility	$1	800-955-4793
New Jersey Resources	NJR			Utility	n/a	800-817-3955
ONEOK	OKE		✓	Utility	$0	800-955-4798
WalMart	WMT	✓	✓	Retail	$1	800-438-6278

DJIA = Dow Jones Industrial Average
S&P 500 = Standard & Poor's 500 Index

TABLE 7.2 Annual Returns of $25 Per Month Stocks, 1995–1999

Company	Total % Return					5 Year Average Return	5 Year Standard Deviation
	1995	1996	1997	1998	1999		
	LUMP SUM INVESTMENT ANNUAL RETURNS						
American Electric Power	31.9	7.5	32.7	-4.1	-27.4	5.6	23.0
CMP Group	13.9	-13.4	41.7	30.1	52.1	22.6	23.0
C R Bard	22.1	-11.4	14.3	61.3	8.8	16.7	24.9
Energen	15.5	31.6	36.3	1.4	-3.9	15.1	15.3
Fannie Mae	75.4	24.3	54.7	31.7	-14.3	30.7	30.2
Goodyear Tire & Rubber	38.2	15.7	26.3	-19.2	-43.0	-1.4	30.2
MCN Energy Group	35.4	28.9	44.2	-51.0	31.3	10.1	34.6
New Jersey Resources	41.6	2.6	43.9	3.2	3.3	17.4	21.0
ONEOK	34.2	37.5	39.8	-7.4	-27.5	11.6	26.5
Wal-Mart	-32.0	-19.8	41.4	79.0	70.4	46.4	41.1

TABLE 7.2 (Continued)

MONTHLY INVESTING ANNUAL RETURNS

American Electric Power	41.8	3.7	45.8	4.0	-23.5	-3.1	26.7
CMP Group	37.0	-17.8	61.6	16.4	56.5	31.9	27.8
C R Bard	24.4	-22.4	4.3	76.1	13.5	19.5	33.7
Energen	24.5	61.9	43.1	7.5	6.4	13.1	24.2
Fannie Mae	84.4	27.8	68.2	37.8	-14.9	21.4	34.4
Goodyear Tire & Rubber	36.1	17.4	20.3	-29.7	-66.6	-19.8	38.0
MCN Energy Group	48.0	33.7	64.1	-42.9	50.5	5.0	38.1
New Jersey Resources	64.0	11.9	68.1	20.2	10.4	15.3	27.9
ONEOK	29.7	43.7	63.0	3.0	-22.8	1.0	30.7
Wal-Mart	-12.9	-8.8	60.0	110.7	105.2	59.9	53.4

Underlined return figures represent DCA returns equal to or greater than LUMP SUM returns.

ingstar) for each stock. Knowing the style box location of each stock allows you to combine stock investments logically and intelligently. For example, if you want to assemble a portfolio of individual stocks, there is logic and wisdom in choosing stocks from different locations in the style box. The same logic holds when combining mutual funds and stocks. If most of your mutual funds have a large-cap orientation, you may want to diversify into some small-cap stocks. In like manner, value stocks would complement growth mutual funds.

For the frugal investor with $50 to spare each month, Table 7.4 lists 18 stocks that can be purchased for at least $50 per month. *These are companies that waive the normal initial investment (ranging from $200 to $500) for investors who commit to an investment of $50 per month, either as an automatic withdrawal*

TABLE 7.3   Style Box Location of $25 Per Month Stocks (as of December 31, 1999)

Large-Cap Value	Large-Cap Blend	Large-Cap Growth
Fannie Mae		*WalMart*
Mid-Cap Value	**Mid-Cap Blend**	**Mid-Cap Growth**
American Electric Power *Goodyear Tire & Rubber*	*C R Bard*	*MCN Energy Group*
Small-Cap Value	**Small-Cap Blend**	**Small-Cap Growth**
CMP Group *Energen* *ONEOK*	*New Jersey Resources*	

Style box location according to Morningstar (1999).

Phone Numbers for Information and Application Forms:

American Electric Power	800-955-4740
CMP Group	800-736-3001
C R Bard	800-828-1639
Energen	800-946-4316
Fannie Mae	888-289-3266
Goodyear Tire & Rubber	800-453-2440
MCN Energy Group	800-955-4793
New Jersey Resources	800-817-3955
ONEOK	800-955-4798
Wal-Mart	800-438-6278

from your checking account or money you mail in. Table 7.5a shows the annual returns for each stock from 1995 to 1999 with lump sum investing, and Table 7.5 b with monthly investing. The style box location of each $50 stock is shown in Table 7.6.

It's important to remember that stocks (and mutual funds) can drift around within the style box. The style box information reported here for $25 and $50 per month stocks is as of late 1999. The most common style drift is horizontal, rather than up or down. For example, Merck might be classified as a large-cap blend for several months or quarters and then drift into the large-cap-growth category. That's a horizontal shift. It would be less common for a stock or fund to drift between the large-cap category and the small-cap category. That would be up/down, or market-cap, style drift. And it is less common than style drift between value, blend, and growth.

So, in addition to the Frugal Forty mutual funds that can be started for $50 per month, you now have 28 individual stocks that can be purchased with a monthly commitment of either $25 or $50. *That's 68 investment choices for $50 a month or less.* Baskin-Robbins has only 31 flavors, so you're way ahead at this point.

For those who would rather make a single, large investment in a stock rather than commit to smaller investments each month, I would call your attention to Table 7.7. It contains a select list of 123 companies with direct stock purchase plans. These are companies with good performance histories (for the most part), relatively low initial investment requirements, and reasonable fees (setup and automatic investment fees). Table 7.7 includes the 28 companies already discussed, plus 95 additional companies, some of which have a monthly investment option of $100 per month. As you can see, many are S&P 500 companies. As already mentioned, *the companies of the S&P 500 represent an excellent list to shop from when buying individual stocks.* The one-, three-, five-, and ten-year performance histories of these companies are reported in Table 7.8. Following that is Table 7.9, which lists each of the companies by five-year return from highest to lowest.

In many cases, the minimum required investment to start an account is waived if the investor will set up an automatic monthly investment.

In the case of *CMP Group* the initial required investment of $25 exceeds the minimum requirement for subsequent investments, which is $10. In a case such as this, an investor could send in the $25 initial deposit and then set up an automatic investment for as little as $10 per month.

TABLE 7.4 Direct Stock Purchase Plans for $50 Per Month

Company (Listed alphabetically)	Ticker Symbol	DJIA Stock	S&P 500 Stock	Industry	Automatic Monthly Investment Fee	Phone Number for Information
Allstate	ALL		✓	Financial	$0	800-448-7007
Avery Dennison	AVY		✓	Consumer Products	$2	800-649-2291
Becton Dickinson	BDX		✓	Health	$0	800-955-4743
Campbell Soup	CPB		✓	Consumer Staples	$2	800-649-2160
Caterpillar	CAT	✓	✓	Heavy Equipment	$2	201-324-0498
Chevron	CHV		✓	Energy	$1.50	800-842-7629
Conoco	COC.B		✓	Energy	$0	800-483-0294
Dayton Hudson	DH		✓	Retail	$2	888-268-0203
Dollar General	DG		✓	Retail	$.75	888-266-6785

TABLE 7.4 (Continued)

Company	Symbol			Sector	Min.	Phone
IBM	IBM	✓	✓	Technology	$1	888-426-6700
Johnson Controls	JCI		✓	Industrial Products	$0	800-524-6220
MDU Resources	MDU		✓	Utility	$0	800-813-3324
Merck	MRK	✓	✓	Health	$2	800-831-8248
Pinnacle West Capital	PNW		✓	Utility	$0	800-457-2983
Providian Financial	PVN		✓	Financial	$2	800-482-8690
SBC Communications	SBC	✓	✓	Services	$1	800-351-7221
Tribune	TRB		✓	Services	$2	800-446-2617
Walgreen	WAG		✓	Retail	$1.50	800-286-9178
Warner-Lambert	WLA		✓	Health	$2	800-446-2617

Two companies, Dollar General and Pinnacle West Capital, require only $50 to open an account. The subsequent monthly contributions to either company could be as little as $1.

TABLE 7.5a Annual Returns of $50 Per Month Stocks (1995–1999) with Lump Sum Investment

| Company | Total % Return | | | | | 5 Year Average Return | 5 Year Standard Deviation |
	1995	1996	1997	1998	1999		
	LUMP SUM INVESTMENT ANNUAL RETURNS						
Allstate	77.6	43.3	58.4	-13.9	-36.4	17.2	43.6
Avery Dennison	45.0	44.2	28.8	2.4	64.6	35.3	20.1
Becton Dickinson	58.5	17.0	16.5	72.2	-36.2	18.9	38.0
Campbell Soup	39.1	36.8	47.9	0.0	-28.2	15.1	28.8
Caterpillar	8.8	31.0	31.3	-3.1	4.7	13.7	15.3
Chevron	22.2	28.5	22.1	11.0	7.4	18.0	10.1
Dayton Hudson	8.6	60.0	74.2	62.1	36.2	46.2	32.4

TABLE 7.5a (*Continued*)

Dollar General	-13.0		78.0	2.3	20.9	30.1	44.8
IBM	25.7	94.1	39.3	77.5	17.6	43.7	23.3
Johnson Controls	44.1	67.7	17.5	25.8	-2.0	20.8	14.2
MDU Resources	16.2	23.4	43.8	28.9	-21.2	15.6	21.6
Merck	76.6	21.7	35.6	41.3	-7.5	31.2	25.0
Pinnacle West Capital	52.5	24.0	38.3	2.9	-25.4	13.1	27.6
Providian Financial	32.0	14.4	-11.8	149.8	21.7	34.9	55.3
SBC Communications	47.0	26.1	45.6	49.7	-7.4	22.7	25.2
Tribune	13.7	-6.3	60.0	7.1	68.3	33.9	26.2
Walgreen	39.2	31.1	57.4	87.8	0.4	41.3	28.7
Warner-Lambert	30.2	36.4	67.9	83.5	10.2	47.6	26.4

111

TABLE 7.5b Annual Returns of $50 Per Month Stocks (1995–1999) with Monthly Investing

| Company | Total % Return | | | | | 5 Year Average Return | 5 Year Standard Deviation |
	1995	1996	1997	1998	1999		
	MONTHLY INVESTING ANNUAL RETURNS						
Allstate	76.0	58.0	58.2	-20.6	-45.6	-1.3	48.7
Avery Dennison	52.7	56.8	29.5	-13.4	60.6	34.2	27.5
Becton Dickinson	64.9	12.3	8.5	42.9	-26.1	8.1	32.0
Campbell Soup	51.1	39.7	46.5	6.6	-19.8	4.7	28.2
Caterpillar	2.5	24.6	10.1	-11.3	-14.8	8.8	14.4
Chevron	24.3	25.7	14.4	9.5	0.0	14.5	11.2
Dayton Hudson	12.3	59.4	75.0	66.2	32.5	52.7	23.2

TABLE 7.5b (*Continued*)

Dollar General	-39.4	56.2	65.4	-20.5	-16.8	27.0	43.1
IBM	5.9	70.0	39.9	119.2	6.6	43.6	45.2
Johnson Controls	49.8	31.8	22.5	22.9	-18.0	15.1	22.2
MDU Resources	13.1	19.9	69.0	29.3	-20.5	11.5	28.8
Merck	83.4	39.3	32.0	37.6	-12.2	22.7	30.3
Pinnacle West Capital	51.5	22.4	71.7	-2.0	-32.5	2.4	37.1
Providian Financial	23.8	31.6	1.4	161.8	-3.1	39.7	60.5
SBC Communications	48.4	6.0	54.6	64.6	-11.7	20.7	30.9
Tribune	5.7	22.9	74.7	9.6	73.8	38.5	33.7
Walgreen	40.1	38.6	59.6	107.9	13.7	41.0	31.5
Warner-Lambert	36.1	73.1	36.2	46.0	33.7	48.4	14.7

Underlined return figures represent DCA returns equal to or greater than LUMP SUM returns.

113

TABLE 7.6   Style Box Location of $50 Per Month Stocks (as of December 31, 1999)

Large-Cap Value	Large-Cap Blend	Large-Cap Growth
Allstate *Caterpillar* *Chevron* *Dayton Hudson* *IBM* *SBC Communications* *Tribune*	*Merck* *Providian Financial* *Walgreen*	*Campbell Soup* *Warner-Lambert*
Mid-Cap Value	**Mid-Cap Blend**	**Mid-Cap Growth**
Johnson Controls *Pinnacle West Capital*	*Becton Dickinson*	*Avery Dennison* *Dollar General*
Small-Cap Value	**Small-Cap Blend**	**Small-Cap Growth**
	MDU Resources	

Style box location according to Morningstar (1999)

Phone Numbers for Information and Application Forms:

Allstate	800-448-7007
Avery Dennison	800-649-2291
Becton Dickinson	800-955-4743
Campbell Soup	800-649-2160
Caterpillar	201-324-0498
Chevron	800-842-7629
Dayton Hudson	888-268-0203
Dollar General	888-266-6785
IBM	888-426-6700
Johnson Controls	800-524-6220
MDU Resources	800-813-3324
Merck	800-831-8248
Pinnacle West Capital	800-457-2983
Providian Financial	800-482-8690
SBC Communications	800-351-7221
Tribune	800-446-2617
Walgreen	800-286-9178
Warner-Lambert	800-446-2617

Now, let's talk about Option B—*purchasing stock via the Internet,* or web. The premier company that makes web-based Investing not only possible, but also affordable, is **ShareBuilder** (http://www.ShareBuilder.com). Some folks may choose not to have Internet access, so this particular investment option isn't for them. No problem. For those who are Internet users, ShareBuilder gives thrifty investors access to the stock market like never before.

Direct stock purchase plans (as just discussed) are popular, but many companies do not offer them. ShareBuilder remedies this problem. Here's how the folks at ShareBuilder describe their service:

What makes ShareBuilder unique is that it makes dollar-based-investing easy and automatic, and it's all done on-line. It gives you the ability to open an on-line account with Netstock and invest in dollar amounts, buying partial shares of stock in the largest and most actively traded stocks on the NYSE and Nasdaq. ShareBuilder features:

- *Automatic and flexible investments—set it up once and let it do the investing.*
- *No account or investment minimums—most brokers have minimums.*
- *On-line account statements—eliminates paper and simplifies tax-basis accounting issues.*
- *Low transaction fees—$2 per transaction, and only $1 for a child's custodial account.*

As of February 2000 there were over 2000 stocks available for purchase through ShareBuilder. I have personally set up a Share-Builder account for my oldest son. His web-based account, for which I act as custodian under the UTMA status, automatically purchases stock in a company I really like but that doesn't offer a direct stock purchase plan. Like clockwork, on the second Tuesday of each month, $50 is withdrawn from my checking account. The money is then used by ShareBuilder to purchase the stock we requested. If $50 won't buy one share, then his account gets credit for the appropriate fractional share that $50 purchased. Buying fractional shares is an everyday occurrence with mutual fund accounts, but is unique in relation to purchasing stock.

So, what's really great about ShareBuilder is the ability to invest whatever you can afford, rather than being required to invest an amount dictated by the share price of the stock. That's what they mean by the term **dollar-based investing.**

The companies available at ShareBuilder.com as of March, 2000 are listed in Appendix D. In all likelihood, by the time you read this the number of stocks available will have grown. Appendices E, F, and G report the one-, three-, five-, and ten-year returns for selected large-cap, mid-cap, and small-cap companies in the U.S. stock market. These data may be helpful should you find a company in the ShareBuilder.com stable that you would like to invest in.

TABLE 7.7 Select List of 123 Companies with Direct Stock Purchase Plans

Brief descriptions for many of these stocks can be found in Appendix A

Company Name	Ticker Symbol	S&P 500 Stock	Industry Sector	Minimum Initial Purchase Requirement	Automatic Monthly Investment Which Waives Initial Purchase Requirement	Minimum Monthly Purchase Requirement	Setup Fee	Automatic Investment Fee	Phone Number for Application Materials to Open a Direct Investment Account
AFLAC	AFL	✓	Financial	1000	--	50	0	0	800-235-2667
Air Products and Chemicals	APD	✓	Industrial	500	100	100	10	2	800-519-3111
Allstate	ALL	✓	Financial	500	50	100	10	0	800-448-7007
American Electric Power	AEP	✓	Utility	250	25	25	10	0	800-955-4740
American Express	AXP	✓	Financial	1000	--	50	6	3	800-842-7629
Arrow Financial	AROW		Financial	300	--	50	0	NA	518-745-1000
Atmos Energy	ATO	✓	Utility	200	--	25	0	0	800-543-3038
Avery Dennison	AVY	✓	Industrial	500	50	100	10	2	800-649-2291
Bank of America	BAC	✓	Financial	1000	--	50	10	0	800-642-9855
Bank of New York	BK	✓	Financial	1000	--	50	7.5	0	800-432-0140
Becton Dickinson	BDX	✓	Health	250	50	50	0	0	800-955-4743
Bell Atlantic	BEL	✓	Services	1000	--	50	5	1	800-631-2355
BellSouth	BLS	✓	Services	500	--	50	10	0	888-266-6778
Blyth Industries	BTH		Consumer	250	50	50		1.5	877-424-1968
Bob Evans Farms	BOBE		Services	100	--	50	0	0	614-492-4952
Borg Warner Automotive	BWA		Consumer	500	--	50	0	0	800-842-7629
Campbell Soup	CPB	✓	Consumer	500	50	50	15	2	800-649-2160
Caterpillar	CAT	✓	Industrial	500	50	50	15	2	201-324-0498
Central Hudson Gas & Elec	CNH		Utility	100	--	50	0	0	888-280-3848
Chevron	CHV	✓	Energy	250	50	50	8	1.5	800-842-7629
Citicorp	CER		Utility	250	--	25	0	NA	800-622-5514

TABLE 7.7 (Continued)

Company Name	Ticker Symbol	S&P 500 Stock	Industry Sector	Minimum Initial Purchase Requirement	Automatic Monthly Investment Which Waives Initial Purchase Requirement	Minimum Monthly Purchase Requirement	Setup Fee	Automatic Investment Fee	Phone Number for Application Materials to Open a Direct Investment Account
CMP Group	CTP		Utility	25	--	10	0	0	800-736-3001
CMS Energy	CMS	✓	Utility	500	100	25	0	0	800-774-4117
Coastal	CGP	✓	Energy	250	--	50			800-788-2500
Compaq Computer	CPQ	✓	Technology	250	--	50	10	2.5	888-218-4373
Connecticut Energy	CNE		Utility	250	--	50	0	0	800-736-3001
Conoco	COC.B	✓	Energy	250	50	50	10	0	800-483-0294
C R Bard	BCR	✓	Health	250	25	25	15	1	800-828-1639
CVS	CVS	✓	Retail	100	--	100	7.5	1	877-287-7526
Dayton Hudson	DH	✓	Retail	500	50	50	10	2	888-268-0203
Deere & Company	DE	✓	Industrial	500	--	100	7.5	1	800-727-7033
Disney, Walt	DIS	✓	Services	1000	100	100	10	1	800-948-2222
Dollar General	DG	✓	Retail	50	--	0	5	0.75	888-266-6785
Dominion Resources	D	✓	Utility	250	--	40	0	0	800-552-4034
Dow Jones & Company	DJ	✓	Services	1000	100	100	5	0	800-842-7629
DQE	DQE		Utility	105	--	10	5	0	800-247-0400
DTE Energy Holding	DTE	✓	Utility	100	--	25	0	NA	800-551-5009
Duke-Weeks Realty	DRE		Financial	250	--	50	0	0	800-937-5449
Eastern	EML		Industrial	250	--	50	5	0	800-633-3455
Eastman Kodak	EK	✓	Industrial	150	--	50	0	0	800-253-6057
Energen	EGN		Energy	250	25	25	0	0	800-946-4316
Enron	ENE		Energy	250	--	25	17	1	800-519-3111
Essex Property Trust	ESS		Financial	100	--	100	5	0	781-575-3120

117

TABLE 7.7 (Continued)

Company Name	Ticker Symbol	S&P 500 Stock	Industry Sector	Minimum Initial Purchase Requirement	Automatic Monthly Investment Which Waives Initial Purchase Requirement	Minimum Monthly Purchase Requirement	Setup Fee	Automatic Investment Fee	Phone Number for Application Materials to Open a Direct Investment Account
ExxonMobil	XOM	✓	Energy	250	--	50	0	0	800-252-1800
Fannie Mae	FNM	✓	Financial	250	25	25	15	2	888-289-3266
Florida Progress	FPC	✓	Utility	100	--	10	0	0	800-352-1121
Ford Motor	F	✓	Consumer	1000	100	50	10	1	800-955-4791
General Electric	GE	✓	Industrial	250	--	10	7.5	1	800-786-2543
General Growth Properties	GGP		Financial	200	50	50	15	3	888-291-3713
Gillette	G	✓	Consumer	1000	--	100	10	2.5	888-218-2841
Goodyear Tire & Rubber	GT	✓	Consumer	250	25	25	10	0	800-453-2440
Guidant	GDT	✓	Health	250	50	50	15	1	800-537-1677
Hawaiian Electric Ind.	HE		Utility	250	--	25	0	0	808-532-5841
Hershey Foods	HSY	✓	Consumer	500	100	100		3	800-842-7629
Home Depot	HD	✓	Retail	250	--	25	5	0	800-928-0380
IBM	IBM	✓	Technology	500	50	50	15	1	888-426-6700
Illinova	ILN		Utility	250	--	25			800-750-7011
Ipalco Enterprises	IPL		Utility	250	--	25			888-847-2526
ITT Industries	IIN	✓	Consumer	500	--	50	7.5	0	800-254-2823
JC Penney	JCP	✓	Retail	250	--	20	10	1.5	800-565-2576
Johnson Controls	JCI	✓	Industrial	50	--	50	0	0	800-524-6220
Justin Industries	JSTN		Industrial	500	--	25	7.5	0	800-727-7033
Lehman Brothers Holdings	LEH	✓	Financial	500	--	50	7.5	0	800-824-5707
Libbey	LBY		Consumer	100	--	20	7.5	0	800-727-7033
Longs Drug Stores	LDG	✓	Retail	500	--	25	5	5	800-842-7629

TABLE 7.7 (Continued)

Company Name	Ticker Symbol	S&P 500 Stock	Industry Sector	Minimum Initial Purchase Requirement	Automatic Monthly Investment Which Waives Initial Purchase Requirement	Minimum Monthly Purchase Requirement	Setup Fee	Automatic Investment Fee	Phone Number for Application Materials to Open a Direct Investment Account
Lucent Technologies	LU	✓	Technology	1000	100	100	7.5	2	800-727-7033
Madison Gas & Electric	MDSN	✓	Utility	50	--	25	0	NA	800-356-6423
Mattel	MAT	✓	Consumer	500	--	100	10	2.5	888-909-9922
McDonald's	MCD	✓	Services	1000	100	100	5	1	800-621-7825
McGraw-Hill Companies	MHP	✓	Services	500	100	100	10	0	800-842-7629
MCN Energy Group	MCN		Utility	250	25	25	10	1	800-955-4793
MDU Resources Group	MDU		Utility	50	--	50		0	800-813-3324
Mellon Financial Corp.	MEL	✓	Financial	500	--	100	6	0	800-842-7629
Merck	MRK	✓	Health	350	50	50	5	2	800-831-8248
Minnesota Power	MPL		Utility	250	--	10			800-535-3056
Montana Power	MTP		Utility	100	--	25			800-245-6767
Morgan Stanley Dean Witter	MWD	✓	Financial	1000	--	100	0	0	800-228-0829
New Jersey Resources	NJR		Utility	25	--	25	0		800-817-3955
Northern States Power	NSP	✓	Utility	100	--	25	0		800-527-4677
Northwestern	NOR		Utility	500	--	10			800-677-6716
OGE Energy Corp	OGE		Utility	250	--	25	0	0	800-842-7629
ONEOK	OKE	✓	Utility	250	25	25	3	0	800-955-4798
Peoples Energy	PGL	✓	Utility	250	--	25	0	0	800-901-8878
Pfizer	PFE	✓	Health	500	--	50	0	0	800-733-9393
Philadelphia Suburban	PSC		Utility	500	--	50	0	0	800-205-8314
Phillips Petroleum	P	✓	Energy	500	--	50	10	0	888-887-2968
Piedmont Natural Gas	PNY		Energy	250	--	25	0	0	800-693-9917

TABLE 7.7 (Continued)

Company Name	Ticker Symbol	S&P 500 Stock	Industry Sector	Minimum Initial Purchase Requirement	Automatic Monthly Investment Which Waives Initial Purchase Requirement	Minimum Monthly Purchase Requirement	Setup Fee	Automatic Investment Fee	Phone Number for Application Materials to Open a Direct Investment Account
Pier 1 Imports	PIR		Retail	500	--	50	10	0	800-842-7629
Pinnacle West Capital	PNW	✓	Utility	50	--	0	0	0	800-457-2983
Popular	BPOP		Financial	100	--	25	5	1	877-764-1893
Procter & Gamble	PG	✓	Consumer	250	--	100	5		800-764-7483
Providian Financial	PVN	✓	Financial	500	50	50	15	2	800-482-8690
Public Service of NC	PGS		Utility	250	--	50			800-774-4117
Public Service of NM	PNM		Utility	50	--	50	0		800-545-4425
Quaker Oats	OAT	✓	Consumer	500	--	50	10	1.5	800-286-9178
Quanex	NX		Industrial	250	--	50		0	800-278-4353
Reliant Energy	REI	✓	Utility	250	--	50	0	0	800-231-6406
Roadway Express	ROAD		Services	250	--	50		1.5	800-286-9178
Rockwell International	ROK	✓	Industrial	1000	--	100	5	5	800-842-7629
SBC Communications	SBC	✓	Services	500	50	50	10	1	800-351-7221
Sears Roebuck	S	✓	Retail	500	100	50	10	1	800-732-7780
Sempra Energy	SRE	✓	Utility	500	50	25	15	0.5	877-773-6772
South Jersey Industries	SJI		Utility	100	--	25	0	NA	888-754-3100
Southern	SO	✓	Utility	250	--	25	10	0	800-554-7626
Southern Union	SUG		Utility	250	--	50	5	NA	781-575-3120
Southwest Gas	SWX		Utility	100	--	25	0	0	702-876-7280
Synovus Financial	SNV	✓	Financial	250	--	50	10	0	800-337-0896
Tandy	TAN	✓	Retail	250	--	50	10	2.5	888-218-4374
Tektronix	TEK	✓	Technology	500	--	100	5	5	800-842-7629

TABLE 7.7 (Continued)

Company Name	Ticker Symbol	S&P 500 Stock	Industry Sector	Minimum Initial Purchase Requirement	Automatic Monthly Investment Which Waives Initial Purchase Requirement	Minimum Monthly Purchase Requirement	Setup Fee	Automatic Investment Fee	Phone Number for Application Materials to Open a Direct Investment Account
Texaco	TX	✓	Energy	250	–	50	0	0	800-283-9785
TNP Enterprises	TNP		Utility	100	–	25	5	0	800-649-0629
Total System Services	TSS		Services	250	–	50	10	0	800-553-0292
Tribune	TRB	✓	Services	500	50	50	10	2	800-446-2617
Unitrin	UNIT		Financial	500	50	50	10	2	888-665-9701
US West	USW	✓	Services	1000	–	25			800-537-0222
UtiliCorp United	UCU	✓	Utility	250	–	50	0	0	800-884-5426
Wal-Mart Stores	WMT	✓	Retail	250	25	25	20	1	800-438-6278
Walgreen	WAG	✓	Retail	50	–	50	10	1.5	800-286-9178
Warner-Lambert	WLA	✓	Health	250	50	50	15	2	800-446-2617
Whirlpool	WHR	✓	Consumer	1000	100	100	10	2	800-446-2617
Wicor	WIC		Utility	500	–	100	0	0	800-842-7629
Wisconsin Energy	WEC		Utility	50	–	25	0	0	800-558-9663
WPS Resources	WPS		Utility	100	–	25	0	0	920-433-1050

TABLE 7.8 Performance History for Selected Companies with Direct Stock Purchase Plans

Company Name	Industry	Total % Return 1 Year 1999	Total % Return 3 Year Ave 1997-99	Total % Return 5 Year Ave 1995-99	Total % Return 10 Year Ave 1990-99
AFLAC	Insurance (Life)	8.18%	31.2%	35.98%	27.28%
Air Products and Chemicals	Chemicals	-14.32	0.82	10.51	13.11
Allstate	Insurance (Property)	-36.39	-4.61	17.17	NA
American Electric Power	Electric Utilities	-27.36	-2.58	5.55	6.67
American Express	Finance	63.39	44.57	43.26	21.51
Arrow Financial	Banks	-3.32	9.46	19.08	10.89
Atmos Energy	Natural Gas Utilities	-33.67	-1.09	8.26	10.96
Avery Dennison	Paper	64.58	29.49	35.34	19.25
Bank of America	Banks	-14	3.49	20.66	11.62
Bank of New York	Banks	0.95	35.89	43.58	27.7
Becton Dickinson	Medical Equipment	-36.2	8.57	18.86	14.91
Bell Atlantic	Telecommunications	16.98	28.12	24.68	13.26
BellSouth	Telecommunications	-4.53	35.42	30.98	13.68
Blyth Industries	Misc. Manufacturing	-21.4	-6.88	20.82	NA
Bob Evans Farms	Restaurants	-39.55	6.57	-3.71	5.71
Borg Warner Automotive	Auto-Parts Makers	-26.8	2.83	11.62	NA
Campbell Soup	Food Manufacturing	-28.21	2.04	15.1	13.09

TABLE 7.8 (Continued)

Caterpillar	Construction Machinery	4.69	10.04	13.68	14.62
Chevron	Oil/Gas	7.36	13.33	17.98	14.11
CMP Group	Electric Utilities	52.11	41	22.56	10.28
CMS Energy	Electric Utilities	-33.35	0.71	9.98	0.91
Coastal	Oil/Gas	1.57	14	23.53	9.12
Compaq Computer	Computer Equipment	-35.35	22.32	28.07	26.23
Connecticut Energy	Natural Gas Utilities	32.5	28.16	21.15	14.81
CR Bard	Medical Equipment	8.76	26.1	16.74	11.39
CVS	Stores (Misc.)	-27.14	25.27	26.82	10.65
Dayton Hudson	Department Stores	36.24	56.68	46.21	23.54
Deere & Company	Agricultural Machinery	34.86	4.36	16.89	10.9
Dollar General	Department Stores	20.9	30.08	30.05	40.82
Dominion Resources	Electric Utilities	-10.97	7.2	8.53	9.06
Dow Jones & Company	Publishing	43.94	28.72	19.69	10.13
DQE	Electric Utilities	-18.02	10.62	16.96	13.53
DTE Energy Holding	Electric Utilities	-22.51	5.11	10.48	8.93
Duke-Weeks Realty	REITS	-10.26	6.54	13.43	12.54
Eastern	Metal Products	-5.2	24.31	16	11.01
Eastman Kodak	Household Products	-5.59	-3.84	9.42	14.12
Energen	Natural Gas Utilities	-3.88	9.9	15.07	11.08
Enron	Natural Gas Utilities	57.66	29.62	26.34	23.16
Essex Property Trust	REITS	22.22	11.62	26.16	NA

TABLE 7.8 (Continued)

Company Name	Industry	Total % Return 1 Year 1999	Total % Return 3 Year Ave 1997-99	Total % Return 5 Year Ave 1995-99	Total % Return 10 Year Ave 1990-99
ExxonMobil	Oil/Gas	12.56	20.95	25.33	16.88
Fannie Mae	Finance	-14.29	20.42	30.66	24.85
Florida Progress	Electric Utilities	-0.66	15.79	12.2	7.18
Ford Motor	Auto Makers	-6.16	41.92	30.5	21.46
General Electric	Electric Equipment	53.56	48.4	46.09	28.43
General Growth Properties	REITS	-21.75	0.21	11.12	NA
Gillette	Household Products	-12.78	3.02	18.41	22.58
Goodyear Tire & Rubber	Rubber Products	-43	-16.51	-1.43	5.09
Guidant	Medical Equipment	-14.55	48.95	63.87	NA
Hawaiian Electric Industries	Electric Utilities	-22.98	-0.73	4.51	3.32
Hershey Foods	Food Manufacturing	-22.34	4.37	16.59	12.62
Home Depot	Home Supply Stores	68.98	84.01	46.93	44.34
IBM	Computer Equipment	17.57	42.72	43.69	19.28
Illinova	Electric Utilities	45.83	13.49	14.84	10.21
Ipalco Enterprises	Electric Utilities	-36.63	9.81	13.88	9.84
ITT Industries	Auto-Parts Makers	-14.49	12.98	17.92	23.17
JC Penney	Department Stores	-55.2	-22.51	-11.24	-1.85

TABLE 7.8 (Continued)

Johnson Controls	Measuring Devices	-1.96	13.16	20.84	16.62
Justin Industries	Building Materials	14.99	10.5	6.09	12.73
Lehman Brothers Holdings	Securities	93.4	40.07	42.86	NA
Libbey	Clay/Glass	0.38	1.98	11.64	NA
Longs Drug Stores	Stores (Misc.)	-30.29	3.43	12.62	4.14
Lucent Technologies	Phone/Network Equipment	36.62	87.01	NA	NA
Madison Gas & Electric	Electric Utilities	-5.75	6.07	4.52	8.89
Mattel	Toys	-43.18	-21.19	-2.98	10.27
McDonald's	Restaurants	5.44	21.8	23.22	17.57
McGraw-Hill Companies	Publishing	22.88	41.55	32.96	19.45
MCN Energy Group	Natural Gas Utilities	31.25	-2.5	10.09	22.27
MDU Resources Group	Electric Utilities	-21.22	13.44	15.6	12.86
Merck	Pharmaceuticals	-7.48	21.03	31.16	20.61
Minnesota Power	Electric Utilities	-18.57	13.51	13.07	9.1
Mobile America	Insurance (Life)	-49.43	-38.58	-15.51	NA
Montana Power	Electric Utilities	30.73	57.14	33	20.18
Morgan Stanley Dean Witter & Co.	Securities	103.1	64.65	55.11	NA
New Jersey Resources	Natural Gas Utilities	3.31	15.33	17.4	13.03
Northern States Power	Electric Utilities	-24.98	0.24	3.38	5.95
Northwestern	Electric Utilities	-13.11	13.65	16.32	14.6
OGE Energy Corp	Electric Utilities	-30.81	2.33	9.28	6.64
ONEOK	Natural Gas Utilities	-27.52	-2.12	11.59	10

TABLE 7.8 (Continued)

Company Name	Industry	Total % Return 1 Year 1999	Total % Return 3 Year Ave 1997-99	Total % Return 5 Year Ave 1995-99	Total % Return 10 Year Ave 1990-99
Peoples Energy	Natural Gas Utilities	-11.32	4.93	11.07	9.06
Pfizer	Pharmaceuticals	-21.5	34.12	40.05	29.89
Philadelphia Suburban	Water Utilities	-27.88	15.25	23.02	17.8
Phillips Petroleum	Oil/Gas	13.5	5.11	10.93	10.27
Piedmont Natural Gas	Natural Gas Utilities	-12.66	13.49	14.88	13.33
Pier 1 Imports	Furniture Retail	-33.22	-5.67	11.46	5.46
Pinnacle West Capital	Electric Utilities	-25.37	2.04	13.13	13.15
Popular	Savings Institutions	-16.14	20.51	34.82	22.03
Procter & Gamble	Household Products	21.56	28.45	30.83	22.49
Providian Financial	Finance	21.69	38.9	34.85	18.14
Quaker Oats	Food Manufacturing	12.33	22.42	19.41	12.45
Quanex	Steel/Iron	16.33	0.14	4.81	8.31
Reliant Energy	Electric Utilities	-25.67	5.88	11.34	9.82
Roadway Express	Truck Transport	51.37	4.82	NA	NA
Rockwell International	Machinery	21.47	5.12	17.85	15.79
SBC Communications	Telecommunications	-7.41	26.38	22.69	15.95
Sears Roebuck	Department Stores	-26.83	-11.21	8.59	22.54
Sempra Energy	Natural Gas Utilities	-26.21	-2.25	5.3	4.33
South Jersey Industries	Natural Gas Utilities	14.46	11.32	16.22	10.25
Southern	Electric Utilities	-15.01	6.82	9.04	11.48

TABLE 7.8 (Continued)

Southern Union	Natural Gas Utilities	-17.61	14.71	24.22	19
Southwest Gas	Natural Gas Utilities	-10.92	10.2	15.37	8.72
Synovus Financial	Banks	-15.66	13.33	32.15	22.32
Tandy	Electronics Stores	139.98	66.19	33.08	19.35
Tektronix	Measuring Devices	31.49	5.97	12.86	14.98
Texaco	Oil/Gas	5.72	6.74	16.79	11.02
TNP Enterprises	Electric Utilities	12.39	18.81	27.48	13.67
Total System Services	Data Processing	-30.42	-2.89	23.67	22.53
Tribune	Publishing	68.32	42.37	33.87	18.63
Unitrin	Insurance (Life)	9.11	15	16.53	NA
US West	Telecommunications	15.9	36.96	35.28	21.95
UtiliCorp United	Electric Utilities	-16.25	8.32	7.94	9.14
Wal-Mart Stores	Department Stores	70.44	83.52	46.41	29.25
Walgreen	Stores (Misc.)	0.37	43.7	41.31	27.56
Walt Disney	Entertainment	-1.68	8.72	14.58	12.82
Warner-Lambert	Pharmaceuticals	10.21	50.3	47.58	26.91
Whirlpool	Electric Equipment	20.23	14.44	7.89	9.92
Wicor	Natural Gas Utilities	38.7	22.31	20.76	14.79
Wisconsin Energy	Electric Utilities	-34.8	-5.1	-0.29	4.54
WPS Resources	Electric Utilities	-23.75	2.37	5.24	7.13

TABLE 7.9   Selected Companies with Direct Stock Purchase Plans

Company Name	Total % Return 5 Year Average 1995-99 Highest to Lowest
Guidant	63.9%
Morgan Stanley Dean Witter & Co.	55.1
Warner-Lambert	47.6
Home Depot	46.9
Wal-Mart Stores	46.4
Dayton Hudson	46.2
General Electric	46.1
IBM	43.7
Bank of New York	43.6
American Express	43.3
Lehman Brothers Holdings	42.9
Walgreen	41.3
Pfizer	40.1
AFLAC	36.0
Avery Dennison	35.3
US West	35.3
Providian Financial	34.9
Popular	34.8
Eli Lilly & Company	34.8
Tribune	33.9
Tandy	33.1
Montana Power	33.0
McGraw-Hill Companies	33.0
Synovus Financial	32.2
Merck	31.2
BellSouth	31.0
Procter & Gamble	30.8
Fannie Mae	30.7
Ford Motor	30.5
Dollar General	30.1
Compaq Computer	28.1
TNP Enterprises	27.5
CVS	26.8
Enron	26.3
Essex Property Trust	26.2

TABLE 7.9 *(Continued)*

Company Name	Total % Return 5 Year Average 1995-99 Highest to Lowest
ExxonMobil	25.3
Bell Atlantic	24.7
Southern Union	24.2
Total System Services	23.7
Coastal	23.5
McDonald's	23.2
Philadelphia Suburban	23.0
SBC Communications	22.7
CMP Group	22.6
Connecticut Energy	21.2
Johnson Controls	20.8
Blyth Industries	20.8
Wicor	20.8
Bank of America	20.7
Dow Jones & Company	19.7
Quaker Oats	19.4
Arrow Financial	19.1
Becton Dickinson	18.9
Gillette	18.4
Chevron	18.0
ITT Industries	17.9
Rockwell International	17.9
New Jersey Resources	17.4
Allstate	17.2
DQE	17.0
Deere & Company	16.9
Texaco	16.8
CR Bard	16.7
Hershey Foods	16.6
Unitrin	16.5
Northwestern	16.3
South Jersey Industries	16.2
Eastern	16.0

TABLE 7.9 (*Continued*)

Company Name	Total % Return 5 Year Average 1995-99 Highest to Lowest
MDU Resources Group	15.6
Southwest Gas	15.4
Campbell Soup	15.1
Energen	15.1
Piedmont Natural Gas	14.9
Illinova	14.8
Walt Disney	14.6
Ipalco Enterprises	13.9
Caterpillar	13.7
Duke-Weeks Realty	13.4
Pinnacle West Capital	13.1
Minnesota Power	13.1
Tektronix	12.9
Longs Drug Stores	12.6
Florida Progress	12.2
Libbey	11.6
Borg Warner Automotive	11.6
ONEOK	11.6
Pier 1 Imports	11.5
Reliant Energy	11.3
General Growth Properties	11.1
Peoples Energy	11.1
Phillips Petroleum	10.9
Air Products and Chemicals	10.5
DTE Energy Holding	10.5
MCN Energy Group	10.1
CMS Energy	10.0
Eastman Kodak	9.4
OGE Energy Corp	9.3
Southern	9.0
Sears Roebuck	8.6
Dominion Resources	8.5
Atmos Energy	8.3
UtiliCorp United	7.9
Whirlpool	7.9

TABLE 7.9 (*Continued*)

Company Name	Total % Return 5 Year Average 1995-99 Highest to Lowest
Justin Industries	6.1
American Electric Power	5.6
Sempra Energy	5.3
WPS Resources	5.2
Quanex	4.8
Madison Gas & Electric	4.5
Hawaiian Electric Industries	4.5
Northern States Power	3.4
Wisconsin Energy	-0.3
Goodyear Tire & Rubber	-1.4
Mattel	-3.0
Bob Evans Farms	-3.7
JC Penney	-11.2
Mobile America	-15.5
Roadway Express	NA
Lucent Technologies	NA

CHAPTER 8

How Much Is Enough?

Okay, you've decided to invest. That's great. From the list of Frugal Funds you've identified a couple that look appealing. Perhaps you also have one or two individual stocks in mind. Now, the question: "How much should I invest?" Here's an obvious answer: "As much as you can!" Frankly, that's a very acceptable answer, even if it's $10 per month.

I find it discouraging (almost depressing) to read about how much I *should* be investing. My wife and I have seven children. I have the good fortune of being a teacher. My spouse is a homemaker. We don't make millions. We never will. We're not financially rich, but we certainly have enough for our needs. So how can I can write a book like this when I'm probably not saving "enough" for my own children? There are a lot of answers to that question. I'll choose this one: We, like you, can only do our best. If a person's best is $10 per month, then do that. If it's $1000 per month, do it. After teaching Personal & Family Finance for over a decade, I have become convinced that the amount a person is saving or investing is not *the* most important issue. The commitment and discipline (and maybe even sacrifice) involved in starting and staying with an investment program is the real benefit.

Certainly there is a day of reckoning when bills must be paid, and we either have the necessary money or we don't. Preparing today for tomorrow is an obvious reality. But even the best laid plans can't guarantee we'll have all the necessary resources at that future day, whether it be for Suzy's college tuition or our much anticipated retirement travel plans. Another reality is that we seldom get everything we want. Plans change. People lose their jobs. And die. Planning, though critically important, can sometimes provide a false sense of security. "True security," suggests Og Mandino, "lies not in what one has, but in what one can do without." I can think of no better advice to consider when pondering one's financial future.

The act of saving/investing involves a certain amount of faith, or at least hope. It is this faith that propels a person who is saving as much as they can but still less than the "necessary amount" to reach a certain future goal. For example, if our goal as a family was to have each of our children attend an Ivy League university, we would need to be saving more each month than we currently earn. That's pretty tough to do. So we clearly don't have that as a goal. I suppose my wife and I have this type of faith. A faith that one's best effort may set into motion a resource ripple effect. "Where there's a will, there's a way," might capture the essence of this type of faith. While to some this may appear naive, what is the alternative? If one should be saving $350 each month for a distant goal (say, a child's college expenses) but can only afford to save $150 per month, should they then not save at all? Of course not. The virtues associated with saving are reaped whether it's $150 a month or $350 per month. Either way, a certain amount of faith is involved in planning for the future. At $150 per month, we simply rely a bit more heavily on faith that other means will materialize to assist us in meeting our future plans and goals. As it relates to planning for the future, the issue is not whether we rely upon faith or not, but rather to what degree. Doing one's best is all that one can do.

Enough. I'll get off the soapbox. Now let's take a look at what modest monthly investments can grow to over time. The information in the following five tables is meant to be encouraging, not discouraging.

One of the most interesting aspects of investing is the impact of time. Growth compounds upon itself over time, as illustrated in Tables 8.1 through 8.6. For instance, notice in the five-year table (Table 8.1) that the difference in the ending account value of a $250 monthly investment between an account that returns 6 percent annually versus 14 percent annually is rather small (about $4000). Now look at the results of a 40-year investment in Table 8.6. The ending account value of a $250 monthly investment after 40 years in an account that averages a 14 percent annual return is $5 million greater than the account

TABLE 8.1   Ending Account Value of Monthly Investments After 5 years

Annual Return	Monthly Investments for 5 Years				
	$10	$25	$50	$100	$250
6%	$698	$1,744	$3,489	$6,977	$17,443
8%	$735	$1,837	$3,674	$7,348	$18,369
10%	$774	$1,936	$3,872	$7,744	$19,359
12%	$817	$2,042	$4,083	$8,167	$20,417
14%	$862	$2,155	$4,310	$8,620	$21,549

TABLE 8.2   Ending Account Value of Monthly Investments After 10 years

Annual Return	Monthly Investments for 10 Years				
	$10	$25	$50	$100	$250
6%	$1,639	$4,097	$8,194	$16,388	$40,970
8%	$1,829	$4,574	$9,147	$18,295	$45,737
10%	$2,048	$5,121	$10,242	$20,484	$51,211
12%	$2,300	$5,751	$11,502	$23,004	$57,510
14%	$2,591	$6,477	$12,953	$25,907	$64,767

TABLE 8.3   Ending Account Value of Monthly Investments After 15 years

Annual Return	Monthly Investments for 15 Years				
	$10	$25	$50	$100	$250
6%	$2,908	$7,270	$14,541	$29,082	$72,705
8%	$3,460	$8,651	$17,302	$34,604	$86,510
10%	$4,145	$10,362	$20,724	$41,447	$103,618
12%	$4,996	$12,490	$24,979	$49,958	$124,895
14%	$6,058	$15,145	$30,289	$60,579	$151,447

TABLE 8.4 Ending Account Value of Monthly Investments After 20 years

Annual Return	Monthly Investments for 20 Years				
	$10	$25	$50	$100	$250
6%	$4,620	$11,551	$23,102	$46,204	$115,510
8%	$5,890	$14,726	$29,451	$58,902	$147,255
10%	$7,594	$18,984	$37,968	$75,937	$189,842
12%	$9,893	$24,731	$49,463	$98,926	$247,314
14%	$13,012	$32,529	$65,058	$130,117	$325,292

TABLE 8.5 Ending Account Value of Monthly Investments After 30 years

Annual Return	Monthly Investments for 30 Years				
	$10	$25	$50	$100	$250
6%	$10,045	$25,113	$50,226	$100,452	$251,129
8%	$14,904	$37,259	$74,518	$149,036	$372,590
10%	$22,605	$56,512	$113,024	$226,049	$565,122
12%	$34,950	$87,374	$174,748	$349,496	$873,741
14%	$54,930	$137,324	$274,649	$549,297	$1,373,243

TABLE 8.6 Ending Account Value of Monthly Investments After 40 years

Annual Return	Monthly Investments for 40 Years				
	$10	$25	$50	$100	$250
6%	$19,915	$49,787	$99,575	$199,149	$497,873
8%	$34,910	$87,275	$174,550	$349,101	$872,752
10%	$63,241	$158,102	$316,204	$632,408	$1,581,020
12%	$117,648	$294,119	$588,239	$1,176,477	$2,941,193
14%	$223,544	$558,860	$1,117,719	$2,235,438	$5,588,596

TABLE 8.7   College Savings Planning Guide

Child's Age in 2001	Number of Years before College	Child Starts College in...	ESTIMATED Future Total Cost of College (4 Year Total at Average Public University)	ESTIMATED Amount Needed at Start of College	ESTIMATED Monthly Investment Needed to Meet Goal
1	17	2018	$ 80,000	$ 73,000	$ 150
3	15	2016	$ 75,000	$ 68,000	$ 180
5	13	2014	$ 68,000	$ 62,000	$ 210
8	10	2011	$ 59,000	$ 54,000	$ 280
12	6	2007	$ 48,000	$ 44,000	$ 460
15	3	2004	$ 42,000	$ 38,000	$ 930

Assumptions: College cost annual inflation of 5%, taxes paid out of pocket, annual investment return of 9%, zero starting balance. Future Total Cost of College includes tuition, room, board, and fees.

that earns 6 percent annually. Over time, differences in the annual rate of return of an investment can produce massive disparities in the account's future value. The key is not the rate of return, but rather the length of the investment period.

Length of investment is more important than rate of return.

So, knowing that length of the investment is the most crucial component of an investment informs us that starting our investments NOW is a really good idea. A thrifty investor who invests $50 per month for 10 years will have $10,000 dollars if the account averages a 10 percent annual return. The same investor will have almost $21,000 after 15 years. After 20 years, nearly $38,000. After 30 years, just over $113,000. Fifty dollars a month invested in an account that averages 10 percent per year will grow into $316,000 after 40 years. Notice in Figure 8.1 how the account grows faster and faster over time—that's the effect of compounded growth. More time is better. That means we need to start sooner. The amount we invest is less important than starting right away.

Many people start investing with very modest amounts ($10 or $20 per month) and increase it as they can. You may hear other people say that it is pointless to invest such a small amount. That's garbage. Don't believe it. Starting your investment program with whatever amount you can will accomplish many things. First off, you'll learn about the logistics of investing, such as how to set up an automatic monthly investment program. Though not hard, it's a mystery to those who haven't worked with it. Second, you'll learn about how investment markets behave. When it comes to learning about investing, there really is no substitute for firsthand experience. Third, you'll experience satisfaction in knowing that you are DOING rather than TALKING. Satisfaction empowers people to endure. Because investing is a long-term process, endurance is critical. In fact, investors who endure are usually the ones who experience megadoses of satisfaction. The amount you invest each month has nothing to do with any of these important lessons.

Now, for just a minute, at the risk of being depressing, we need to talk about saving "enough." How do you know if you're saving "enough"? Well, what are you saving for? The question "What's the goal?" must precede the issue of "How much is enough?" Let's use an example of saving for college. Here's the scenario: two children, ages three and five. For the oldest child (the five-year-old) there are about 13 years prior to college starting, 15 years for the youngest. The average cost per year at a public university in the United States was about $7000 in 1999 (remember, that's the cost per year!).

The five-year-old will most likely start college first, somewhere around the year 2014. By that time, college will cost more—probably around $68,000 for the four-year stay (see Table 8.7).

FIGURE 8.1 Growth of $50 Monthly Investment

Ending Account Value—$50 Per Month at 10% Annual Return

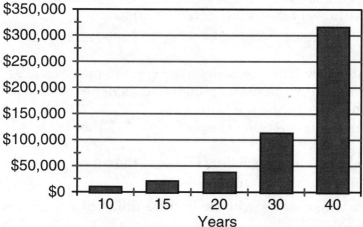

That's assuming that college costs increase at about 5 percent per year. Therefore, your five-year-old needs about $62,000 saved up by the year 2014. (The full $68,000 isn't needed by 2014 because the investment account can continue to grow *during* college.) To have $62,000 saved up will require a monthly investment of $210, starting now. These projections assume an annual return of 9 percent, a zero starting balance in the child's account, and that taxes are paid out of pocket and not with money withdrawn from the account. Your three-year-old will have "enough" if you start saving about $180 per month. (By the time the three-year-old starts college it will cost about $75,000 at the average public university.)

Now, these projections are obviously filled with assumptions. But one thing is certain: The earlier you start saving for children's college expenses (or whatever else you're saving for), the less you need to save each month. So we see it again, *length of investment is more critical than amount invested or rate of return earned.*

College savings plans (officially known as **Section 529** plans) may also be worth looking into. Section 529 plans are also known as qualified state tuition programs or prepaid tuition programs. As of early 2000, 41 states had operating plans. The best resource for more information about college savings plans around the country is on Joseph Hurley's web site at http://www.savingforcollege.com. Or you can get Joseph Hurley's book, *The Best Way to Save for College—A Complete Guide to Section 529 Plans.*

In Missouri (where my family and I live) the Section 529 plan is referred to as MO$T, which stands for Missouri Saving for Tuition. MO$T utilizes **TIAA-CREF** as the investment manager. TIAA-CREF, which manages over $250 billion, stands for *Teachers Insurance Annuity Association—College Retirement Equities Fund.* Key features of the MO$T program are:

- Missouri state tax deduction of up to $8000 in annual contributions
- Earnings are federal tax-deferred and exempt from Missouri state taxes if used for qualified higher education expenses
- Minimum contribution of only $25, or $15 through payroll deduction
- Use of funds at any eligible school in the country
- No application or maintenance fees

Plans in other states will likely have different guidelines.

But a common thread through all Section 529 plans is preferential tax treatment of the invested money (at the federal and/or state level), removal of assets from taxable estate, open to all people regardless of their income level, the option to invest as much as $100,000 in a child's account in a single year, and when money is withdrawn from the account it is taxed at the child's tax rate.

Another source for information about tuition savings options in other states is the College Savings Plans Network at (877) 277-6496, or their web site at http://www.collegesavings.org.

Prepaid tuition plans are another version of Section 529 plans. They are more conservative than college savings plans. The idea is that you invest a certain amount of money for your child that is guaranteed to be enough to pay for college. In essence, you "lock-in" the cost of college 10 or 15 years down the road. It's a good plan if (1) you are worried about college costs spiraling out of control in the future, and (2) you're reasonably certain that your child will eventually be attending college. The down side is that your investments might have done better in a college savings plan, but the performance of a college savings plan is not guaranteed.

Obviously there are a lot of reasons to save money for the future. Saving for college expenses is just one example. Another common purpose for saving is for a retirement nest egg. As people are living longer, this becomes a more compelling issue. Sixty years ago retirement planning was less common. Back in 1940 men didn't live much past age 61, and women lived, on average, about 65 years. Today, men and women often live well into their eighties and beyond. Better health care and nutrition has produced longer lives. But the meter continues to run. Living longer requires money. The need for retirement planning (the financial aspect) becomes a more critical issue as our longevity increases.

Here's a very simplified way to look at retirement planning. Let's assume 20 years of retirement (from age 65 to 85). Let's also assume that you will need $25,000 of annual income during the 20-year retirement period. The $25,000 is to supplement other income sources, such as a pension and social security. This annual income is *real income,* meaning it goes up each year by the rate of inflation (annual inflation during retirement is estimated at 5 percent in this example). "Real" income is income with constant purchasing power. If we don't use real income figures in our retirement planning estimations, it assumes that our retirement income is a constant $25,000 each year, which means

TABLE 8.8   Monthly Investment Required to Meet Retirement Goal of $375,000*

Current Age	Monthly Investment Needed to Reach Goal Assuming a 9% Annual Return
25	$80
30	$130
35	$205
40	$335
45	$560
50	$991

* $375,000 in an investment account at age 65 will allow you to receive $25,000 of "real" income (i.e. income that increases at a 5% rate each year) for 20 years. This assumes the investment account can earn an average return of 8% during retirement.

that inflation erodes the purchasing power of our fixed retirement income.

To crank out a real income of $25,000 each year during 20 years of retirement will require that $375,000 is saved up by age 65. In other words, an account with a balance of $375,000 at the start of retirement will allow you to withdraw $25,000 in real dollars each year if the account earns at least 8 percent annually. So, after the first year of retirement you will withdraw $26,250 (or 5 percent added to $25,000). The following year you will be able to withdraw $27,560, and on it goes.

Now, the big question. "How much must I invest to reach that goal of $375,000 by the age of 65?" The answer depends entirely upon how old you are now. As shown in Table 8.8, the advantage of starting early is easy to see. A 25-year-old needs to invest about $80 each month into an account (i.e., mutual fund) which averages a 9 percent annual return to reach the goal of $375,000 by the age of 65. In contrast, if you're currently 50 years old, you'll need to plow nearly $1000 each month into an investment account to meet the same goal.

Of course, the information in Table 8.8 is a rough approximation. The only way to really know "how much is enough" requires a lot more information that is highly person-specific. A certified financial planner might be needed to fine-tune the answers to your specific "How much is enough?" questions.

CHAPTER 9

Don't Mess with Taxes

I'm not suggesting that you avoid taxes, just don't mess them up. And that's easy to do. But if you really don't want to mess with taxes, there is a way, and it's called the **Roth IRA.** More about that in a moment.

If you decide to start a monthly investment program, you will want to keep good records of all your purchases and subsequent sales. This is required whether you're buying shares of a mutual fund or a stock. Yes, record keeping takes time. Yes, it's a pain. But there isn't a good alternative. Of course, you could hire a tax consultant (which isn't a bad idea). A good tax consultant will probably save you more money than you pay in consulting fees. But even if you hire a tax consultant, you still need to keep good records.

Tax laws and investment advice are both moving targets—which makes writing a book (like this one) somewhat challenging. Nevertheless, I've given you my best shot with regard to the best thrifty investments available today.

Offering specific tax guidance is even harder. Because tax law is cluttered with a zillion rules, many of which can change annually, it may be one area where buying professional help is the best approach. I'll attempt to give you an overview of the basic tax issues that are relevant to investors. Beyond that, you might need to consult a qualified tax preparer.

The Internal Revenue Service allows *mutual fund investors* to average out the price of mutual fund shares purchased. This considerably simplifies your record keeping. Additionally, many mutual fund companies will automatically calculate your average cost basis for you, so that when you sell shares, the mutual fund company can determine your capital gain (or loss) for you.

There are actually four different IRS-approved methods for determining your cost basis. Your mutual fund will most likely be using the "Average-Cost Method—Single Category" method.

If you sell shares of a mutual fund within one year of buying them, your gain or loss is considered short-term, and if you have a capital gain it will be taxed at your ordinary income tax rate. If you sell shares after holding them for at least 366 days, any capital gain will be taxed at 10 percent for those in the 15 percent tax bracket, and 20 percent for taxpayers in higher tax brackets. (Remember, these are the rules applying to 1999 tax returns. The rules can change.)

Dividends and capital gain distributions declared by your mutual fund and paid to you during a year are taxable whether you actually receive them or have them reinvested. It's important to keep track of these because you don't want to pay taxes on them twice. You need to add reinvested dividends and capital gain distributions to your *cost basis* (the average purchase price of the mutual fund). This raises your cost basis, which in turn lowers your capital gain when you later sell shares of the fund. If you don't do this, you'll end up paying taxes on reinvested distributions twice. Another little detail: Brokerage fees paid by the company are treated as taxable dividends to you.

> Keep track of reinvested distributions. They raise your cost basis, which will lower your capital gain—thus lowering the tax you owe when you sell shares.

Of course, if your account is a tax-deferred account—such as an IRA, 401(k), 403(b), Keogh, etc.—you do not owe taxes in the current year, but only when you withdraw the money during retirement. Here's the logic: Your investments into a tax-deferred retirement account lower your gross income, which reduces the amount of federal tax withheld from your paycheck. For example, if you authorize your employer to take $100 out of your monthly paycheck and invest it into a mutual fund that has been set up as a 401(k) account, your take-home pay may only be reduced by $87. This means it only cost you $87 to invest $100, the difference being the amount by which your federal withholding taxes were reduced. The deal gets even sweeter if your employer matches (fully or partially) your contribution into your 401(k) or 403(b) account.

Ask at work. If your employer is 401(k) friendly, start as soon as possible. Your employer's contribution is pure profit to you.

The logic continues: When you withdraw the money from your account during retirement, you will pay taxes on your withdrawals. However, it's probable that your tax bracket will be lower in retirement than it was while you were working. But if your tax bracket is higher in retirement, then the classic logic doesn't exactly work for you. However, having a high marginal tax bracket during retirement is hardly a terrible problem! A lot of folks would be delighted to have sufficient income in retirement so as to have a tax "problem."

One final note regarding 401(k) or 403(b) tax-deferred retirement accounts. One reason they are so popular is because they have higher contribution limits than Individual Retirement Accounts (IRAs). As of 2000, a maximum of $10,500 can be contributed annually to a 401(k) plan compared to $2000 per person for IRAs.

If the mutual fund belongs to your child (using the UTMA option), he or she can annually receive up to $700 of unearned income (interest, dividends, capital gains) without owing tax ($700 is a figure determined by the IRS, so it may change). Assuming a $50 per month investment into one of the Frugal Forty mutual funds, your child's account won't generate over $700 of taxable distributions (dividends and capital gains) for probably six or seven years. For some funds (particularly small-cap funds) it may be more than ten years before taxable distributions exceed $700.

Unlike mutual fund shares, the cost of *stocks purchased directly* cannot be averaged out. So, this is where record keeping is really important. If you're handy with a spreadsheet (Lotus, Excel, Quattro, etc.), you may want to set up a template to keep track of each purchase and each reinvested dividend. Alternatively, a ledger sheet and a sharp pencil are known to work; not as sexy as a computerized spreadsheet, but still very functional. Every purchase (including reinvested dividends) has its own unique cost basis and specific holding period. When you later sell shares of stock, you will use the FIFO (first in, first out) method to determine the length of the holding period and amount of gain for each share sold.

The only way to totally eliminate the hassle of taxation is to set up your mutual fund and/or direct stock purchase account as a *Roth IRA*. Mutual funds, almost without exception, can be established as regular accounts or IRA accounts. Within the IRA format there are three options: traditional (or contributory) IRA,

Roth IRA, and Education IRA. Contributions to the traditional IRA account are tax-deductible; when money is withdrawn during retirement, taxes will be owed. The Roth IRA is just the opposite. Contributions are not tax-deductible, but no federal income tax is owed on money withdrawn starting at age 59½. Contributions (money you invested) can be withdrawn tax-free at any time. *Earnings* in a Roth IRA account (dividends and capital gains) can be withdrawn prior to age 59½ and still be tax-free under certain conditions. First, the account needs to have been established for at least five years. Second, the money can only be used for certain purposes, such as purchasing your first home ($10,000 limit per person) or to pay for higher education expenses for yourself, spouse, or children. Bingo! If you really want to avoid keeping tax records on your investments, the Roth IRA may be for you. However, if you are a single tax filer with an Adjusted Gross Income (AGI) in excess of $110,000, you can't contribute to a Roth IRA. For married filing jointly, the AGI limit is $160,000. Final caveat: As with any investment plan that may involve a complicated tax situation, you are encouraged to consult a tax adviser before signing on the dotted line.

The other option to avoid the hassle of keeping tax records is an *Education IRA*. The down side there is the annual contribution limit is $500, but the money grows tax-free if it is used for education expenses. Many mutual funds offer the Education IRA, though it's often not their favorite type of account because the maximum that can be invested into the account is limited to $500 per year. Clearly, they would prefer to have larger amounts invested into their funds.

When used according to their respective rules, money withdrawn from a Roth IRA or Education IRA is tax-free, therefore keeping track of the cost basis of each purchase is irrelevant. The down side is that money deposited into a Roth or Education IRA does not lower your taxable income each year. If you want to do that, set up your account as a traditional IRA. As money is withdrawn from a traditional IRA (during retirement), it is taxed as ordinary income, therefore it isn't necessary to keep track of your cost basis for a traditional IRA either. The cost basis is only needed to compute capital gains, and IRA withdrawals are treated as ordinary income, not as capital gains. Therefore, the IRA format is a good one if you want to eliminate the need for keeping track of each and every purchase.

Each type of IRA has advantages and disadvantages. It's always a good idea to seek out qualified tax advice as you chart your course through the maze of tax-deferred and tax-exempt investment options.

Direct stock purchase plans can also be set up as IRA accounts, either as a traditional IRA, Roth IRA, or Education IRA. However, at this writing there are probably less than 50 companies that provide the IRA option. In all likelihood, that number will increase over time, as direct stock purchase plans become more popular.

Fannie Mae is one company with a direct stock purchase plan that can be set up as a regular account or as an IRA. They offer the traditional IRA, the Roth IRA, and the Education IRA. Here's how Fannie Mae described the details of their IRA options in 1999:

". . . Save for Retirement, or borrow from your Retirement Savings to help purchase your first home or to fund a child's college education."

The Taxpayer Relief Act of 1997 has expanded the options available for retirement saving, and you can establish an Individual Retirement Account (IRA) which invests in Fannie Mae common stock. Consult your financial or tax adviser to fully understand and determine which, if any, of these options is best for you. Call First Chicago for registration materials and specific information on the IRAs described.

Regular IRA—$35 Annual Fee

Regular IRA contributions are allowed for individuals under age 70½ who have earned income. Tax-deductible contributions are subject to new adjusted gross income (AGI) phase-out levels, while non-deductible contributions are allowed regardless of income level. Maximum individual contribution is $2000 annually, with tax-deferred growth of investment. Beginning in 1998, penalty-free withdrawals can be made to help pay for first home purchases or higher education expenses. (Maximum annual contribution between Regular and Roth IRA is $2000.)

Roth IRA—$35 Annual Fee

Contributions are allowed for individuals of any age with (AGI) below $160,000 (joint) or $110,000 (single), but allowed contributions begin to phase out at an AGI of $150,000 (joint) and $95,000 (single). Maximum individual contribution is $2000 annually. Investments and earnings grow tax-free. Contributions are not tax-deductible but if the investment stays in the Roth IRA for five years or more, qualified withdrawals are distributed tax-free (and free of penalty in most cases). There are no requirements to begin distributions at age 70½. Beginning in 1998, penalty-free withdrawals can be made to help pay for first home purchases or higher education expenses.

Education IRA—$35 Annual Fee

Any individual of any age may contribute, subject to the same income ranges as the Roth IRA, to an Education IRA for a child. Contributions of up to $500 annually can be made for secondary education expenses for a child beneficiary under age 18. Contributions are not deductible, but investments grow tax-free and are not taxed when withdrawn for higher education expenses, including tuition, room and board, books, and supplies. Withdrawals must be made by age 30 or the investment will be taxed to the child and will be subject to a 10% penalty. Unused account balances may be transferred to another family member's Educational IRA.

The annual fees incurred when setting up your Fannie Mae direct stock purchase plan as an IRA account may be a deterrent to thrifty investors. Nevertheless, it's still worth knowing that for the record-keeping impaired there are tax-exempt solutions. Table 9.1

TABLE 9.1   Direct Stock Purchase Plans Offering IRA Accounts

Allstate
American Electric Power
Atmos Energy
Bell Atlantic
Campbell Soup
ExxonMobil
Fannie Mae
Ford Motor
Hershey Foods
Lucent Technologies
McDonald's
MCN Energy Group
ONEOK
Philadelphia Suburban Corp.
Reliant Energy
SBC Communications
Sears Roebuck
Total System Services
UtiliCorp United
Wal-Mart

lists additional companies that offer direct stock purchase plans which can be set up as IRA accounts.

Additional information (investment requirements, phone, performance history, etc.) for each of the companies listed in Table 9.1 can be found in Tables 7.7 and 7.8.

CHAPTER 10

Battle Plan

The logistics of investing have never been easier. Coming up with the money to invest is about the only obstacle now. Below is a plan of attack for the Thrifty Investor.

Step 1: Decide *how much* you *can* invest. That will probably require a careful look at your budget. If you're not budgeting, you might want to start. It might also require that you study the information in Tables 8.1 through 8.8 if you're interested in determining how much you "should be" investing.

Step 2: Decide *how* you are going to invest:

- *Tax-deferred annuity at work, such as a 401(k) or 403(b)*
- *Regular investment account on your own*
- *UTMA account for a child*
- *Traditional IRA*
- *Roth IRA*
- *Education IRA*
- *Education Savings Plan (Section 529 plans)*

If you're not sure which type of account to establish, consult a tax adviser or financial planner. Generally, you should start with a tax-deferred annuity at work, such as a 401(k) or 403(b). Beyond that, your own unique situation will determine which type of account(s) you establish.

If you just want to get something started, don't want to talk with a tax adviser or financial planner, and don't need the tax deduction of a Regular IRA, then you should start a *Roth IRA* using mutual funds and/or individual stocks. You can withdraw your *contributions* at any time without owing tax, so the money is not tied up as it is in a regular IRA, and it's not earmarked for a specific purpose, as is money in an Education IRA or Education Savings Plan.

Step 3: Decide *which* investments to select. Look at the list of Frugal Forty Funds in Table 5.1. Pick one or two. Or check out the Balanced Mutual Fund Portfolios in Table 6.4. Pick one. Or two. Intelligently integrated mutual fund portfolios will incorporate large U.S. stock, small U.S. stock, and non-U.S. stock. Mutual funds represent the *core* of your investment plan.

Step 4: If you want to *explore* into some individual stocks, start your search using the information in Tables 7.1, 7.4, and 7.7. If you want to go beyond the direct stock purchase plans listed in those tables, cast around among S&P 500 stocks. The information in Appendices A, B, and C will help. If you want to expand your horizons beyond stocks in the S&P 500, you'll want to search through Appendix D or hop on the web and go to http://www.ShareBuilder.com. Once you pick a company, you'll likely find its recent performance history in Appendix E, F, or G. Several examples of direct stock purchase plan applications can be found in Appendix J.

Step 5: Be patient. Investing is like rearing children—the "payoff" may take a while.

Step 6: Monitor the performance of your investments, but be reasonable. For long-term investments, you certainly DO NOT need to be checking the account balances everyday. Your mental hygiene is more important than that. For those of you who must check your investments often, a good web resource is http://www.quicken.com.

Step 7: Keep good records, particularly if you're using a direct stock purchase plan.

Step 8: Enjoy the process. Thrifty doesn't imply being stingy. Share. Investing isn't a goal, but rather a means to many important ends.

Step 9: Teach someone else what you have learned. We're all
         better off if we help each other plan for tomorrow.
         Uncle Sam is a great guy, but our financial future is
         really our own responsibility.

Step 10: Do what you do. If you're a poet, do that. If you're an
         engineer, do that. If you're a mom or dad, you have
         the best job of all. Don't let investing consume your
         thinking. Don't become a day-trader. Don't put a price
         tag on everything. Don't second-guess yourself every
         time an investment doesn't turn out to be a winner.

Set your investment plans in motion, and then get back to your life.
And, by all means, have a good life.

Brief Descriptions of S&P 500 Companies that Offer Direct Stock Purchase Plans

AFLAC Inc. (AFL)   Writes supplemental health insurance, mainly limited to reimbursement for medical, nonmedical, and surgical expenses of cancer; sells individual and group life, and accident and health insurance.

Air Products & Chemicals (APD)   Recovers and distributes industrial gases and a variety of medical and specialty gases; produces and markets polymer chemicals, performance chemicals and chemical intermediates; supplies cryogenic and other process equipment and related engineering services.

Allstate Corp (ALL)   Writes property-liability insurance, primarily private passenger automobile and homeowners' policies; offers life insurance, annuity, and group pension products.

American Electric Power (AEP)   Operates one of the nation's largest energy companies, providing electric service to almost three million people in parts of Michigan, Indiana, Ohio, Kentucky, Virginia, West Virginia, and Tennessee.

American Express (AXP)   Provides travel-related services, including travelers' cheques, American Express cards, consumer lending, tour packages and itineraries, and publications; investors' diversified financial products and services; international banking services through offices in 37 countries.

Avery Dennison Corp (AVY)   Produces self-adhesive materials. Company also makes and sells a variety of office products and other items, including notebooks, three-ring binders, organizing systems, felt-tip markers, glues, fasteners, business forms, tickets, tags, and imprinting equipment.

Bank of America Corp (BAC)   Conducts a general banking business through some 5000 banking offices in 22 states and the District of Columbia. BankAmerica, with total assets exceeding $570 billion, has a relationship with 30 million American households. It also has offices in nearly 40 countries overseas.

Bank of New York (BK)   Conducts a general banking business through 363 offices in New York, New Jersey, Connecticut, and numerous international offices; and provides cash management services, investment management, securities servicing, and equipment leasing.

C R Bard (BCR)   Designs, makes, packages, distributes, and sells medical, surgical, diagnostic, and patient care devices to hospitals, physicians, and nursing homes. The company's products consist of urological, cardiovascular, and surgical items.

151

Becton, Dickinson (BDX)   Makes and sells a broad line of medical supplies and devices, and diagnostic systems used by health care professionals, medical research institutions, and the general public.

Bell Atlantic Corp (BEL)   Operates a diversified telecommunications concern that provides voice and data transport and calling services network access, directory publishing, and public telephone services to customers in the Mid-Atlantic and New England regions.

BellSouth Corp (BLS)   Provides wire-line telecommunications to approximately two-thirds of the population and one-half of the territory within Alabama, Kentucky, Louisiana, Mississippi, Tennessee, Florida, Georgia, North Carolina, and South Carolina; provides wireless and international communications services, and advertising and publishing products.

Campbell Soup (CPB)   Makes and markets soups and sauces, biscuits and confectionery products; distributes products to the food service and home meal replacement markets.

Caterpillar Inc. (CAT)   Makes earth-moving, construction, and materials handling machinery, equipment, and diesel engines; provides various financial products and services.

Chevron Corp (CHV)   Explores for, develops, and produces crude oil and natural gas; refines crude oil into finished petroleum products; transports and markets crude oil, natural gas, and petroleum products; makes chemicals for industrial uses.

CMS Energy (CMS)   Supplies electricity and natural gas in Michigan; explores and produces oil and natural gas; invests in, develops, converts, constructs, operates, and acquires nonutility power generation projects; owns, develops, and manages natural gas transmission, processing, and storage projects.

Coastal Corp (CGP)   Supplies natural gas; refines, markets, and distributes petroleum and chemical products; explores and produces oil and natural gas; mines coal; provides independent power production.

Compaq Computer (CPQ)   Makes and markets desktop personal computers, portable computers, workstations, communications products, tower PC servers, and peripheral products that store and manage data in network environments. Products are marketed mainly to business, home, government, and education customers.

Conoco (COC.B)   An integrated energy company; headquartered in Houston, Texas.

CVS Corp (CVS)   Operates 4000 prescription drugs, health, and beauty care stores in the Northeast and Mid-Atlantic regions under the name CVS, substantially all of which have pharmacies.

Dayton Hudson (DH)   Operates department stores under the names Hudson's, Marshall Field's, and Dayton's; Target discount stores selling everyday needs, apparel, and recreational items; retail stores under the name Mervyn's California, selling mainly apparel and soft goods.

Deere & Co. (DE)   Makes and distributes agricultural, industrial, commercial, and consumer equipment. Company also provides credit services, property and casualty insurance, and health management programs.

Disney (Walt) Co. (DIS)   Diversified international entertainment company with operations in filmed entertainment, theme parks and resorts, and consumer products; broadcasting (including Capital Cities/ABC, Inc.) and publishing operations.

Dollar General (DG)   Owns and operates 3169 retail general merchandise stores in 24 states located predominantly in small towns in the midwestern and southeastern United States, operating under the name Dollar General Stores.

Dominion Resources (D)   Supplies electricity in Virginia and North Carolina; participates in independent power production projects; through ventures, acquires and develops natural gas reserves.

Dow Jones & Co. (DJ)   Publishes *The Wall Street Journal* and other business and community newspapers and business publications; provides financial information services.

DTE Energy (DTE)   Supplies electricity in Detroit and the surrounding areas and in industrial and agricultural sections outside Detroit; provides financial services for nonutility affiliates; holds real estate investments; provides specialty engineering services for industrial and utility clients.

Eastman Kodak (EK)   Develops, makes, and sells consumer and commercial photographic imaging products. Products include films, photographic papers and chemicals, cameras, projectors, processing equipment, audiovisual equipment, copiers, microfilm products, applications software, and printers.

Exxon Mobil Corp (XOM)   Explores, produces, transports, and sells crude oil and natural gas petroleum products; explores for and mines coal and other mineral properties; makes and sells petrochemicals; owns interests in electrical power generation facilities.

Federal National Mortgage (FNM) "Fannie Mae"   Provides ongoing assistance to the secondary market for residential mortgages by providing liquidity for residential mortgage investments, thereby improving the distribution of investment capital available for such mortgage financing.

Florida Progress (FPC)   Supplies electricity in Florida; mines, procures, and transports coal; transports bulk commodities.

Ford Motor (F)   Makes, assembles, and sells cars, vans, trucks, tractors, and their related parts and accessories; provides financing operations, vehicle and equipment leasing, and insurance operations. Ford is the second largest producer of cars and trucks in the world.

General Electric (GE)   Makes major appliances, industrial and power systems, aircraft engines, engineered plastics, silicones, superabrasives, laminates, and technical products; furnishes TV network services, produces programs, operates VHF and UHF TV stations; provides financial services.

Gillette Co. (G)   A leading manufacturer of male and female grooming products; top seller of writing instruments and correction products; oral care products.

Goodyear Tire & Rubber (GT)   Develops, makes, and sells tires and related transportation products; participates in various crude oil transportation and gathering activities; makes various industrial rubber and chemical products.

Guidant Corp (GDT)   A leading provider of medical devices for use in cardiac rhythm management, vascular intervention, and other forms of minimally invasive surgery; implantable pacemaker systems used in the treatment of slow or irregular arrhythmias.

Hershey Foods (HSY)   Makes and sells chocolate and nonchocolate confectionery products, grocery and pasta products.

Home Depot (HD)   Operates 690 do-it-yourself warehouse stores in the United States, Canada, and Chile, which sell a wide assortment of building material, home improvement, lawn and garden products; 6 EXPO Design Centers in Florida, Texas, Georgia, California, and New York, which mainly offer interior design and renovation products.

International Business Machines (IBM) Provides customer solutions through the use of advanced information technologies; offers a variety of solutions that include services, software, systems, products, financing, and technologies.

ITT Industries (IIN) Develops, makes, and supports high-technology electronic systems and components for defense and commercial markets worldwide; supplies systems and components to vehicle manufacturers worldwide; designs, makes, and sells products and systems used to move and contain liquids.

J.C. Penney (JCP) Operates a nationwide chain of department stores under the J.C. Penney name, augmented by the JC Penney Catalog, selling mainly apparel, accessories, and home furnishings; retail drugstores; markets group life and health insurance.

Johnson Controls (JCI) Makes automobile batteries, interior and seating systems; makes, installs, and services control systems for nonresidential buildings to manage energy use, temperature, ventilation, security, and fire safety.

Lehman Br Holdings (LEH) Provides securities underwriting, financial advisory, investment, and merchant banking services; securities and commodities trading as principal and agent; asset management to institutional, corporate, government, and high-net-worth individual clients throughout the United States and the world.

Longs Drug Stores (LDG) Operates 349 self-service drug stores in California, Hawaii, Nevada, and Colorado.

Lucent Technologies (LU) One of the world's leading designers, developers, and manufacturers of telecommunications systems, software, and products; a leading global marketer of business communications systems and computers.

Mattel, Inc. (MAT) Designs, makes, and sells Barbie fashion dolls and doll clothing and accessories, Fisher-Price toys and juvenile products, die-cast Hot Wheels vehicles and playsets, Cabbage Patch Kids dolls and other large dolls, Scrabble, card games, preschool and Disney-licensed toys.

McDonald's Corp (MCD) Develops, franchises, operates, and services a worldwide system of approximately 23,300 quick-service restaurants under the name McDonald's.

McGraw-Hill Companies (MHP) Provides informational products and services for business and industry, with a focus on such markets as finance, business, education, construction, communications, medical and health, aerospace, and defense.

Mellon Financial Corp (MEL) Provides domestic retail banking through 1183 locations; worldwide commercial banking; trust banking and investment management services, mutual fund activities, real estate financing, mortgage servicing, and securities-related activities.

Merck & Co (MRK) A leading pharmaceutical concern that discovers, develops, makes, and markets a broad range of human and animal health products and services; administers managed prescription drug programs.

Morgan Stanley Dean Witter (MWD) Provides a broad range of nationally marketed credit and investment products, with a principal focus on individual customers; provides investment banking, transaction processing, private-label credit card, and various other investment advice services.

Northern States Pwr (NSP) Generates, transmits, and distributes electricity throughout a 49,000-square-mile service area, and distributes natural gas in about 151 communities in Minnesota, Wisconsin, North Dakota, South Dakota, and the upper peninsula of Michigan.

ONEOK Inc. (OKE)   Supplies natural gas to retail and wholesale customers in Oklahoma; leases pipeline capacity to customers for their use in transporting natural gas to their facilities; transports gas for others; explores and produces natural gas and oil; extracts and sells natural gas liquids.

Peoples Energy (PGL)   Distributes natural gas in Chicago and various other communities in Illinois. Other operations include management-related services and, through a partnership, on-site fueling services for natural gas-powered fleet vehicles.

Pfizer, Inc. (PFE)   Produces and distributes anti-infectives, anti-inflammatory agents, cardiovascular agents, antifungal drugs, central nervous system agents, orthopedic implants, food science products, animal health products, toiletries, baby care products, dental rinse, and other proprietary health items.

Phillips Petroleum (P)   Refines, transports, and markets crude oil, natural gas liquids and petroleum products; provides feedstock for the production of petrochemicals; makes intermediate and finished chemical products; explores for and produces petroleum liquids; acquires, gathers, and processes raw natural gas.

Pinnacle West Capital (PNW)   Supplies electricity to the state of Arizona with the exception of Tucson and one-half of the Phoenix area; owns, holds, and develops real property in Arizona; makes equity investments in other concerns.

Procter & Gamble (PG)   Makes detergents, fabric conditioners, and hard surface cleaners; products for personal cleansing, oral care, digestive health, hair and skin; paper tissue, disposable diapers, and pharmaceuticals; shortenings, oils, snacks, baking mixes, peanut butter, coffee, drinks, and citrus products.

Providian Financial (PVN)   Provides consumer loans, deposit products, and other banking services to consumers nationwide, including credit cards, revolving lines of credit, home loans, secured credit cards, and fee-based services.

Quaker Oats (OAT)   Makes hot cereals, pancake mixes, grain-based snacks, cornmeal, hominy grits and value-added rice products, ready-to-eat cereals, syrups and dry pasta products, biscuits, cookies; sports and single-serve alternative beverages.

Reliant Energy (REI)   Operates as a diversified international energy services company with 3.8 million electric and natural gas customers in the United States, and ownership interests in international utilities serving over seven million customers.

Rockwell International Corp (ROK)   Researches, develops, and makes automation equipment and systems, avionics and communications products and systems; and electronic commerce equipment. Its products are sold to customers in both commercial and government markets.

SBC Communications (SBC)   Provides land-line and wireless telecommunications services and equipment, directory advertising, publishing and cable television services in Texas, Missouri, Oklahoma, Kansas, Arkansas, California, Nevada, and Connecticut.

Sears Roebuck (S)   Operates a chain of 833 retail stores in the United States; operates hardware superstores and auto supply and specialty stores.

Sempra Energy (SRE)   Supplies electricity and natural gas in San Diego and 24 other cities, and provides energy management services, equipment leasing, and real estate investments; supplies natural gas in southern and central California.

Southern Co. (SO)   Supplies electricity in Alabama, Georgia, Florida, and Mississippi; owns generating units at a large electric generating station that supplies power to certain utility subsidiaries.

Synovus Financial (SNV)   Conducts a banking business through 34 banks in Georgia, Alabama, Florida, and South Carolina; provides bank-card data processing services, mortgage servicing throughout the Southeast, trust and brokerage services.

Tandy Corp (TAN)   Sells consumer electronic products through its RadioShack and Computer City store chains. Products include private label electronic parts and accessories, audio/video equipment, digital satellite systems, personal computers, telephones, scanners, electronic toys, batteries.

Tektronix Inc. (TEK)   Makes a wide variety of electronic test and measurement instruments, including oscilloscopes, cable testers, analyzers, probes, and general purpose test instruments; makes color printing and imaging products, video and networking products.

Texaco Inc. (TX)   Explores for, produces, transports, refines, and markets crude oil, natural gas, and petroleum products. Conducts its operations in the United States, Europe, and elsewhere throughout the Eastern and Western Hemispheres.

Tribune Co. (TRB)   Publishes daily newspapers and community publications in several states; operates 16 television and four radio stations; provides television program production and syndication; owns the Chicago Cubs major league baseball team; publishes educational materials.

U S West (USW)   Operates a telephone business; provides cellular advanced communications services; publishes telephone directories and marketing reference guides; operates cable television networks.

Wal-Mart Stores (WMT)   Largest retailer in the United States, measured by total revenues. Operates 1921 Wal-Mart retail discount department stores, 441 Wal-Mart Supercenters, and 443 Sam's wholesale clubs in the United States, and 601 units in Puerto Rico, Canada, Germany, Mexico, China, and Brazil.

Walgreen Co. (WAG)   Operates nationwide chain of 2356 retail Walgreen's drugstores in 34 states and Puerto Rico. Merchandise includes prescription and nonprescription drugs, general merchandise, cosmetics, toiletries, liquor, beverages, and tobacco products; also operates two mail-order facilities.

Warner-Lambert (WLA)   Makes consumer health care products including over-the-counter health, shaving products, and pet care products; confectionery products, including chewing gums, breath mints and hard candies; ethical pharmaceuticals, biologicals, and empty gelatin capsules.

Whirlpool Corp (WHR)   Makes and markets major home appliances, including home laundry appliances, home refrigeration and room air-conditioning equipment, and other home appliances, products, and services.

Alphabetical Listing of All 500 Companies in the Standard & Poor's 500 Index as of December 31, 1999

Ticker	COMPANY	INDUSTRY
COMS	3Com Corp.	Networking Equipment
ABT	Abbott Labs	Pharmaceuticals
ADPT	Adaptec, Inc.	Semiconductors
ADCT	ADC Telecommunications	Telecommunications Equipment
ADBE	Adobe Systems	Systems Software
AMD	Advanced Micro Devices	Semiconductors
AES	AES Corp.	Electric Utilities
AET	Aetna Inc.	Managed Health Care
AFL	AFLAC Inc.	Life & Health Insurance
APD	Air Products & Chemicals	Industrial Gases
ACV	Alberto-Culver	Personal Products
ABS	Albertson's	Food Retail
AL	Alcan Aluminium Ltd.	Aluminum
AA	Alcoa Inc.	Aluminum
ATI	Allegheny Technologies	Steel
AGN	Allergan, Inc.	Health Care Supplies
AW	Allied Waste Industries	Environmental Services
ALL	Allstate Corp.	Property & Casualty Insurance
AT	ALLTEL Corp.	Integrated Telecommunication Serv
AZA	ALZA Corp. Cl. A	Pharmaceuticals
AHC	Amerada Hess	Integrated Oil & Gas
AEE	Ameren Corp.	Electric Utilities
AOL	America Online	Internet Software & Services
AEP	American Electric Power	Electric Utilities
AXP	American Express	Diversified Financial Services
AGC	American General	Life & Health Insurance
AM	American Greetings Cl. A	Housewares & Specialties
AHP	American Home Products	Pharmaceuticals
AIG	American Int'l Group	Multiline Insurance
AMGN	Amgen	Biotechnology
AMR	AMR Corp.	Airlines
ASO	AmSouth Bancorporation	Banks
APC	Anadarko Petroleum	Oil & Gas Exploration & Production
ADI	Analog Devices	Semiconductors
ANDW	Andrew Corp.	Telecommunications Equipment
BUD	Anheuser-Busch	Brewers
AOC	Aon Corp.	Insurance Brokers
APA	Apache Corp.	Oil & Gas Exploration & Production
AAPL	Apple Computer	Computer Hardware
AMAT	Applied Materials	Semiconductor Equipment
ADM	Archer-Daniels-Midland	Agricultural Products
ACK	Armstrong World	Building Products
ASH	Ashland Inc.	Oil & Gas Refining & Marketing
AFS	Associates First Capital	Diversified Financial Services
T	AT&T Corp.	Integrated Telecommunication Serv
ARC	Atlantic Richfield	Integrated Oil & Gas

ADSK	Autodesk, Inc.	Application Software
AUD	Automatic Data Processing	Data Processing Services
AZO	AutoZone Inc.	Specialty Stores
AVY	Avery Dennison Corp.	Office Services & Supplies
AVP	Avon Products	Personal Products
BHI	Baker Hughes	Oil & Gas Equipment & Services
BLL	Ball Corp.	Metal & Glass Containers
BAC	Bank of America Corp.	Banks
BK	Bank of New York	Banks
ONE	Bank One Corp.	Banks
BCR	Bard (C.R.) Inc.	Health Care Equipment
ABX	Barrick Gold Corp.	Gold
BOL	Bausch & Lomb	Health Care Supplies
BAX	Baxter International Inc	Health Care Equipment
BBT	BB&T Corporation	Banks
BSC	Bear Stearns Cos.	Diversified Financial Services
BDX	Becton, Dickinson	Health Care Equipment
BBBY	Bed Bath & Beyond	Specialty Stores
BEL	Bell Atlantic	Integrated Telecommunication Serv
BLS	BellSouth	Integrated Telecommunication Serv
BMS	Bemis Company	Paper Packaging
BBY	Best Buy Co., Inc.	Computer & Electronics Retail
BFO	BestFoods Inc.	Packaged Foods
BS	Bethlehem Steel	Steel
BMET	Biomet, Inc.	Health Care Equipment
BDK	Black & Decker Corp.	Household Appliances
HRB	Block H&R	Diversified Commercial Service
BMCS	BMC Software	Systems Software
BA	Boeing Company	Aerospace & Defense
BCC	Boise Cascade	Paper Products
BSX	Boston Scientific	Health Care Equipment
BGG	Briggs & Stratton	Industrial Machinery
BMY	Bristol-Myers Squibb	Pharmaceuticals
BF.B	Brown-Forman Corp.	Brewers
BC	Brunswick Corp.	Leisure Products
BNI	Burlington Northern Santa	Railroads
BR	Burlington Resources	Oil & Gas Exploration & Production
CS	Cabletron Systems	Networking Equipment
CPB	Campbell Soup	Packaged Foods
COF	Capital One Financial	Consumer Finance
CAH	Cardinal Health, Inc.	Health Care Distributors & Service
CCL	Carnival Corp.	Hotels
CPL	Carolina Power & Light	Electric Utilities
CAT	Caterpillar Inc.	Construction & Farm Machinery
CBS	CBS Corp.	Broadcasting & Cable TV
CD	Cendant Corporation	Diversified Commercial Services
CTX	Centex Corp.	Homebuilding
CSR	Central & South West	Electric Utilities
CTL	CenturyTel, Inc.	Integrated Telecommunication Serv
CEN	Ceridian Corp.	IT Consulting & Services
CHA	Champion International	Paper Products
SCH	Charles Schwab	Diversified Financial Services
CMB	Chase Manhattan	Banks
CHV	Chevron Corp.	Integrated Oil & Gas
CB	Chubb Corp.	Property & Casualty Insurance
CI	CIGNA Corp.	Managed Health Care
CINF	Cincinnati Financial	Property & Casualty Insurance
CIN	CINergy Corp.	Electric Utilities

CC	Circuit City Group	Computer & Electronics Retail
CSCO	Cisco Systems	Networking Equipment
C	Citigroup Inc.	Diversified Financial Services
CTXS	Citrix Systems	Application Software
CCU	Clear Channel Commun	Broadcasting & Cable TV
CLX	Clorox Co.	Household Products
CMS	CMS Energy	Electric Utilities
CGP	Coastal Corp.	Integrated Oil & Gas
KO	Coca Cola Co.	Soft Drinks
CCE	Coca-Cola Enterprises	Soft Drinks
CL	Colgate-Palmolive	Household Products
CG	Columbia Energy Group	Gas Utilities
COL	Columbia/HCA Healthcare	Health Care Facilities
CMCSK	Comcast Class A Special	Broadcasting & Cable TV
CMA	Comerica Inc.	Banks
CPQ	COMPAQ Computer	Computer Hardware
CA	Computer Associates Int'l	Systems Software
CSC	Computer Sciences Corp.	IT Consulting & Services
CPWR	Compuware Corp.	Systems Software
CMVT	Comverse Technology	Telecommunications Equipment
CAG	ConAgra Inc.	Packaged Foods
COC.B	Conoco Inc.	Integrated Oil & Gas
CNC	Conseco Inc.	Life & Health Insurance
ED	Consolidated Edison Hldg	Electric Utilities
CNG	Consolidated Natural Gas	Gas Utilities
CNS	Consolidated Stores	General Merchandise Stores
CEG	Constellation Energy Gro	Electric Utilities
CBE	Cooper Industries	Electrical Components & Equipment
CTB	Cooper Tire & Rubber	Tires & Rubber
RKY	Coors (Adolph)	Brewers
GLW	Corning Inc.	Electrical Components & Equipment
COST	Costco Wholesale Corp.	General Merchandise Stores
CCR	Countrywide Credit Indus	Consumer Finance
CR	Crane Company	Building Products
CCK	Crown Cork & Seal	Metal & Glass Containers
CSX	CSX Corp.	Railroads
CUM	Cummins Engine Co., Inc.	Construction & Farm Machinery
CVS	CVS Corp.	Drug Retail
DCN	Dana Corp.	Auto Parts & Equipment
DHR	Danaher Corp.	Industrial Machinery
DRI	Darden Restaurants	Restaurants
DH	Dayton Hudson	General Merchandise Stores
DE	Deere & Co.	Construction & Farm Machinery
DELL	Dell Computer	Computer Hardware
DPH	Delphi Automotive System	Auto Parts & Equipment
DAL	Delta Air Lines	Airlines
DLX	Deluxe Corp.	Diversified Commercial Service
DDS	Dillard Inc.	Department Stores
DG	Dollar General	General Merchandise Stores
D	Dominion Resources	Electric Utilities
DNY	Donnelley (R.R.) & Sons	Commercial Printing
DOV	Dover Corp.	Industrial Machinery
DOW	Dow Chemical	Diversified Chemicals
DJ	Dow Jones & Co.	Publishing & Printing
DTE	DTE Energy Co.	Electric Utilities
DD	Du Pont (E.I.)	Diversified Chemicals
DUK	Duke Energy	Electric Utilities
DNB	Dun & Bradstreet Corp.	Diversified Commercial Service

EFU	Eastern Enterprises	Gas Utilities
EMN	Eastman Chemical	Diversified Chemicals
EK	Eastman Kodak	Photographic Products
ETN	Eaton Corp.	Industrial Machinery
ECL	Ecolab Inc.	Diversified Commercial Service
EIX	Edison Int'l	Electric Utilities
EDS	Electronic Data Systems	IT Consulting & Services
EPG	El Paso Energy	Gas Utilities
EMC	EMC Corp.	Computer Storage & Peripherals
EMR	Emerson Electric	Electrical Components & Equipment
EC	Engelhard Corp.	Diversified Chemicals
ENE	Enron Corp.	Multi-Utilities
ETR	Entergy Corp.	Electric Utilities
EFX	Equifax Inc.	Diversified Commercial Service
XOM	Exxon Mobil Corp.	Integrated Oil & Gas
FNM	Fannie Mae	Diversified Financial Services
FDX	FDX Holding Corp.	Air Freight & Couriers
FRE	Federal Home Loan Mtg.	Diversified Financial Services
FD	Federated Dept. Stores	Department Stores
FITB	Fifth Third Bancorp	Banks
FDC	First Data	Data Processing Services
FTU	First Union Corp.	Banks
FSR	Firstar Corporation	Banks
FE	FirstEnergy Corp.	Electric Utilities
FBF	FleetBoston Financial	Banks
FLE	Fleetwood Enterprises	Homebuilding
FPC	Florida Progress	Electric Utilities
FLR	Fluor Corp.	Construction & Engineering
FMC	FMC Corp.	Diversified Chemicals
F	Ford Motor	Automobile Manufacturers
FJ	Fort James Corp.	Household Products
FO	Fortune Brands, Inc.	Housewares & Specialties
FWC	Foster Wheeler	Construction & Engineering
FPL	FPL Group	Electric Utilities
BEN	Franklin Resources Inc	Diversified Financial Services
FCX	Freeport-McMoran Copper	Diversified Metals & Mining
GCI	Gannett Co.	Publishing & Printing
GPS	Gap (The)	Apparel Retail
GTW	Gateway, Inc.	Computer Hardware
GD	General Dynamics	Aerospace & Defense
GE	General Electric	Industrial Conglomerates
GIC	General Instrument Corp.	Telecommunications Equipment
GIS	General Mills	Packaged Foods
GM	General Motors	Automobile Manufacturers
GPC	Genuine Parts	Trading Companies & Distributors
GP	Georgia-Pacific Group	Forest Products
G	Gillette Co.	Personal Products
GBLX	Global Crossing	Alternative Carriers
GDW	Golden West Financial	Banks
GR	Goodrich (B.F.)	Aerospace & Defense
GT	Goodyear Tire & Rubber	Tires & Rubber
GPU	GPU Inc.	Electric Utilities
GRA	Grace (W.R.) & Co.(New)	Specialty Chemicals
GWW	Grainger (W.W.) Inc.	Trading Companies & Distributors
GAP	Great A & P	Food Retail
GLK	Great Lakes Chemical	Specialty Chemicals
GTE	GTE Corp.	Integrated Telecommunication Serv
GDT	Guidant Corp.	Health Care Equipment

HAL	Halliburton Co.	Oil & Gas Equipment & Services
H	Harcourt General Inc.	Publishing & Printing
HET	Harrah's Entertainment	Casinos & Gaming
HIG	Hartford Financial Svc.	Multiline Insurance
HAS	Hasbro Inc.	Leisure Products
HRC	HEALTHSOUTH Corp.	Health Care Facilities
HNZ	Heinz (H.J.)	Packaged Foods
HPC	Hercules, Inc.	Diversified Chemicals
HSY	Hershey Foods	Packaged Foods
HWP	Hewlett-Packard	Computer Hardware
HLT	Hilton Hotels	Hotels
HD	Home Depot	Home Improvement Retail
HM	Homestake Mining	Gold
HON	Honeywell International	Aerospace & Defense
HI	Household International	Consumer Finance
HUM	Humana Inc.	Managed Health Care
HBAN	Huntington Bancshares	Banks
IKN	IKON Office Solutions	Office Electronics
ITW	Illinois Tool Works	Industrial Machinery
RX	IMS Health Inc.	Diversified Commercial Services
IN	Inco, Ltd.	Diversified Metals & Mining
IR	Ingersoll-Rand	Industrial Machinery
INTC	Intel Corp.	Semiconductors
IBM	International Bus. Mach	Computer Hardware
IFF	International Flav/Frag	Specialty Chemicals
IP	International Paper	Paper Products
IPG	Interpublic Group	Advertising
IIN	ITT Industries, Inc.	Industrial Conglomerates
JP	Jefferson-Pilot	Life & Health Insurance
JNJ	Johnson & Johnson	Pharmaceuticals
JCI	Johnson Controls	Auto Parts & Equipment
JOS	Jostens Inc.	Apparel & Accessories
KM	K mart	General Merchandise Stores
KSU	Kansas City Southern Ind	Railroads
KBH	Kaufman & Broad Home	Homebuilding
K	Kellogg Co.	Packaged Foods
KMG	Kerr-McGee	Oil & Gas Exploration & Production
KEY	KeyCorp	Banks
KMB	Kimberly-Clark	Household Products
KLAC	KLA-Tencor Corp.	Semiconductor Equipment
KRI	Knight-Ridder Inc.	Publishing & Printing
KSS	Kohl's Corp.	Department Stores
KR	Kroger Co.	Food Retail
LEG	Leggett & Platt	Home Furnishings
LEH	Lehman Bros. Hldgs.	Diversified Financial Services
LXK	Lexmark Int'l. Group A	Computer Storage & Peripherals
LLY	Lilly (Eli) & Co.	Pharmaceuticals
LTD	Limited, Inc.	Apparel Retail
LNC	Lincoln National	Life & Health Insurance
LIZ	Liz Claiborne, Inc.	Apparel & Accessories
LMT	Lockheed Martin Corp.	Aerospace & Defense
LTR	Loews Corp.	Multiline Insurance
LDG	Longs Drug Stores	Drug Retail
LPX	Louisiana Pacific	Forest Products
LOW	Lowe's Cos.	Home Improvement Retail
LSI	LSI Logic	Semiconductors
LU	Lucent Technologies	Telecommunications Equipment
MKG	Mallinckrodt Inc.	Health Care Equipment

HCR	Manor Care Inc.	Health Care Facilities
MAR	Marriott Int'l (New)	Hotels
MMC	Marsh & McLennan	Insurance Brokers
MAS	Masco Corp.	Building Products
MAT	Mattel, Inc.	Leisure Products
MAY	May Dept. Stores	Department Stores
MYG	Maytag Corp.	Household Appliances
MBI	MBIA Inc.	Property & Casualty Insurance
KRB	MBNA Corp.	Consumer Finance
MDR	McDermott International	Construction & Engineering
MCD	McDonald's Corp.	Restaurants
MHP	McGraw-Hill	Publishing & Printing
WCOM	MCI WorldCom	Integrated Telecommunication Serv
MCK	McKesson HBOC Inc.	Health Care Distributors & Service
MEA	Mead Corp.	Paper Products
UMG	MediaOne Group Inc.	Broadcasting & Cable TV
MDT	Medtronic Inc.	Health Care Equipment
MEL	Mellon Financial Corp.	Banks
MRK	Merck & Co.	Pharmaceuticals
MDP	Meredith Corp.	Publishing & Printing
MER	Merrill Lynch	Diversified Financial Services
MTG	MGIC Investment	Property & Casualty Insurance
MU	Micron Technology	Semiconductors
MSFT	Microsoft Corp.	Systems Software
MZ	Milacron Inc.	Industrial Machinery
MIL	Millipore Corp.	Electronic Equipment & Instrum
MMM	Minn. Mining & Mfg.	Industrial Conglomerates
MIR	Mirage Resorts	Casinos & Gaming
MOLX	Molex Inc.	Electrical Components & Equipment
MTC	Monsanto Company	Diversified Chemicals
JPM	Morgan (J.P.) & Co.	Banks
MWD	Morgan Stanley, Dean Witter	Diversified Financial Services
MOT	Motorola Inc.	Telecommunications Equipment
NGH	Nabisco Group Hldgs.	Packaged Foods
NC	NACCO Ind. Cl. A	Construction & Farm Machinery
NCC	National City Corp.	Banks
NSM	National Semiconductor	Semiconductors
NSI	National Service Ind.	Electrical Components & Equipment
NAV	Navistar International	Construction & Farm Machinery
NTAP	Network Appliance	Computer Storage & Peripherals
NCE	New Century Energies	Electric Utilities
NYT	New York Times Cl. A	Publishing & Printing
NWL	Newell Rubbermaid Inc.	Housewares & Specialties
NEM	Newmont Mining	Gold
NXTL	NEXTEL Communications	Wireless Telecommunication Service
NMK	Niagara Mohawk Hldgs Inc	Electric Utilities
GAS	NICOR Inc.	Gas Utilities
NKE	NIKE Inc.	Footwear
JWN	Nordstrom	Department Stores
NSC	Norfolk Southern Corp.	Railroads
NT	Nortel Networks Corp.	Telecommunications Equipment
NSP	Northern States Power	Electric Utilities
NTRS	Northern Trust Corp.	Banks
NOC	Northrop Grumman Corp.	Aerospace & Defense
NOVL	Novell Inc.	Systems Software
NUE	Nucor Corp.	Steel
OXY	Occidental Petroleum	Integrated Oil & Gas
ODP	Office Depot	Specialty Stores

OK	Old Kent Financial	Banks
OMC	Omnicom Group	Advertising
OKE	ONEOK Inc.	Gas Utilities
ORCL	Oracle Corp.	Systems Software
OWC	Owens Corning	Building Products
OI	Owens-Illinois	Metal & Glass Containers
PCAR	PACCAR Inc.	Construction & Farm Machinery
PTV	Pactiv Corporation	Paper Packaging
PWJ	PaineWebber Group	Diversified Financial Services
PLL	Pall Corp.	Industrial Machinery
PMTC	Parametric Technology	Application Software
PH	Parker-Hannifin	Industrial Machinery
PAYX	Paychex Inc.	Data Processing Services
PEB	PE Corp.-PE Biosystems	Electronic Equipment & Instrum
PE	PECO Energy Co.	Electric Utilities
JCP	Penney (J.C.)	Department Stores
PGL	Peoples Energy	Gas Utilities
PSFT	PeopleSoft Inc.	Application Software
PBY	Pep Boys	Specialty Stores
PEP	PepsiCo Inc.	Soft Drinks
PKI	PerkinElmer, Inc.	Electronic Equipment & Instrum
PFE	Pfizer, Inc.	Pharmaceuticals
PCG	PG&E Corp.	Electric Utilities
PNU	Pharmacia & Upjohn, Inc.	Pharmaceuticals
PD	Phelps Dodge	Diversified Metals & Mining
MO	Philip Morris	Tobacco
P	Phillips Petroleum	Integrated Oil & Gas
PNW	Pinnacle West Capital	Electric Utilities
PBI	Pitney-Bowes	Office Services & Supplies
PDG	Placer Dome Inc.	Gold
PNC	PNC Bank Corp.	Banks
PRD	Polaroid Corp.	Photographic Products
PCH	Potlatch Corp.	Paper Products
PPL	PP & L Resources	Electric Utilities
PPG	PPG Industries	Specialty Chemicals
PX	Praxair, Inc.	Industrial Gases
PG	Procter & Gamble	Household Products
PGR	Progressive Corp.	Property & Casualty Insurance
PVN	Providian Financial Corp	Consumer Finance
PEG	Public Serv. Enterprise	Electric Utilities
PHM	Pulte Corp.	Homebuilding
OAT	Quaker Oats	Packaged Foods
QCOM	QUALCOMM Inc.	Telecommunications Equipment
QTRN	Quintiles Transnational	Health Care Distributors & Service
RAL	Ralston-Ralston Purina	Packaged Foods
RTN.B	Raytheon Co.	Aerospace & Defense
RBK	Reebok International	Footwear
RGBK	Regions Financial Corp.	Banks
REI	Reliant Energy	Electric Utilities
RLM	Reynolds Metals	Aluminum
RAD	Rite Aid	Drug Retail
ROK	Rockwell International	Electrical Components & Equipment
ROH	Rohm & Haas	Specialty Chemicals
RDC	Rowan Cos.	Oil & Gas Drilling
RD	Royal Dutch Petroleum	Integrated Oil & Gas
RML	Russell Corp.	Apparel & Accessories
R	Ryder System	Trucking
SAFC	SAFECO Corp.	Property & Casualty Insurance

SWY	Safeway Inc.	Food Retail
SLE	Sara Lee Corp.	Packaged Foods
SBC	SBC Communications Inc.	Integrated Telecommunication Serv
SGP	Schering-Plough	Pharmaceuticals
SLB	Schlumberger Ltd.	Oil & Gas Equipment & Services
SFA	Scientific-Atlanta	Telecommunications Equipment
SEG	Seagate Technology	Computer Storage & Peripherals
VO	Seagram Co. Ltd.	Movies & Entertainment
SEE	Sealed Air Corp.(New)	Paper Packaging
S	Sears Roebuck & Co.	Department Stores
SRE	Sempra Energy	Gas Utilities
SRV	Service Corp. Int'l.	Health Care Facilities
SMS	Shared Medical Systems	IT Consulting & Services
SHW	Sherwin-Williams	Home Improvement Retail
SIAL	Sigma-Aldrich	Specialty Chemicals
SGI	Silicon Graphics	Computer Hardware
SLM	SLM Holding Corp.	Diversified Financial Services
SNA	Snap-On Inc.	Auto Parts & Equipment
SLR	Solectron Corp.	Electronic Equipment & Instrum
SO	Southern Co.	Electric Utilities
SOTR	SouthTrust Corp.	Banks
LUV	Southwest Airlines	Airlines
SMI	Springs Industries Inc.	Home Furnishings
FON	Sprint Corp. FON Group	Integrated Telecommunication Serv
PCS	Sprint Corp. PCS Group	Wireless Telecommunication Serv
STJ	St Jude Medical	Health Care Equipment
SPC	St. Paul Cos.	Property & Casualty Insurance
SWK	Stanley Works	Household Appliances
SPLS	Staples Inc.	Specialty Stores
STT	State Street Corp.	Diversified Financial Services
SUB	Summit Bancorp	Banks
SUNW	Sun Microsystems	Computer Hardware
SUN	Sunoco Inc.	Oil & Gas Refining & Marketing
STI	SunTrust Banks	Banks
SVU	Supervalu Inc.	Food Distributors
SNV	Synovus Financial	Banks
SYY	Sysco Corp.	Food Distributors
TROW	T.Rowe Price Associates	Diversified Financial Services
TAN	Tandy Corp.	Computer & Electronics Retail
TEK	Tektronix Inc.	Electronic Equipment & Instrum
TLAB	Tellabs, Inc.	Telecommunications Equipment
TIN	Temple-Inland	Paper Packaging
THC	Tenet Healthcare Corp.	Health Care Facilities
TER	Teradyne, Inc.	Semiconductor Equipment
TX	Texaco Inc.	Integrated Oil & Gas
TXN	Texas Instruments	Semiconductors
TXU	Texas Utilities Hldg.Cos	Electric Utilities
TXT	Textron Inc.	Industrial Conglomerates
TMO	Thermo Electron	Electrical Components & Equipm
TNB	Thomas & Betts	Electrical Components & Equipm
TWX	Time Warner Inc.	Movies & Entertainment
TMC	Times Mirror	Publishing & Printing
TKR	Timken Co.	Industrial Machinery
TJX	TJX Companies Inc.	Apparel Retail
TMK	Torchmark Corp.	Life & Health Insurance
TOS	Tosco Corp.	Oil & Gas Refining & Marketing
TOY	Toys 'R' Us Hldg. Cos.	Specialty Stores
RIG	Transocean Sedco Forex	Oil & Gas Drilling

TRB	Tribune Co.	Publishing & Printing
YUM	TRICON Global Restaurant	Restaurants
TRW	TRW Inc.	Auto Parts & Equipment
TUP	Tupperware Corp.	Housewares & Specialties
TYC	Tyco International	Industrial Conglomerates
USB	U.S. Bancorp	Banks
UCM	Unicom Corp.	Electric Utilities
UN	Unilever N.V.	Packaged Foods
UK	Union Carbide	Diversified Chemicals
UNP	Union Pacific	Railroads
UPR	Union Pacific Resources	Oil & Gas Exploration & Production
UPC	Union Planters	Banks
UIS	Unisys Corp.	IT Consulting & Services
UNH	United HealthCare Corp.	Managed Health Care
UTX	United Technologies	Aerospace & Defense
UCL	Unocal Corp.	Oil & Gas Exploration & Production
UNM	UNUMProvident Corp.	Life & Health Insurance
USW	US West Inc.	Integrated Telecommunication Serv
U	USAirways Group Inc.	Airlines
UST	UST Inc.	Tobacco
MRO	USX-Marathon Group	Integrated Oil & Gas
X	USX-U.S. Steel Group	Steel
VFC	V.F. Corp.	Apparel & Accessories
VIA.B	Viacom Inc.	Movies & Entertainment
VMC	Vulcan Materials	Construction Materials
WB	Wachovia Corp.	Banks
WMT	Wal-Mart Stores	General Merchandise Stores
WAG	Walgreen Co.	Drug Retail
DIS	Walt Disney Co.	Movies & Entertainment
WLA	Warner-Lambert	Pharmaceuticals
WM	Washington Mutual, Inc.	Banks
WMI	Waste Management (New)	Environmental Services
WPI	Watson Pharmaceuticals	Pharmaceuticals
WLP	WellPoint Health Network	Managed Health Care
WFC	Wells Fargo & Co. (New)	Banks
WEN	Wendy's International	Restaurants
W	Westvaco Corp.	Paper Products
WY	Weyerhaeuser Corp.	Forest Products
WHR	Whirlpool Corp.	Household Appliances
WLL	Willamette Industries	Paper Products
WMB	Williams Cos.	Multi-Utilities
WIN	Winn-Dixie	Food Retail
WTHG	Worthington Ind.	Steel
WWY	Wrigley (Wm) Jr.	Packaged Foods
XRX	Xerox Corp.	Office Electronics
XLNX	Xilinx Inc.	Semiconductors
YHOO	Yahoo! Inc.	Internet Software & Services

Historical Performance of S&P 500 Companies

Companies of the S&P 500

Historical Returns as of December 31, 1999

Company	1 Year % Return	3 Year Average % Return	5 Year Average % Return	10 Year Average % Return
3Com	4.88	-13.8	12.76	29.89
Abbott Laboratories	-24.79	14.49	19.52	17.93
Adaptec	183.98	7.63	33.38	36.51
ADC Telecommunications	108.81	32.6	42.15	41.24
Adobe Systems	188.35	54.43	36.13	30.44
Adolph Coors B	-5.83	42.51	28.22	16.39
Advanced Micro Devices	-0.21	3.97	3.07	13.9
AES	57.78	47.59	50.29	NA
Aetna	-28.24	-10.38	5.62	3.96
AFLAC	8.18	31.2	35.98	27.28
Air Products and Chemicals	-14.32	0.82	10.51	13.11
Alberto-Culver B	-2.26	3.35	14.67	9.21
Albertson's	-48.64	-1.79	3.74	10.44
Alcan Aluminium	55.95	9.29	12.28	8.65
Alcoa	125.88	39.79	33.20	18.78
Allegheny Technologies	-35.32	-15.15	-5.45	0.49
Allergan	54.58	43.04	30.62	20.98
Allied Waste Industries	-62.7	-1.60	17.12	NA
Allstate	-36.39	-4.61	17.17	NA
Alltel	40.66	41.67	25.97	19.4
Alza	-33.73	11.00	14.48	4.90
Amerada Hess	15.27	0.44	5.63	2.74
Ameren	-18.01	1.21	5.14	8.32
America Online	95.18	231.7	144.13	NA
American Electric Power	-27.36	-2.58	5.55	6.67
American Express	63.39	44.57	43.26	21.51
American General	-0.56	26.04	25.92	22.09
American Greetings A	-40.86	-3.86	-0.46	5.14
American Home Products	-29.16	12.40	23.15	15.12
American International Group	40.16	41.46	36.43	24.02
Amgen	129.77	64.09	52.11	50.30
AMR	12.84	14.99	20.27	8.73
AmSouth Bancorporation	-34.55	13.38	24.34	19.93
Anadarko Petroleum	11.18	2.33	12.77	7.11
Analog Devices	196.41	54.12	51.36	39.85

Companies of the S&P 500

Historical Returns as of December 31, 1999

Company	1 Year Return	3 Year Average Return	5 Year Average Return	10 Year Average Return
Andrew	14.78	-18.8	4.11	22.84
Anheuser-Busch Companies	9.77	23.52	26.23	17
Aon	10.72	15.45	26.03	15.96
Apache	47.1	2.55	9.09	8.51
Apple Computer	151.14	70.14	21.76	12.1
Applied Materials	196.78	91.75	64.36	53.17
Archer Daniels Midland	-24.62	-12.93	-4.61	3.27
Armstrong World Industries	-42.42	-19.26	0.19	2.21
Ashland	-29.99	-6.88	1.73	0.98
Associates First Capital A	-34.87	8.21	NA	NA
AT&T	2.39	25.53	20.32	13.23
Atlantic Richfield	37.07	13.52	15.94	9.24
Autodesk	-20.29	7.2	-2.46	6.52
Automatic Data Processing	35.36	37.1	30.99	25.54
AutoZone	-1.9	5.52	5.91	NA
Avery Dennison	64.58	29.49	35.34	19.25
Avon Products	-24.06	6.88	19.82	17.43
B.F. Goodrich	-20.67	-9.47	8.35	7.24
Baker Hughes	21.7	-13.89	4.63	-0.1
Ball	-12.71	16.37	6.48	5.69
Bank of America	-14	3.49	20.66	11.62
Bank of New York	0.95	35.89	43.58	27.7
Bank One	-34.8	-3.31	12.72	10.77
Barrick Gold	-8.29	-14.16	-3.78	9.04
Bausch & Lomb	15.91	27.73	17.85	10.02
Baxter International	-0.59	17.6	21.85	13.41
BB&T	-30.65	17.37	26.95	18.73
Bear Stearns Companies	27.72	22.89	31.24	23.64
Becton Dickinson	-36.2	8.57	18.86	14.91
Bed Bath & Beyond	1.83	42.04	35.89	NA
Bell Atlantic	16.98	28.12	24.68	13.26
BellSouth	-4.53	35.42	30.98	13.68
Bemis	-5.62	0.38	10.22	9.76
Best Buy	63.74	166.43	45.1	58.57
BestFoods	0.74	15.58	18.72	14.6
Bethlehem Steel	0	-1.91	-14.19	-7.12
Biomet	-0.22	38.89	23.84	19.48
Black & Decker	-5.93	21.44	18.44	12.26
BMC Software	79.38	56.92	62.25	41.23
Boeing	28.74	-6.88	13.52	9.62
Boise Cascade	32.8	10.41	10.57	1.73

Companies of the S&P 500

Historical Returns as of December 31, 1999

Company	1 Year Return	3 Year Average Return	5 Year Average Return	10 Year Average Return
Boston Scientific	-18.42	-9.99	20.28	NA
Briggs & Stratton	9.79	9.32	13.08	18.56
Bristol-Myers Squibb	-2.82	34.99	37.88	20.31
Brown-Forman B	-22.9	9.93	16.19	9.9
Brunswick	-8.16	-0.57	5.54	7.34
Burlington Northern Santa Fe	-28.07	-4.19	10.28	11.19
Burlington Resources	-6.34	-11.91	0.21	-0.83
Cabletron Systems	210.45	-7.87	2.26	30.08
Campbell Soup	-28.21	2.04	15.1	13.09
Capital One Financial	26	59.69	56.41	NA
Cardinal Health	-36.79	7.39	18.56	24.25
Carnival	0.45	43.98	36.7	27.37
Carolina Power & Light	-32.01	-1.19	8.14	8.76
Caterpillar	4.69	10.04	13.68	14.62
CBS	94.86	48.17	40.17	8
Cendant	37.54	3.08	12.44	30.01
Centex	-44.92	10.01	17.41	13.15
Central and South West	-21.56	-1.02	4.63	3.53
Centurytel	5.73	52.17	30.39	17.33
Ceridian	-38.23	2.12	9.92	9.05
Champion International	53.63	13.22	11.65	7.81
Charles Schwab	36.34	75.83	72.3	56.79
Chase Manhattan	11.65	23.01	37.58	22.89
Chevron	7.36	13.33	17.98	14.11
Chubb	-11.14	3.47	9.97	11.37
Cigna	5.71	22.98	33.54	19.62
Cincinnati Financial	-12.9	15.18	17.36	16.54
Cinergy	-26.18	-5.4	6.33	8.12
Circuit City Group	80.79	44.52	32.73	24.03
Cisco Systems	130.84	96.41	93.95	NA
Citigroup	70.08	41.78	52.59	35.12
Citrix Systems	153.44	111.39	NA	NA
Clear Channel Communications	63.76	70.32	69.69	64.26
Clorox	-12.48	28.23	30.63	20.41
CMS Energy	-33.35	0.71	9.98	0.91
Coastal	1.57	14	23.53	9.12
Coca-Cola	-12.17	4.4	18.97	21.31
Coca-Cola Enterprises	-43.38	8.08	27.85	14.61
Colgate-Palmolive	41.7	43.28	35.11	26.14
Columbia Energy Group	11.25	15.91	33.65	6.78
Columbia/HCA Healthcare	25.18	-8.55	5.18	15.94

Companies of the S&P 500

Historical Returns as of December 31, 1999

Company	1 Year Return	3 Year Average Return	5 Year Average Return	10 Year Average Return
Comcast	72.37	78.82	45.68	25.74
Comerica	-29.75	12.77	27.11	20.1
Compaq Computer	-35.35	22.32	28.07	26.23
Computer Associates International	64.31	28.44	37.48	34.76
Computer Sciences	47.28	32.08	29.98	25.68
Compuware	-4.64	81.15	52.61	NA
Comverse Technology	205.81	79.07	78.82	47.78
ConAgra	-25.95	-0.78	10.26	11.53
Conoco A	22.52	NA	NA	NA
Conseco	-40.21	-16.39	11.68	27.69
Consolidated Edison	-31.41	11.68	12.63	8.5
Consolidated Natural Gas	24.39	9.27	17.34	6.92
Consolidated Stores	-19.51	-14.28	6.39	20.68
Constellation Energy Group	-0.43	8.76	12.24	9.09
Cooper Industries	-12.81	1.31	6.62	3.53
Cooper Tire & Rubber	-21.22	-5.48	-6.27	8.19
Corning	189.74	51.52	41.44	24.51
Costco Wholesale	26.41	53.71	47.94	24.59
Countrywide Credit Industries	-49.2	-3.22	15.63	23.83
CR Bard	8.76	26.1	16.74	11.39
Crane	-29.71	4.01	13.7	9.9
Crown Cork & Seal	-24.8	-23.66	-8.12	3.39
CSX	-22.28	-7.2	0.27	8.54
Cummins Engine	39.39	3.87	3.61	8.84
CVS	-27.14	25.27	26.82	10.65
Dana	-24.32	-0.07	8.11	9.48
Danaher	-11.06	27.63	30.1	29.1
Darden Restaurants	1.09	28.23	NA	NA
Dayton Hudson	36.24	56.68	46.21	23.54
Deere & Company	34.86	4.36	16.89	10.9
Dell Computer	39.37	148.56	139.96	96.98
Delphi Automotive Systems	NA	NA	NA	NA
Delta Air Lines	-4.04	12.23	14.82	4.64
Deluxe	-21.5	-1.42	5.47	1.84
Dillard's	-28.37	-12.74	-5.01	-1.22
Dollar General	20.9	30.08	30.05	40.82
Dominion Resources	-10.97	7.2	8.53	9.06
Dover	25.32	23	30.24	19.86
Dow Chemical	51.48	23.71	19.42	11.18
Dow Jones & Company	43.94	28.72	19.69	10.13

Companies of the S&P 500

Historical Returns as of December 31, 1999

Company	1 Year Return	3 Year Average Return	5 Year Average Return	10 Year Average Return
DTE Energy Holding	-22.51	5.11	10.48	8.93
Du Pont De Nemours E.I.	26.87	14.27	21.56	15.88
Duke Energy	-19.43	6.45	9.67	10.81
Dun & Bradstreet	-4.27	10.56	13.59	14.88
Eastern Enterprises	36.58	22.52	22.04	10.25
Eastman Chemical	10.57	-1.67	1.9	NA
Eastman Kodak	-5.59	-3.84	9.42	14.12
Eaton	5.05	3.59	10.62	12.87
Ecolab	9.33	29.29	32.23	20.85
Edison International	-2.9	13.74	17.52	8.81
El Paso Energy	17.37	19.34	24.97	NA
Electronic Data Systems	34.82	17.25	13.2	18.78
Eli Lilly & Company	-24.24	23.69	34.81	17.54
EMC	157.06	136.28	81.85	95.2
Emerson Electric	-3.08	7.99	14.89	12.34
Engelhard	-1.17	1.56	7.08	15.06
Enron	57.66	29.62	26.34	23.16
Entergy	-13.89	3.25	9.8	6.92
Equifax	-30.27	-3.6	16.59	15.27
ExxonMobil	12.56	20.95	25.33	16.88
Fannie Mae	-14.29	20.42	30.66	24.85
FDX	-8.2	22.54	22.14	13.6
Federated Department Stores	16.07	14	21.31	NA
Fifth Third Bancorp	4.25	39.77	40.96	28.38
First Data	54.98	10.8	16.04	NA
First Union	-43.48	-0.62	13.55	16.79
Firstar	-30.57	29.58	42.23	27.91
FirstEnergy	-26.58	NA	NA	NA
FleetBoston Financial	-19.92	14.89	20.5	14.72
Fleetwood Enterprises	-39.28	-7.21	3.79	6.61
Florida Progress	-0.66	15.79	12.2	7.18
Fluor	10.43	-8.22	2.84	3.53
FMC	2.34	-6.5	-0.15	4.98
Ford Motor	-6.16	41.92	30.5	21.46
Fort James	-30.29	-4.56	9.99	3
Fortune Brands	7.11	4.54	11.87	10.35
Foster Wheeler	-29.8	-35.69	-19.13	-5.04
FPL Group	-27.73	1.34	8.23	7.31
Franklin Resources	0.9	12.68	22.78	22.01
Freddie Mac	-26.15	20.77	31.92	25.89

Companies of the S&P 500

Historical Returns as of December 31, 1999

Company	1 Year Return	3 Year Average Return	5 Year Average Return	10 Year Average Return
Freeport-McMoRan Copper & Gold A	91.61	-11.54	-0.57	16.93
Gannett	27.95	31.35	27.22	16.73
Gap	23.21	73.49	60.2	38.72
Gateway	181.56	75.24	67.86	NA
General Dynamics	-9.22	16.39	22.11	32.76
General Electric	53.56	48.4	46.09	28.43
General Instrument	150.46	NA	NA	NA
General Mills	-5.47	7.09	12.31	13.02
General Motors	26.54	22.93	21.39	12.84
Genuine Parts	-23.13	-2.75	3.86	6.22
Georgia-Pacific Group	75.44	27.22	15.7	11.82
Gillette	-12.78	3.02	18.41	22.58
Global Crossing	121.6	NA	NA	NA
Golden West Financial	10.24	17.45	24.1	14.83
Goodyear Tire & Rubber	-43	-16.51	-1.43	5.09
GPU	-28.88	1.4	8.58	8.42
Great A & P Tea	-4.7	-3.1	10.22	-5.48
Great Lakes Chemical	-3.75	-1.01	-4.1	7.3
GTE	11.53	19.81	23.07	12.38
Guidant	-14.55	48.95	63.87	NA
H & R Block	-0.62	17.19	6.14	12.39
Halliburton	37.69	11.6	22.62	9.57
Harcourt General	-8.88	2.87	8.13	9.89
Harrah's Entertainment	68.52	9.98	3.68	NA
Hartford Financial Services Group	-12.51	13.86	NA	NA
Hasbro	-20.63	4.12	8.98	14.01
Healthsouth	-65.18	-34.71	-10.03	6.46
Heinz HJ	-27.46	6.5	13.5	8.76
Hercules	6.17	-11.05	-3.94	11.57
Hershey Foods	-22.34	4.37	16.59	12.62
Hewlett-Packard	67.7	32.47	36.68	26.73
Hilton Hotels	-24.57	-17.11	-1.68	-0.91
Home Depot	68.98	84.01	46.93	44.34
Homestake Mining	-13.68	-17.39	-13.64	-7.6
Honeywell International	31.8	21.48	29.57	23.61
Household International	-4.44	8.22	26.89	19.28
Humana	-54.03	-24.47	-18.39	-10.46
Huntington Bancshares	-10.23	9.24	19.85	17.9
IBM	17.57	42.72	43.69	19.28
Ikon Office Solutions	-19.25	-44.66	-22.06	-4.9

Companies of the S&P 500

Historical Returns as of December 31, 1999

Company	1 Year Return	3 Year Average Return	5 Year Average Return	10 Year Average Return
Illinois Tool Works	17.6	20.25	26.55	21.13
IMS Health	-19.55	NA	NA	NA
Inco	125.14	-9.06	-2.98	0.43
Ingersoll-Rand	17.89	24.56	23.2	14.84
Intel	39.06	36.18	59.76	44.2
International Flavors & Fragrances	-11.35	-2.4	-0.91	8.48
International Paper	28.49	14.04	10.83	9.81
Interpublic Group of Companies	45.88	55.41	41.75	28.55
ITT Industries	-14.49	12.98	17.92	23.17
J.P. Morgan & Co.	24.32	12.7	21.93	15.5
JC Penney	-55.2	-22.51	-11.24	-1.85
Jefferson-Pilot	-7.32	24.35	27.25	21.92
Johnson & Johnson	12.47	24.9	29.64	22.32
Johnson Controls	-1.96	13.16	20.84	16.62
Jostens	-3.19	8.95	9.6	2.38
Kansas City Southern Industries	52.15	71.48	49.49	36.26
Kaufman & Broad Home	-14.79	25.11	15.38	7.96
Kellogg	-7.24	0.35	3.61	8.75
Kerr-McGee	68.72	-1.48	9.48	5.39
KeyCorp	-28.61	-1.34	16.1	13.9
Kimberly-Clark	22.31	13.34	23.72	16.33
KLA-Tencor	156.77	46.39	35.37	38.22
Kmart	-34.28	-1.01	-4.07	-2.7
Knight-Ridder	18.42	17.83	20.91	9.83
Kohl's	17.5	54.37	48.67	NA
Kroger	-37.6	17.53	25.63	17.74
Leggett & Platt	-1.01	8.91	21.47	21.21
Lehman Brothers Holdings	93.4	40.07	42.86	NA
Lexmark International	80.1	87.12	NA	NA
Limited	59.73	39.17	23.38	12.27
Lincoln National	0.19	18.27	21.87	14.68
Liz Claiborne	20.72	0.24	18.82	5.97
Lockheed Martin	-46.91	-20.21	NA	NA
Loews	-37.39	-12.66	8.14	0.84
Longs Drug Stores	-30.29	3.43	12.62	4.14
Louisiana-Pacific	-20.71	-10.12	-10.06	2.13
Lowe's Companies	16.98	50.28	28.62	33.33
LSI Logic	318.6	36.14	27.35	34.22
Lucent Technologies	36.62	87.01	NA	NA
Mallinckrodt	5.16	-8.57	3.1	7.94

Companies of the S&P 500

Historical Returns as of December 31, 1999

Company	1 Year Return	3 Year Average Return	5 Year Average Return	10 Year Average Return
Manor Care	-45.53	-17.63	-4.44	NA
Marriott International A	9.55	NA	NA	NA
Marsh & McLennan Companies	67.72	44.12	33.37	17.61
Masco	-10.34	13.89	19.88	10.1
Mattel	-43.18	-21.19	-2.98	10.27
May Department Stores	-18.03	3.43	12.35	11.83
Maytag	-21.95	36.73	28.95	12.61
MBIA	-18.24	2.78	15.23	14.37
MBNA	11.03	15.11	44.91	NA
McDermott International	-62.83	-17.99	-16.41	-5.99
McDonald's	5.44	21.8	23.22	17.57
McGraw-Hill Companies	22.88	41.55	32.96	19.45
MCI Worldcom	10.93	45.08	52.28	52.92
McKesson HBOC	-71.34	-6.14	8.15	NA
Mead	50.81	16.55	14.54	11.58
MediaOne Group	63.43	61.09	NA	NA
Medtronic	-1.5	29.52	39.93	34.22
Mellon Financial	1.31	27.35	39.32	26.4
Merck	-7.48	21.03	31.16	20.61
Meredith	11.01	17.45	30.26	18.77
Merrill Lynch & Company	26.6	28.61	38.23	31.74
MGIC Investment	51.51	16.8	29.75	NA
Micron Technology	54.51	38.94	28.91	44.86
Microsoft	68.36	78.13	72.51	57.94
Milacron	-18.02	-9.21	-6.52	1.24
Millipore	38.17	-1	11.06	12.66
Minnesota Mining & Manufacturing (3M)	41.08	8.29	16.88	13.29
Mirage Resorts	1.25	-11.23	8.09	10.7
Molex	48.93	31.54	26.48	33.26
Monsanto	-25.2	0.5	24.18	15.96
Morgan Stanley Dean Witter & Co.	103.1	64.65	55.11	NA
Motorola	142.46	34.98	21.39	27.04
Nabisco Group Holdings	-42.24	-15	-2.24	NA
Nacco Industries	-38.84	2.33	4.01	1.27
National City	-32.49	5.02	16.98	13.95
National Semiconductor	217.13	20.45	17.03	19.43
National Service Industries	-19.48	-4.93	6.1	4.23
Navistar International	64.91	72.7	25.45	1.95
NCR	-9.28	4.05	NA	NA

Companies of the S&P 500

Historical Returns as of December 31, 1999

Company	1 Year Return	3 Year Average Return	5 Year Average Return	10 Year Average Return
Network Appliance	270.45	135.5	NA	NA
New Century Energies	-33.66	-2.64	6.69	8.59
New York Times A	43.27	38.91	36.83	16.19
Newell Rubbermaid	-28.32	-1.03	8.58	12.07
Newmont Mining	35.08	-17.6	-6.61	-3.24
Nextel Communications	350.7	101.25	49.25	NA
Niagara Mohawk Holdings	-13.56	12.17	1.23	0.53
Nicor	-19.63	0.75	11.94	8.46
Nike	23.32	-5.26	22.74	23.57
Nordstrom	-23.39	15.22	5.74	4.57
Norfolk Southern	-33.45	-8.9	3.04	7.38
Nortel Networks	305.5	87.91	65.85	34.27
Northern States Power	-24.98	0.24	3.38	5.95
Northern Trust	22.73	44.76	45.75	28.68
Northrop Grumman	-24.19	-11.46	7.6	16.13
Novell	120.35	61.57	18.45	26.27
Nucor	28.11	3.43	0.61	14.54
Occidental Petroleum	34.82	1.91	7.01	2.24
Office Depot	-55.48	-2.63	-6.85	15.22
Old Kent Financial	-18.55	22.24	27.73	20.16
Omnicom Group	73.82	65.31	52.68	34.78
Oneok	-27.52	-2.12	11.59	10
Oracle	289.78	82.11	66.66	47.44
Owens-Corning	-44.84	-22.48	-8.97	-2.3
Owens-Illinois	-18.16	3.28	17.9	NA
Paccar	13.58	14.55	21.26	12.24
Pactiv	NA	NA	NA	NA
PaineWebber Group	1.61	29.08	33.39	25.38
Pall	-12.24	-2.93	5.36	8.71
Parametric Tech	66.54	1.75	25.7	40.94
Parker Hannifin	59.17	27.68	22.54	19.21
Paychex	17.58	38.97	50.71	43.82
PE Corp - PE Biosystems	148.01	61.17	58.31	28.89
PECO Energy	-14.71	16.57	12.73	10.03
Peoples Energy	-11.32	4.93	11.07	9.06
PeopleSoft	12.54	-3.84	35.19	NA
Pep Boys	-42.04	-32.9	-21.2	-1.93
PepsiCo	-12.47	11.04	17.98	15.51
Perkinelmer	52.55	30.37	27.42	12.19
Pfizer	-21.5	34.12	40.05	29.89
PG & E Corp	-32.03	3.58	2.09	5.36

	1 Year Return	3 Year Average Return	5 Year Average Return	10 Year Average Return
Companies of the S&P 500				
Historical Returns as of December 31, 1999				
Company				
Pharmacia & Upjohn	-18.99	6.9	NA	NA
Phelps Dodge	37.31	3.19	4.95	12.49
Philip Morris Companies	-54.66	-11.45	8.39	9.65
Phillips Petroleum	13.5	5.11	10.93	10.27
Pinnacle West Capital	-25.37	2.04	13.13	13.15
Pitney Bowes	-25.58	23.18	27.81	17.8
Placer Dome	-5.64	-19.98	-12	-3.64
PNC Bank	-15.03	9.2	20.78	12.83
Polaroid	3.4	-22.93	-8.79	-6.79
Potlatch	26.36	5.49	7.96	5.9
PP and L Resources	-14.71	5.67	10.67	7.49
PPG Industries	10.22	6.13	13.76	15.36
Praxair	44.55	4.1	21	NA
Procter & Gamble	21.56	28.45	30.83	22.49
Progressive	-56.72	3.01	16.27	19.71
Providian Financial	21.69	38.9	34.85	18.14
Public Service Enterprise Group	-7.99	15.94	12.88	9.29
Pulte	-18.52	14.28	15.22	15.98
Quaker Oats	12.33	22.42	19.41	12.45
Qualcomm	2619.24	230.52	126.79	NA
Quintiles Transnational	-64.99	-17.37	20.64	NA
Ralston Purina	-12.01	7.07	16.06	14.66
Raytheon B	-49.21	-16.53	-1.91	6.7
Reebok International	-44.95	-42.02	-26.74	-7.33
Regions Financial	-35.74	1.66	13.28	16.07
Reliant Energy	-25.67	5.88	11.34	9.82
Reynolds Metals	49.16	13.46	12	6.37
Rite Aid	-77.09	-16.1	1.08	5.44
Rockwell International	21.47	5.12	17.85	15.79
Rohm and Haas	37.74	16.71	19.08	16.3
Rowan Companies	119.63	-1.4	28.25	6.78
Royal Dutch Petroleum ADR	29.81	15.58	21.57	16.87
RR Donnelley & Sons	-41.83	-5.37	-1.25	1.82
Russell	-15.01	-15.49	-9.94	-2.72
Ryder System	-3.64	-2.55	4.37	7.72
SAFECO	-40.61	-11.89	1.92	5.81
Safeway	-41.33	18.7	35.01	NA
Sara Lee	-20.06	7.88	14.34	12.82
SBC Communications	-7.41	26.38	22.69	15.95
Schering-Plough	-22.57	39.45	37.87	25.69
Schlumberger	38.03	9.64	22.51	12.14

Companies of the S&P 500

Historical Returns as of December 31, 1999

Company	1 Year Return	3 Year Average Return	5 Year Average Return	10 Year Average Return
Scientific-Atlanta	145.28	55.41	21.97	22.17
Seagate Technology	53.93	5.64	31.15	20.03
Seagram	18.95	6.53	10.47	8.92
Sealed Air	1.47	7.57	23.38	26.11
Sears Roebuck	-26.83	-11.21	8.59	22.54
Sempra Energy	-26.21	-2.25	5.3	4.33
Service Corp International	-81.31	-36.29	-11.79	4.75
Shared Medical Systems	3.75	2.65	11	18.11
Sherwin-Williams	-27.14	-7.68	6.4	10.96
Sigma-Aldrich	3.36	-0.37	13.72	8.41
Silicon Graphics	-24.75	-27.57	-20.83	2.85
SLM Holding	-10.77	18.32	37.93	14.18
Snap-On	-21.56	-7.15	6.27	4.98
Solectron	104.71	92.46	69.12	70.4
Southern	-15.01	6.82	9.04	11.48
Southtrust	4.73	20.17	28.9	22.74
Southwest Airlines	6.73	35.44	26.79	26.43
Springs Industries	-0.11	0.58	4.66	3.82
Sprint	61.57	52.25	45.71	19.41
Sprint PCS Group	343.24	NA	NA	NA
St. Jude Medical	10.09	-10.2	2.98	7
St. Paul	-0.03	7.68	11.7	12.24
Stanley Works	11.9	6.17	13.88	7.55
Staples	-28.76	37.24	33.52	34.63
State Street	5.03	32.35	40.12	23.88
Summit Bancorp	-27.55	4.63	17.22	13.63
Sun Microsystems	261.74	129.31	103.5	53.32
Sunoco	-32.63	1.79	-0.54	-0.8
SunTrust Banks	-8.17	13.7	25.96	22.64
SuperValu	-26.82	14.99	13.58	6.14
Synovus Financial	-15.66	13.33	32.15	22.32
Sysco	45.62	36.18	27.2	18.98
T Rowe Price Associates	9.24	20.67	39.44	28.11
Tandy	139.98	66.19	33.08	19.35
Tektronix	31.49	5.97	12.86	14.98
Tellabs	87.24	50.54	55.9	66.54
Temple-Inland	13.48	9.16	10.39	8.98
Tenet Healthcare	-10.48	2.42	10.72	3.71
Teradyne	211.5	75.61	50.78	37.41
Texaco	5.72	6.74	16.79	11.02

Companies of the S&P 500

Historical Returns as of December 31, 1999

Company	1 Year Return	3 Year Average Return	5 Year Average Return	10 Year Average Return
Texas Instruments	126.32	83.21	60.69	37.61
Texas Utilities	-19.32	1.04	8.42	7.33
Textron	2.64	19.56	27.32	23.07
Thermo Electron	-11.44	-28.62	-5.54	5.15
Thomas & Betts	-24.51	-8.23	1.67	6.25
Time Warner	16.85	57.59	33.59	17.89
Times Mirror	21.23	11.73	26.74	14.54
Timken	12.4	-0.92	5.95	7.24
TJX Companies	-29.18	20.64	41.17	20.54
Torchmark	-16.77	11.58	16.58	9.02
Tosco	6.21	1.95	24.33	15.8
Toys "R" Us	-15.5	-21.75	-14.11	-5.04
Transocean Sedco Forex	26.21	2.86	31.23	NA
Tribune	68.32	42.37	33.87	18.63
Tricon Global Restaurants	-22.94	NA	NA	NA
TRW	-4.81	4.14	12.32	9.1
Tupperware	7.66	-29.27	NA	NA
Tyco International	3.51	43.69	46.2	20.82
Unicom	-9.26	12.98	12.81	5.41
Unilever NV ADR	-39.76	5.58	13.33	11.33
Union Carbide	59.74	19.84	20.03	38.81
Union Pacific	-1.51	-8.28	10.4	9.77
Union Pacific Resources Group	42.81	-23	NA	NA
Union Planters	-9.87	3.83	17.58	17.66
Unisys	-7.26	67.88	29.93	8.41
United HealthCare	23.44	5.75	3.37	33.24
United Technologies	20.96	27	35.2	20.1
Unocal	17.54	-4.28	6.69	3.77
Unumprovident	-44.3	-2.65	12.96	12.13
US Airways Group	-38.34	11.11	49.8	-0.36
US Bancorp	-31.29	3.7	19.44	19.42
US West	15.9	36.96	35.28	21.95
UST, Inc.	-23.53	-2.84	3.32	9.73
USX-Marathon Group	-15.55	3.89	11.87	NA
USX-US Steel Group	48.79	5.16	1.85	NA
VF	-34.5	-1.93	6.61	9.38
Viacom A	64.31	51.88	23.76	NA
Vulcan Materials	-7.31	27.83	21.57	13.32
W.R. Grace	-9.96	NA	NA	NA
Wachovia	-20.31	8.97	19.42	16.42
Wal-Mart Stores	70.44	83.52	46.41	29.25

Companies of the S&P 500

Historical Returns as of December 31, 1999

Company	1 Year Return	3 Year Average Return	5 Year Average Return	10 Year Average Return
Walgreen	0.37	43.7	41.31	27.56
Walt Disney	-1.68	8.72	14.58	12.82
Warner-Lambert	10.21	50.3	47.58	26.91
Washington Mutual	-30.78	-1.48	21.18	19.74
Waste Management	-63.12	-18.58	8.63	27.11
Watson Pharmaceuticals	-43.04	16.81	22.23	NA
Wellpoint Health Networks	-24.21	24.25	12.42	NA
Wells Fargo	3.26	25.47	31.35	25.33
Wendy's International	-3.68	1.58	8.58	16.71
Westvaco	25.73	7.59	7.73	8.33
Weyerhaeuser	45.16	18.46	17.62	13.98
Whirlpool	20.23	14.44	7.89	9.92
Willamette Industries	41	12.1	16.54	15.43
Williams Companies	-0.51	20	32.62	20.57
Winn-Dixie Stores	-45.05	-6.34	1.34	6.9
Wm. Wrigley Jr.	-5.91	15.67	12.88	18.97
Worthington Industries	38.31	0.59	-0.73	7.72
WW Grainger	16.51	7.4	12.11	13.03
Xerox	-60.82	-3.18	8.69	12.64
Xilinx	179.26	70.31	55.9	NA
Yahoo!	265.23	434.47	NA	NA

Stocks Available at ShareBuilder.com as of January 2000

Company	Ticker Symbol	Company	Ticker Symbol
1 800 FLOWERS COM INC	FLWS	ADFORCE INC	ADFC
20TH CENTURY INDS	TW	ADOBE SYS INC	ADBE
24 / 7 MEDIA INC	TFSM	ADTRAN INC	ADTN
3COM CORP	COMS	ADVANCED DIGITAL INFORMATION	ADIC
4 KIDS ENTMT INC	KIDE	ADVANCED ENERGY INDS INC	AEIS
7-ELEVEN INC	SVEV	ADVANCED FIBRE COMMUNICATIONS	AFCI
99 CENTS ONLY STORES	NDN	ADVANCED MICRO DEVICES INC	AMD
ABBOTT LABS	ABT	ADVANTAGE LEARNING SYS INC	ALSI
ABERCROMBIE & FITCH CO	ANF	ADVENT SOFTWARE INC	ADVS
ABGENIX INC	ABGX	AERIAL COMMUNICATIONS INC	AERL
ABOUT COM INC	BOUT	AES CORP	AES
ACCRUE SOFTWARE INC	ACRU	AETHER SYSTEMS INC	AETH
ACKERLEY GROUP INC	AK	AETNA INC	AET
ACME COMMUNICATIONS INC	ACME	AFFILIATED COMPUTER SVCS INC	ACS
ACNIELSEN CORP	ART	AFFILIATED MANAGERS GROUP	AMG
ACTEL CORP	ACTL	AFFYMETRIX INC	AFFX
ACTIVE SOFTWARE INC	ASWX	AFLAC INC	AFL
ACTUATE CORP	ACTU	AGCO CORP	AG
ACTV INC	IATV	AGILE SOFTWARE CORP DEL	AGIL
ACXIOM CORP	ACXM	AGL RES INC	ATG
ADAPTEC INC	ADPT	AIR EXPRESS INTL CORP	AEIC
ADAPTIVE BROADBAND CORP	ADAP	AIR PRODS & CHEMS INC	APD
ADC TELECOMMUNICATIONS INC	ADCT	AIRBORNE FGHT CORP	ABF
ADELPHIA BUSINESS SOLUTIONS	ABIZ	AIRGAS INC	ARG
ADELPHIA COMMUNICATIONS CORP	ADLAC	AIRGATE PCS INC	PCSA

180

AIRONET WIRELESS COMMUNICATION	AIRO
AK STL HLDG CORP	AKS
ALASKA AIR GROUP INC	ALK
ALBEMARLE CORP	ALB
ALBERTO CULVER CO	ACV
ALBERTSONS INC	ABS
ALCOA INC	AA
ALEXANDER & BALDWIN INC	ALEX
ALFA CORP	ALFA
ALKERMES INC	ALKS
ALLAIRE CORP	ALLR
ALLEGHANY CORP DEL	Y
ALLEGHENY ENERGY INC	AYE
ALLEGHENY TECH	ATI
ALLEGIANCE TELECOM INC	ALGX
ALLERGAN INC	AGN
ALLIANCE SEMICONDUCTOR CORP	ALSC
ALLIANT ENERGY CORP	LNT
ALLIANT TECHSYSTEMS INC	ATK
ALLIED CAP CORP NEW	ALLC
ALLIED RISER COMM CORP	ARCC
ALLIED WASTE INDUSTRIES	AW
ALLMERICA FINL CORP	AFC
ALLSCRIPTS INC	MDRX
ALLSTATE CORP	ALL
ALLTEL CORP	AT
ALPHA INDS INC	AHAA
ALPHARMA INC	ALO
ALTERA CORP	ALTR
ALZA CORPORATION	AZA
AMAZON COM INC	AMZN

AMB PPTY CORP	AMB
AMBAC FINL GROUP INC	ABK
AMCORE FINL INC	AMFI
AMERADA HESS CORP	AHC
AMERCO	UHAL
AMEREN CORP	AEE
AMERICA ONLINE INC DEL	AOL
AMERICA WEST HLDGS CORP	AWA
AMERICAN ANNUITY GROUP INC	AAG
AMERICAN AXLE & MFG HLDGS	AXL
AMERICAN EAGLE OUTFITTERS	AEOS
AMERICAN ELEC PWR INC	AEP
AMERICAN EXPRESS CO	AXP
AMERICAN FINL GROUP INC OHIO	AFG
AMERICAN FREIGHTWAYS CORP	AFWY
AMERICAN GEN CORP	AGC
AMERICAN GREETINGS CORP	AM
AMERICAN HOME PRODS CORP	AHP
AMERICAN INTL GROUP INC	AIG
AMERICAN ITALIAN PASTA CO	PLB
AMERICAN MGMT SYS INC	AMSY
AMERICAN MOBILE SATELLITE CORP	SKYC
AMERICAN NATIONAL CAN GROUP	CAN
AMERICAN NATL INS CO	ANAT
AMERICAN PWR CONVERSION CORP	APCC
AMERICAN STD COS INC DEL	ASD
AMERICAN TOWER CORP	AMT
AMERICAN WTR WKS INC	AWK
AMERICREDIT CORP	ACF
AMERISOURCE HEALTH CORP	AAS
AMERITRADE HLDG CORP	AMTD

AMERUS LIFE HLDGS INC	AMH
AMES DEPT STORES INC	AMES
AMETEK INC NEW	AME
AMFM INC	AFM
AMGEN INC	AMGN
AMKOR TECHNOLOGY INC	AMKR
AMPHENOL CORP NEW	APH
AMR CORP DEL	AMR
AMSOUTH BANCORPORATION	ASO
ANADARKO PETE CORP	APC
ANADIGICS INC	ANAD
ANALOG DEVICES INC	ADI
ANCHOR GAMING	SLOT
ANCOR COMMUNICATIONS INC	ANCR
ANDREW CORP	ANDW
ANDRX CORP	ADRX
ANHEUSER BUSCH COS INC	BUD
ANIXTER INTL INC	AXE
ANNTAYLOR STORES CORP	ANN
ANSWERTHINK CONSULTING GROUP	ANSR
ANTEC CORP	ANTC
AON CORP	AOC
APACHE CORP	APA
APEX INCORPORATED	APEX
APOLLO GROUP INC	APOL
APPLE COMPUTER INC	AAPL
APPLEBEES INTL INC	APPB
APPLIED MATLS INC	AMAT
APPLIED MICRO CIRCUITS CORP	AMCC
APPLIED PWR INC	APW
APPNET INC	APNT
APRIA HEALTHCARE GROUP INC	AHG
APTARGROUP INC	ATR
ARCHER DANIELS MIDLAND CO	ADM
ARCHSTONE CMNTYS TR	ASN
ARDEN RLTY INC	ARI
ARDENT SOFTWARE INC	ARDT
ARGONAUT GROUP INC	AGII
ARIBA INC	ARBA
ARIZONA PUB SVC CO	AZD
ARMSTRONG WORLD INDS INC	ACK
ARROW ELECTRS INC	ARW
ARROW INTL INC	ARRO
ART TECHNOLOGY GROUP	ARTG
ARTESYN TECHNOLOGIES INC	ATSN
ARTHROCARE CORP	ARTC
ARVIN INDS INC	ARV
ASHLAND INC	ASH
ASK JEEVES	ASKJ
ASPECT COMMUNICATIONS INC	ASPT
ASPECT DEV INC	ASDV
ASPEN TECHNOLOGY INC	AZPN
ASSOCIATED BANC CORP	ASBC
ASSOCIATED GROUP INC	AGRPA
ASSOCIATES FIRST CAP CORP	AFS
ASTORIA FINL CORP	ASFC
ASYST TECHNOLOGIES INC	ASYT
AT HOME CORP	ATHM T
AT&T CORP	T
AT&T LIBERTY MEDIA GRP INC CLA	LMGA
ATLANTIC RICHFIELD CO	ARC
ATLAS AIR INC	CGO

Company	Ticker	Company	Ticker
ATMEL CORP	ATML	BANK ONE CORP	ONE
ATMI INC	ATMI	BANK UTD CORP	BNKU
ATMOS ENERGY CORP	ATO	BANKNORTH GROUP INC DEL	BKNG
ATWOOD OCEANICS INC	ATW	BANTA CORP	BN
AUDIOVOX CORP	VOX	BARD C R INC	BCR
AURORA FOODS INC	AOR	BARNES & NOBLE INC	BKS
AUTODESK INC	ADSK	BARR LABS INC	BRL
AUTOMATIC DATA PROCESSING INC	AUD	BARRETT RES CORP	BRR
AUTOZONE INC	AZO	BATTLE MTN GOLD CO	BMG
AVALONBAY CMNTYS INC	AVB	BAUSCH & LOMB INC	BOL
AVANT CORP	AVNT	BAXTER INTL INC	BAX
AVERY DENNISON CORP	AVY	BB & T CORP	BBT
AVIS RENT A CAR INC	AVI	BE FREE INC	BFRE
AVISTA CORP	AVA	BEA SYS INC	BEAS
AVNET INC	AVT	BEAR STEARNS COS INC	BSC
AVON PRODS INC	AVP	BEBE STORES INC	BEBE
AVT CORP	AVTC	BECKMAN COULTER INC	BEC
AVX CORP NEW	AVX	BECTON DICKINSON & CO	BDX
AWARE INC MASS	AWRE	BED BATH BEYOND INC	BBBY
AXA FINANCIAL INC	AXF	BELL & HOWELL CO NEW	BHW
AXENT TECHNOLOGIES INC	AXNT	BELL ATLANTIC CORP	BEL
AZURIX CORP	AZX	BELLSOUTH CORP	BLS
BAKER FENTRESS & CO	BKF	BELO A H CORP	BLC
BAKER HUGHES INC	BHI	BEMIS INC	BMS
BALDOR ELEC CO	BEZ	BERGEN BRUNSWIG CORP	BBC
BALL CORP	BLL	BERINGER WINE ESTATES HLDGS	BERW
BANCORPSOUTH INC	BXS	BERKLEY W R CORP	BKLY
BANCWEST CORP NEW	BWE	BEST BUY INC	BBY
BANDAG INC	BDG	BESTFOODS	BFO
BANK NEW YORK INC	BK	BETHLEHEM STL CORP	BS
BANK OF AMERICA CORP	BAC	BHC COMMUNICATIONS INC	BHC

CACHEFLOW INC	CFLO
CADENCE DESIGN SYS INC	CDN
CAL DIVE INTL INC	CDIS
CALICO COMM INC	CLIC
CALLAWAY GOLF CO	ELY
CALPINE CORP	CPN
CAMBREX CORP	CBM
CAMBRIDGE TECHNOLOGY PARTNERS	CATP
CAMDEN PPTY TR	CPT
CAMPBELL SOUP CO	CPB
CANANDAIGUA BRANDS INC	CDB
CAPITAL ONE FINL CORP	COF
CAPITAL RE CORP	KRE
CAPITOL FED FINL	CFFN
CAPROCK COMMUNICATIONS CORP	CPRK
CARAUSTAR INDS INC	CSAR
CARDINAL HEALTH INC	CAH
CAREINSITE INC	CARI
CARLISLE COS INC	CSL
CARNIVAL CORP	CCL
CAROLINA FIRST CORP	CAFC
CAROLINA PWR & LT CO	CPL
CARPENTER TECHNOLOGY CORP	CRS
CARRAMERICA RLTY CORP	CRE
CARRIER ACCESS CORP	CACS
CARTER WALLACE INC	CAR
CASEYS GEN STORES INC	CASY
CATALINA MARKETING CORP	POS
CATALYTICA INC	CTAL
CATELLUS DEVELOPMENT CORP	CDX
CATERPILLAR INC	CAT
CBL & ASSOC PPTYS INC	CBL
CBRL GROUP INC	CBRL
CBS CORP	CBS
CCB FINANCIAL CORP	CCB
CEC ENTMT INC	CEC
CEDAR FAIR L P	FUN
CELGENE CORP	CELG
CELLSTAR CORP	CLST
CENDANT CORPORATION	CD
CENTENNIAL CELLULAR CL A	CYCL
CENTERPOINT PPTYS TR	CNT
CENTEX CONSTR PRODS INC	CXP
CENTEX CORP	CTX
CENTRAL & SOUTH WEST CORP	CSR
CENTRAL HUDSON GAS & ELEC	CHG
CENTRAL NEWSPAPERS INC	ECP
CENTRAL PKG CORP	CPC
CENTURA BKS INC	CBC
CENTURY BUSINESS SVCS INC	CBIZ
CENTURYTEL INC	CTL
CEPHALON INC	CEPH
CERIDIAN CORP	CEN
CERNER CORP	CERN
CHAMPION INTL CORP	CHA
CHARLES E SMITH REALTY	SRW
CHARMING SHOPPES INC	CHRS
CHARTER COMMUNICATIONS INC DEL	CHTR
CHARTER ONE FINL INC	CF
CHASE MANHATTAN CORP NEW	CMB
CHATEAU CMNTYS INC	CPJ
CHECKFREE HLDGS CORP	CKFR

185

Company	Symbol	Company	Symbol
COMMERCE BANCORP INC N J	CBH	CONSOLIDATED NAT GAS CO	CNG
COMMERCE BANCSHARES INC	CBSH	CONSOLIDATED PAPERS INC	CDP
COMMERCE GROUP INC	CGI	CONSOLIDATED STORES CORP	CNS
COMMERCE ONE INC	CMRC	CONSTELLATION ENERGY GROUP INC	CEG
COMMERCIAL FED CORP	CFB	CONTINENTAL AIRLS INC	CAL
COMNET CELLULAR INC	CELS	CONVERGYS CORP	CVG
COMMONWEALTH TEL ENTERPRISES	CTCO	COOPER CAMERON CORP	CAM
COMMSCOPE INC	CTV	COOPER TIRE & RUBR CO	CTB
COMMUNITY FIRST BANKSHARES INC	CFBX	COORS ADOLPH CO	RKY
COMPAQ COMPUTER CORP	CPQ	COPART INC	CPRT
COMPASS BANCSHARES INC	CBSS	COPPER MTN NETWORKS INC	CMTN
COMPLETE BUSINESS SOLUTIONS	CBSI	COR-THERAPEUTICS INC	CORR
COMPUCREDIT CORP	CCRT	CORDANT TECHNOLOGIES INC	CDD
COMPUSA INC	CPU	COREL CORP	CORL
COMPUTER ASSOC INTL INC	CA	CORN PRODS INTL INC	CPO
COMPUTER SCIENCES CORP	CSC	CORNERSTONE PPTYS INC	CPP
COMPUWARE CORP	CPWR	CORNING INC	GLW
COMSAT CORP	CQ	CORPORATE EXECUTIVE BRD CO	EXBD
COMVERSE TECHNOLOGY INC	CMVT	COST PLUS INC CALIF	CPWM
CONAGRA INC	CAG	COSTCO WHOLESALE CORP	COST
CONCENTRIC NETWORK CORP DEL	CNCX	COUNTRYWIDE CR INDS INC	CCR
CONCORD COMMUNICATIONS INC	CCRD	COUSINS PPTYS INC	CUZ
CONCUR TECHNOLOGIES INC	CNQR	COVAD COMMUNICATIONS GROUP INC	COVD
CONCURRENT COMPUTER CORP NEW	CCUR	COVANCE INC	CVD
CONECTIV INC	CIV	COX COMMUNICATIONS INC NEW	COX
CONEXANT SYS INC	CNXT	COX RADIO INC	CXR
CONOCO INC CL A	COCA	CRANE CO	CR
CONOCO INC CL B	COCB	CRAWFORD & CO CL B	CRDB
CONSECO INC	CNC	CREDENCE SYSTEMS CORP	CMOS
CONSOL ENERGY INC	CNX	CREE INC	CREE
CONSOLIDATED EDISON INC	ED	CRESCENT REAL ESTATE EQUITIES	CEI

CRITICAL PATH INC	CPTH
CROSSROADS SYS INC	CRDS
CROWN CASTLE INTL CORP	TWRS
CROWN CORK & SEAL INC	CCK
CSG SYS INTL INC	CSGS
CSK AUTO CORP	CAO
CSX CORP	CSX
CTS CORP	CTS
CULLEN FROST BANKERS INC	CFR
CUMMINS ENGINE INC	CUM
CUMULUS MEDIA INC	CMLS
CURAGEN CORP	CRGN
CVS CORP	CVS
CYBERSOURCE CORP DEL	CYBS
CYBEX COMPUTER PRODS CORP	CBXC
CYMER INC	CYMI
CYPRESS SEMICONDUCTOR CORP	CY
CYSIVE INC	CYSV
CYTEC INDS INC	CYT
CYTYC CORP	CYTC
D R HORTON INC	DHI
DAIMLERCHRYSLER AG	DCX
DAIN RAUSCHER CORP	DRC
DAL-TILE INTL INC	DTL
DALEEN TECHNOLOGIES INC	DALN
DALLAS SEMICONDUCTOR CORP	DS
DANA CORP	DCN
DANAHER CORP	DHR
DARDEN RESTAURANTS INC	DRI
DATA RETURN CORP	DRTN
DATASCOPE CORP	DSCP
DAYTON HUDSON CORP	DH
DEAN FOODS CO	DF
DEERE & CO	DE
DEL MONTE FOODS CO	DLM
DELHAIZE AMERICA INC CL B	D2B
DELL COMPUTER CORP	DELL
DELPHI AUTOMOTIVE SYS CORP	DPH
DELPHI FINL GROUP INC	DFG
DELTA & PINE LD CO	DLP
DELTA AIR LINES INC DEL	DAL
DELUXE CORP	DLX
DENDRITE INTL INC	DRTE
DENTSPLY INTL INC	XRAY
DEVELOPERS DIVERSIFIED RLTY	DDR
DEVON ENERGY CORP	DVN
DEVRY INC DEL	DV
DEXTER CORP	DEX
DIAL CORP NEW	DL
DIAMOND OFFSHORE DRILLING INC	DO
DIAMOND TECHNOLOGY PARTNERS	DTPI
DIAMONDS TR	DIA
DIEBOLD INC	DBD
DIGEX INC DEL	DIGX
DIGIMARC CORP	DMRC
DIGITAL IMPACT INC	DIGI
DIGITAL INSIGHT CORP	DGIN
DIGITAL IS INC DEL	ISLD
DIGITAL LIGHTWAVE INC	DIGL
DIGITAL MICROWAVE CORP	DMIC
DIGITAL RIV INC	DRIV
DII GROUP INC	DIIG

DILLARDS INC	DDS	DUKE-WEEKS RLTY CORP	DRE
DIME BANCORP INC NEW	DME	DUN & BRADSTREET CORP	DNB
DIONEX CORP	DNEX	DUPONT PHOTOMASKS INC	DPMI
DISNEY WALT CO	DIS	DURA PHARMACEUTICALS INC	DURA
DISNEY WALT CO - GO.COM	GO	DYCOM INDS INC	DY
DITECH CORP	DITC	DYNATECH CORP	DYNA
DLJ DIRECT	DIR	DYNEGY INC	DYN
DOCUMENTUM INC	DCTM	E PIPHANY INC	EPNY
DOLE FOOD INC	DOL	E TOWN CORP	ETW
DOLLAR GEN CORP	DG	E TRADE GROUP INC	EGRP
DOLLAR TREE STORES INC	DLTR	E-LOAN INC	EELN
DOMINION RES INC VA	D	EAGLE USA AIRFREIGHT INC	EUSA
DONALDSON INC	DCI	EARTHGRAINS CO	EGR
DONALDSON LUFKIN & JENRETTE	DLJ	EARTHLINK NETWORK INC	ELNK
DONNELLEY R R & SONS CO	DNY	EASTERN ENTERPRISES	EFU
DOUBLECLICK INC	DCLK	EASTERN UTILS ASSOC	EUA
DOVER CORP	DOV	EASTMAN CHEMICAL CO	EMN
DOVER DOWNS ENTMT INC	DVD	EASTMAN KODAK CO	EK
DOW CHEM CO	DOW	EATON CORP	ETN
DOW JONES & CO INC	DJ	EATON VANCE CORP	EV
DOWNEY FINL CORP	DSL	EBAY INC	EBAY
DPL INC	DPL	ECHOSTAR COMMUNICATIONS CORP	DISH
DQE INC	DQE	ECLIPSYS CORP	ECLP
DRKOOP COM INC	KOOP	ECOLAB INC	ECL
DRUGSTORE COM INC	DSCM	EDISON INTL	EIX
DSL NET INC	DSLN	EDISON SCHS INC	EDSN
DSP GROUP INC	DSPG	EDWARDS A G INC	AGE
DST SYS INC DEL	DST	EDWARDS J D & CO	JDEC
DTE ENERGY CO	DTE	EFFICIENT NETWORKS INC	EFNT
DU PONT E I DE NEMOURS & CO	DD	EGGHEAD.COM INC	EGGS
DUKE ENERGY CORP	DUK	EL PASO ELEC CO	EE

Company	Symbol	Company	Symbol
EL PASO ENERGY CORP	EPG	ESS TECHNOLOGY INC	ESST
ELCOR CORP	ELK	ESSEX PPTY TR INC	ESS
ELECTRIC LIGHTWAVE INC	ELIX	ETEC SYS INC	ETEC
ELECTRO SCIENTIFIC INDS INC	ESIO	ETHAN ALLEN INTERIORS INC	ETH
ELECTROGLAS INC	EGLS	ETOYS INC	ETYS
ELECTRONIC ARTS	ERTS	EVEREST REINS HLDGS INC	RE
ELECTRONIC DATA SYS CORP NEW	EDS	EXCHANGE APPLICATIONS INC	EXAP
ELECTRONICS FOR IMAGING INC	EFII	EXODUS COMMUNICATIONS INC	EXDS
EMC CORP	EMC	EXPEDIA INC CL A	EXPE
EMERGING MKTS TELECOM	ETF	EXPEDITORS INTL WASH INC	EXPD
EMERSON ELEC CO	EMR	EXPRESS SCRIPTS INC	ESRX
EMMIS COMMUNICATIONS CORP	EMMS	EXTENDED STAY AMER INC	ESA
EMULEX CORP	EMLX	EXTREME NETWORKS INC	EXTR
ENERGEN CORP	EGN	EXXON MOBIL CORP	XOM
ENERGY EAST CORP	NEG	F & M NATL CORP	FMN
ENGAGE TECHNOLOGIES INC	ENGA	FACTSET RESH SYS INC	FDS
ENHANCE FINL SVCS GROUP INC	EFS	FAIR ISAAC & CO INC	FIC
ENRON CORP	ENE	FAIRCHILD SEMICONDUCTOR INTL	FCS
ENSCO INTL INC	ESV	FAMILY DLR STORES INC	FDO
ENTERCOM COMMUNICATIONS CORP	ETM	FASTENAL CO	FAST
ENTERGY CORP	ETR	FBL FINL GROUP INC	FFG
ENTRUST TECHNOLOGIES INC	ENTU	FEDERAL EXPRESS CORP	FDX
ENZO BIOCHEM INC	ENZ	FEDERAL MOGUL CORP	FMO
ENZON INC	ENZN	FEDERAL NATL MTG ASSN	FNM
EOG RESOURCES INC	EOG	FEDERAL RLTY INVT TR	FRT
EQUIFAX INC	EFX	FEDERAL SIGNAL CORP	FSS
EQUITABLE RES INC	EQT	FEDERATED DEPT STORES INC DEL	FD
EQUITY INCOME FD	ATF	FEDERATED INVS INC PA	FII
EQUITY OFFICE PPTYS TR	EOP	FELCOR LODGING TR INC	FCH
EQUITY RESIDENTIAL PPTYS TR	EQR	FERRO CORP	FOE
ERIE INDTY CO	ERIE	FIFTH THIRD BANCORP	FITB

190

FILENET CORP	FILE
FINANCIAL SEC ASSURN HLDGS LTD	FSA
FINISAR CORP	FNSR
FINOVA GROUP INC	FNV
FIRST AMERN FINL CORP CALIF	FAF
FIRST BANCORP P R	FBP
FIRST COMMLTH FINL CORP PA	FCF
FIRST CTZNS BANCSHARES INC N C	FCNCA
FIRST DATA CORP	FDC
FIRST FINL BANCORP OHIO	FFBC
FIRST HEALTH GROUP CORP	FHCC
FIRST INDL RLTY TR INC	FR
FIRST MIDWEST BANCORP INC DEL	FMBI
FIRST NATL NEB INC	FINN
FIRST SEC CORP	FSCO
FIRST TENN NATL CORP	FTN
FIRST UN CORP	FTU
FIRST VA BKS INC	FVB
FIRSTAR CORP NEW WIS	FSR
FIRSTCOM CORP	FCLX
FIRSTENERGY CORP	FE
FIRSTMERIT CORP	FMER
FISERV INC	FISV
FISHER COS INC	FSCI
FISHER SCIENTIFIC INTL INC	FSH
FLEETBOSTON FINANCE CORP	FBF
FLEETWOOD ENTERPRISES INC	FLE
FLORIDA EAST COAST INDS INC	FLA
FLORIDA PROGRESS CORP	FPC
FLORIDA ROCK INDS INC	FRK
FLOWERS INDS INC	FLO
FLOWSERVE CORP	FLS
FLUOR CORP	FLR
FLYCAST COMMUNICATIONS CORP	FCST
FMC CORP	FMC
FOCAL COMMUNICATIONS CORP	FCOM
FOOTSTAR INC	FTS
FORD MTR CO DEL	F
FOREST LABS INC	FRX
FOREST OIL CORP	FST
FORRESTER RESH INC	FORR
FORT JAMES CORP	FJ
FORTUNE BRANDS INC	FO
FOSSIL INC	FOSL
FOUNDATION HEALTH SYS INC	FHS
FOUNDRY NETWORKS INC	FDRY
FOX ENTMT GROUP INC	FOX
FPL GROUP INC	FPL
FRANCHISE FIN CORP AMER	FFA
FRANKLIN RES INC	BEN
FREDDIE MAC	FRE
FREEPORT-MCMORAN COPPER & GOLD	FCX
FULLER H B CO	FULL
FULTON FINL CORP PA	FULT
FURNITURE BRANDS INTL INC	FBN
G & K SVCS INC	GKSRA
GABELLI ASSET MGMT	GBL
GABLES RESIDENTIAL TR	GBP
GADZOOX NETWORKS INC	ZOOX
GALILEO INTL INC	GLC
GALLAGHER ARTHUR J & CO	AJG
GANNETT INC	GCI

Company	Ticker	Company	Ticker
GAP INC	GPS	GOLDEN WEST FINL CORP DEL	GDW
GARTNER GROUP INC NEW	IT	GOLDMAN SACHS GROUP INC	GS
GATEWAY INC	GTW	GOODRICH B F CO	GR
GATX CORP	GMT	GOODYEAR TIRE & RUBR CO	GT
GAYLORD ENTMT CO NEW	GET	GOTO COM INC	GOTO
GENENTECH INC	DNA	GPU INC	GPU
GENERAL DYNAMICS CORP	GD	GRACE W R & CO	GRA
GENERAL ELEC CO	GE	GRACO INC	GGG
GENERAL GROWTH PPTYS INC	GGP	GRAINGER W W INC	GWW
GENERAL INSTR CORP DEL	GIC	GREAT ATLANTIC & PAC TEA INC	GAP
GENERAL MLS INC	GIS	GREAT LAKES CHEM CORP	GLK
GENERAL MTRS CORP	GM	GREAT PLAINS SOFTWARE INC	GPSI
GENERAL MTRS CORP	GMH	GREATER BAY BANCORP	GBBK
GENERAL SEMICONDUCTOR INC	SEM	GREENPOINT FINL CORP	GPT
GENESYS TELECOMMUNICATIONS	GCTI	GTE CORP	GTE
GENRAD INC	GEN	GTECH HLDGS CORP	GTK
GENTEX CORP	GNTX	GUESS INC	GES
GENUINE PARTS CO	GPC	GUIDANT CORP	GDT
GENZYME CORP	GENZ	HADCO CORP	HDC
GEON CO	GON	HAEMONETICS CORP MASS	HAE
GEORGIA GULF CORP	GGC	HALLIBURTON CO	HAL
GEORGIA PAC CORP	GP	HANNA M A CO	MAH
GEORGIA PAC CORP-TIMBER GRP	TGP	HANNAFORD BROS CO	HRD
GETTY IMAGES INC	GETY	HANOVER COMPRESSOR CO	HC
GILLETTE CO	G	HANOVER DIRECT INC	HNV
GLATFELTER P H CO	GLT	HARBINGER CORP	HRBC
GLOBAL MARINE INC	GLM	HARCOURT GEN INC	H
GLOBAL TELESYSTEMS GRP INC	GTS	HARLAND JOHN H CO	JH
GLOBESPAN INC	GSPN	HARLEY DAVIDSON INC	HDI
GO2NET INC	GNET	HARMAN INTL INDS INC	HAR
GOLDEN ST BANCORP INC	GSB	HARMONIC INC	HLIT

HORACE MANN EDUCATORS CORP NEW	HMN
HORMEL FOODS CORP	HRL
HOSPITALITY PPTYS TR	HPT
HOTJOBS COM LTD	HOTJ
HOUGHTON MIFFLIN CO	HTN
HOUSEHOLD INTL INC	HI
HOWMET INTL INC	HWM
HRPT PPTYS TR	HRP
HSB GROUP INC	HSB
HUBBELL INC CL B	HUBB
HUDSON CITY BANCORP INC	HCBK
HUDSON UTD BANCORP	HU
HUGHES SUPPLY INC	HUG
HUMAN GENOME SCIENCES INC	HGSI
HUMANA INC	HUM
HUNTINGTON BANCSHARES INC	HBAN
HYPERION SOLUTIONS CORP	HYSL
I2 TECHNOLOGIES INC	ITWO
IBASIS INC	IBAS
IBP INC	IBP
ICG COMMUNICATIONS INC	ICGX
ICN PHARMACEUTICALS INC NEW	ICN
ICOS CORP	ICOS
IDACORP INC	IDA
IDEC PHARMACEUTICALS CORP	IDPH
IDEXX LABS INC	IDXX
IDT CORP	IDTC
IDX SYS CORP	IDXC
IKON OFFICE SOLUTIONS INC	IKN
ILLINOIS TOOL WKS INC	ITW
ILLINOVA CORP	ILN

HARRAHS ENTMT INC	HET
HARRIS CORP DEL	HRS
HARSCO CORP	HSC
HARTE-HANKS COMM INC	HHS
HARTFORD FINL SVCS GROUP INC	HIG
HARTFORD LIFE INC	HLI
HASBRO INC	HAS
HAWAIIAN ELEC INDS INC	HE
HCC INS HLDGS INC	HCC
HEALTH CARE PPTY INVS INC	HCP
HEALTHEON / WEBMD CORP	HLTH
HEINZ H J CO	HNZ
HERCULES INC	HPC
HERSHEY FOODS CORP	HSY
HERTZ CORP	HRZ
HEWLETT PACKARD CO	HWP
HIBERNIA CORP	HIB
HIGH SPEED ACCESS CORP	HSAC
HILLENBRAND INDS INC	HB
HISPANIC BROADCASTING CORP	HBCCA
HNC SOFTWARE INC	HNCS
HOLLINGER INTL INC	HLR
HOLLYWOOD ENTMT CORP	HLYW
HOLLYWOOD PK INC NEW	HPK
HOME DEPOT INC	HD
HOME PPTYS N Y INC	HME
HOMESTAKE MNG CO	HM
HOMESTORE COM INC	HOMS
HON INDS INC	HNI
HONEYWELL INC	HON
HOOPER HOLMES INC	HH

ILLUMINET HLDGS INC	ILUM
IMANAGE INC	IMAN
IMATION CORP	IMN
IMC GLOBAL INC	IGL
IMCLONE SYS INC	IMCL
IMMUNEX CORP NEW	IMNX
IMPERIAL BANCORP	IMP
IMS HEALTH INC	RX
IN FOCUS SYS INC	INFS
INCYTE PHARMACEUTICALS INC	INCY
INDIANA ENERGY INC	IEI
INDYMAC MTG HLDGS INC	NDE
INET TECHNOLOGIES INC	INTI
INFINITY BROADCASTING CORP	INF
INFORMATICA CORP	INFA
INFORMIX CORP	IFMX
INFOSPACE COM INC	INSP
INGERSOLL RAND CO	IR
INGRAM MICRO INC	IM
INHALE THERAPEUTIC SYS INC	INHL
INKTOMI CORP	INKT
INPRISE CORP	INPR
INSIGHT COMM INC CL A	ICCI
INSIGHT ENTERPRISES INC	NSIT
INSITUFORM TECH INC CL-A	INSUA
INSWEB CORP	INSW
INTEGRATED DEVICE TECHNOLOGY	IDTI
INTEGRATED SYS INC	INTS
INTEL CORP	INTC
INTER TEL INC	INTL
INTERIM SVCS INC	IS
INTERLEAF INC	LEAF
INTERLIANT INC	INIT
INTERMEDIA COMMUNICATIONS INC	ICIX
INTERNATIONAL BANCSHARES CORP	IBOC
INTERNATIONAL BUSINESS MACHS	IBM
INTERNATIONAL FLAVORS &	IFF
INTERNATIONAL GAME TECHNOLOGY	IGT
INTERNATIONAL HOME FOODS INC	IHF
INTERNATIONAL PAPER CO	IP
INTERNATIONAL RECTIFIER CORP	IRF
INTERNATIONAL SPECIALTY PRODS	ISP
INTERNATIONAL SPEEDWAY CORP	ISCA
INTERNET CAP GROUP INC	ICGE
INTERNET COM CORP	INTM
INTERPUBLIC GROUP COS INC	IPG
INTERSTATE BAKERIES CORP DEL	IBC
INTERTAPE POLYMER GROUP INC	ITP
INTERTRUST TECHNOLOGIES CORP	ITRU
INTERVU INC	ITVU
INTERWORLD CORP	INTW
INTERWOVEN INC	IWOV
INTIMATE BRANDS INC	IBI
INTRAWARE INC	ITRA
INTUIT	INTU
INVACARE CORP	IVC
INVESTMENT TECH GRP INC	ITG
INVESTORS FINL SVCS CORP DEL	IFIN
INVITROGEN CORP	IVGN
IOMEGA CORP	IOM
IPALCO ENTERPRISES INC	IPL
IRON MOUNTAIN INC	IRM

KAISER ALUM CORP	KLU
KANA COMMUNICATIONS INC	KANA
KANSAS CITY PWR & LT CO	KLT
KANSAS CITY SOUTHN INDS INC	KSU
KAUFMAN & BROAD HOME CORP	KBH
KAYDON CORP	KDN
KEANE INC	KEA
KEEBLER FOODS CO	KBL
KELLOGG CO	K
KELLWOOD CO	KWD
KELLY SVCS INC	KELYA
KEMET CORP	KEM
KENNAMETAL INC	KMT
KENT ELECTRS CORP	KNT
KERR MCGEE CORP	KMG
KEYCORP NEW	KEY
KEYNOTE SYS INC	KEYN
KEYSPAN CORP	KSE
KEYSTONE FINL INC	KSTN
KILROY RLTY CORP	KRC
KIMBALL INTL INC	KBALB
KIMBERLY CLARK CORP	KMB
KIMCO RLTY CORP	KIM
KING PHARMACEUTICALS INC	KING
KLA-TENCOR CORP	KLAC
KNIGHT RIDDER INC	KRI
KNIGHT/TRIMARK GROUP INC	NITE
KOHLS CORP	KSS
KOPIN CORP	KOPN
KORN / FERRY INTL	KFY
KROGER CO	KR

ISS GROUP INC	ISSX
ITC DELTACOM INC	ITCD
ITT INDS INC IND	IIN
ITXC CORP	ITXC
IVAX CORP	IVX
IVILLAGE INC	IVIL
IXL ENTERPRISES INC	IIXL
IXNET INC	EXNT
JABIL CIRCUIT INC	JBL
JACK HENRY & ASSOCS	JKHY
JACK IN THE BOX INC	JBX
JACOBS ENGR GROUP INC	JEC
JDN RLTY CORP	JDN
JDS UNIPHASE CORP	JDSU
JEFFERSON PILOT CORP	JP
JLG INDS INC	JLG
JNI CORP	JNIC
JOHN NUVEEN CO	JNC
JOHNS-MANVILLE CORP NEW	JM
JOHNSON & JOHNSON	JNJ
JOHNSON CTLS INC	JCI
JONES APPAREL GROUP INC	JNY
JONES INTERCABLE INC	JOINA
JONES PHARMA INC	JMED
JOSTENS INC	JOS
JOURNAL REGISTER CO	JRC
JSB FINL INC	JSB
JUNIPER NETWORKS INC	JNPR
JUNO ONLINE SVCS INC	JWEB
JUPITER COMMUNICATIONS INC	JPTR
K MART CORP	KM

Company	Ticker	Company	Ticker
KRONOS INC	KRON	LIGAND PHARMACEUTICALS INC	LGND
KULICKE & SOFFA INDS INC	KLIC	LILLY ELI & CO	LLY
L-3 COMMUNICATIONS HLDGS INC	LLL	LIMITED INC	LTD
LA Z BOY INC	LZB	LINCARE HLDGS INC	LNCR
LABOR READY INC	LRW	LINCOLN ELEC HLDGS INC	LECO
LAFARGE CORP	LAF	LINCOLN NATL CORP IND	LNC
LAM RESH CORP	LRCX	LINEAR TECHNOLOGY CORP	LLTC
LAMAR ADVERTISING CO	LAMR	LINENS N THINGS INC	LIN
LANCASTER COLONY CORP	LANC	LIQUID AUDIO INC	LQID
LANDS END INC	LE	LITTON INDS INC	LIT
LATTICE SEMICONDUCTOR CORP	LSCC	LIZ CLAIBORNE INC	LIZ
LAUDER ESTEE COS INC	EL	LNR PROP CORP	LNR
LEAP WIRELESS INTL INC	LWIN	LOCKHEED MARTIN CORP	LMT
LEAR CORP	LEA	LOEWS CORP	LTR
LEE ENTERPRISES INC	LEE	LOISLAW COM INC	LOIS
LEGATO SYS INC	LGTO	LONE STAR TECHNOLOGIES INC	LSS
LEGG MASON INC	LM	LONGS DRUG STORES CORP	LDG
LEGGETT & PLATT INC	LEG	LONGVIEW FIBRE CO	LFB
LEHMAN BROTHERS HLDGS INC	LEH	LOTUS PACIFIC INC	LPFC
LENNAR CORP	LEN	LOUIS DREYFUS NAT GAS CORP	LD
LENNOX INTL INC	LII	LOUISIANA PAC CORP	LPX
LEUCADIA NATL CORP	LUK	LOWES COS INC	LOW
LEUKOSITE INC	LKST	LSI LOGIC CORP	LSI
LEVEL 3 COMMUNICATIONS INC	LVLT	LTX CORP	LTXX
LEXMARK INTL GROUP INC	LXK	LUBRIZOL CORP	LZ
LG&E ENERGY CORP	LGE	LUCENT TECHNOLOGIES INC	LU
LHS GROUP INC	LHSG	LYCOS INC	LCOS
LIBERATE TECHNOLOGIES	LBRT	LYONDELL CHEMICAL CO	LYO
LIBERTY FINL COS INC	L	M & T BK CORP	MTB
LIBERTY CORP S C	LC	MACDERMID INC	MRD
LIBERTY PPTY TR	LRY	MACERICH COMPANY	MAC

Company	Ticker	Company	Ticker
MACK CALI RLTY CORP	CLI	MAXTOR CORP	MXTR
MACROMEDIA INC	MACR	MAY DEPT STORES CO	MAY
MACROVISION CORP	MVSN	MAYTAG CORP	MYG
MAF BANCORP INC	MAFB	MBIA INC	MBI
MAIL COM INC	MAIL	MBNA CORP	KRB
MAIL-WELL INC	MWL	MCAFEE COM CORP	MCAF
MALLINCKRODT INC NEW	MKG	MCCLATCHY CO	MNI
MANDALAY RESORT GROUP	MBG	MCCORMICK & CO INC	MKC
MANITOWOC INC	MTW	MCDONALDS CORP	MCD
MANOR CARE INC	HCR	MCGRAW-HILL COS INC	MHP
MANPOWER INC WIS	MAN	MCI WORLDCOM INC	WCOM
MANUFACTURED HOME CMNTYS INC	MHC	MCK COMMUNICATIONS INC	MCKC
MANUGISTICS GROUP INC	MANU	MCKESSON HBOC INC	MCK
MAPQUEST COM INC	MQST	MCLEODUSA INC	MCLD
MARIMBA INC	MRBA	MCN ENERGY GROUP INC	MCN
MARINE DRILLING COS INC	MRL	MDU RES GROUP INC	MDU
MARK IV INDS INC	IV	MEAD CORP	MEA
MARKEL CORP	MKL	MEDAREX INC	MEDX
MARKETWATCH COM INC	MKTW	MEDIA GEN INC CL A	MEGA
MARRIOTT INTL INC	MAR	MEDIA METRIX INC	MMXI
MARSH & MCLENNAN COS INC	MMC	MEDIAONE GROUP INC	UMG
MARSHALL INDS	MI	MEDICAL MANAGER CORP	MMGR
MARTHA STEWART LIVING	MSO	MEDICIS PHARMACEUTICAL CORP	MRX
MARTIN MARIETTA MATLS INC	MLM	MEDIMMUNE INC	MEDI
MASCO CORP	MAS	MEDITRUST CORP	MT
MASCOTECH INC	MSX	MEDQUIST INC	MEDQ
MASTEC INC	MTZ	MEDTRONIC INC	MDT
MASTECH CORP	MAST	MELLON FINANCIAL CORP	MEL
MATTEL INC	MAT	MEMC ELECTR MATLS INC	WFR
MAXIM INTEGRATED PRODS INC	MXIM	MENS WEARHOUSE INC	SUIT
MAXIMUS INC	MMS	MENTOR CORP MINN	MNTR

MENTOR GRAPHICS CORP	MENT
MERCANTILE BANKSHARES CORP	MRBK
MERCK & CO INC	MRK
MERCURY COMPUTER SYS INC	MRCY
MERCURY GEN CORP NEW	MCY
MERCURY INTERACTIVE	MERQ
MEREDITH CORP	MDP
MERISTAR HOSPITALITY CORP	MHX
MERITOR AUTOMOTIVE INC	MRA
MERRILL LYNCH & CO INC	MER
MESSAGEMEDIA INC	MESG
METAMOR WORLDWIDE INC	MMWW
METASOLV SOFTWARE INC	MSLV
METHODE ELECTRS INC	METHA
METRICOM INC	MCOM
METRIS COS INC	MXT
METRO-GOLDWYN-MAYER INC NEW	MGM
METROMEDIA FIBER NETWORK INC	MFNX
MGC COMMUNICATIONS INC	MGCX
MGIC INVT CORP WIS	MTG
MGM GRAND INC	MGG
MICHAELS STORES INC	MIKE
MICREL INC	MCRL
MICROCHIP TECHNOLOGY INC	MCHP
MICROMUSE INC	MUSE
MICRON ELECTRONICS INC	MUEI
MICRON TECHNOLOGY INC	MU
MICROS SYS INC	MCRS
MICROSOFT CORP	MSFT
MICROSTRATEGY INC	MSTR
MIDAMERICAN ENERGY	MEC
MIDCAP SPDR TR	MDY
MIDWAY GAMES INC	MWY
MILACRON INC	MZ
MILLENNIUM CHEMICALS INC	MCH
MILLENNIUM PHARMACEUTICALS INC	MLNM
MILLER HERMAN INC	MLHR
MILLIPORE CORP	MIL
MINDSPRING ENTERPRISES INC	MSPG
MINERALS TECHNOLOGIES INC	MTX
MINIMED INC	MNMD
MINNESOTA MNG & MFG CO	MMM
MINNESOTA PWR INC	MPL
MIPS TECHNOLOGIES INC	MIPS
MIRAGE RESORTS INC	MIR
MISSION CRITICAL SOFTWARE INC	MCSW
MITCHELL ENRGY & DVLP CORP C A	MNDA
MKS INSTRS INC	MKSI
MMC NETWORKS INC	MMCN
MODEM MEDIA POPPE TYSON INC	MMPT
MODINE MFG CO	MODI
MODIS PROFESSIONAL SVCS INC	MPS
MOHAWK INDS INC	MHK
MOLEX INC	MOLX
MONDAVI ROBERT CORP	MOND
MONSANTO CO	MTC
MONTANA PWR CO	MTP
MONY GROUP INC	MNY
MOORE BENJAMIN & CO	MBEN
MORGAN J P & CO INC	JPM
MORGAN STANLEY DEAN WITTER	MWD
MOTOROLA INC	MOT

Company	Ticker	Company	Ticker
MP3 COM INC	MPPP	NCO GROUP INC	NCOG
MRV COMMUNICATIONS INC	MRVC	NCR CORP NEW	NCR
MSC INDL DIRECT INC	MSM	NEIMAN MARCUS GROUP	NMGA
MTI TECHNOLOGY CORP	MTIC	NET PERCEPTIONS INC	NETP
MUELLER INDS INC	MLI	NET2PHONE INC	NTOP
MULTEX COM INC	MLTX	NETBANK INC	NTBK
MURPHY OIL CORP	MUR	NETCENTIVES INC	NCNT
MYLAN LABORATORIES	MYL	NETEGRITY INC	NETE
MYPOINTS COM INC	MYPT	NETIQ CORP	NTIQ
NABISCO HLDGS CORP CL-A	NA	NETOPIA INC	NTPA
NABORS INDS INC	NBR	NETRO CORP	NTRO
NALCO CHEM CO	NLC	NETSCOUT SYS INC	NTCT
NASDAQ 100 TR	QQQ	NETWORK ACCESS SOLUTIONS CORP	NASC
NATIONAL BANCORP ALASKA INC	NBAK	NETWORK APPLIANCE INC	NTAP
NATIONAL CITY BANCSHARES INC	NCBE	NETWORK PLUS CORP	NPLS
NATIONAL CITY CORP	NCC	NETWORK SOLUTIONS INC DEL	NSOL
NATIONAL COMM BANCORPORATION	NCBC	NETWORKS ASSOCS INC	NETA
NATIONAL COMPUTER SYS INC	NLCS	NETZERO INC	NZRO
NATIONAL DATA CORP	NDC	NEUBERGER BERMAN INC	NEU
NATIONAL DISC BROKERS GROUP	NDB	NEW CENTY ENERGIES INC	NCE
NATIONAL INFORMATION	EGOV	NEW ENGLAND ELEC SYS	NES
NATIONAL INSTRS CORP	NATI	NEW ERA OF NETWORKS INC	NEON
NATIONAL SEMICONDUCTOR CORP	NSM	NEW JERSEY RES CORP	NJR
NATIONAL SVC INDS INC	NSI	NEW PLAN EXCEL RLTY TR INC	NXL
NATIONAL-OILWELL INC	NOI	NEW YORK TIMES CO	NYT
NATIONWIDE FINL SVCS INC	NFS	NEWELL RUBBERMAID INC	NWL
NATIONWIDE HEALTH PPTYS INC	NHP	NEWFIELD EXPL CO	NFX
NAVISITE INC	NAVI	NEWHALL LD & FARMING CO CALIF	NHL
NAVISTAR INTL CORP NEW	NAV	NEWMONT MNG CORP	NEM
NBC INTERNET INC CL-A	NBCI	NEWPORT NEWS SHIPBUILDING INC	NNS
NBTY INC	NBTY	NEXT LEVEL COMMUNICATIONS INC	NXTV

NEXTCARD INC — NXCD
NEXTEL COMMUNICATIONS INC — NXTL
NEXTLINK COMMUNICATIONS INC — NXLK
NIAGARA MOHAWK HODGS — NMK
NICOR INC — GAS
NIKE INC — NKE
NISOURCE INC COM — NI
NL INDS INC — NL
NOBLE AFFILIATES INC — NBL
NOBLE DRILLING CORP — NE
NORDSON CORP — NDSN
NORDSTROM INC — JWN
NORFOLK SOUTHN CORP — NSC
NORTEL NETWORKS CORP — NT
NORTH FORK BANCORPORATION INC — NFB
NORTHEAST OPTIC NETWORK INC — NOPT
NORTHEAST UTILS — NU
NORTHERN STS PWR CO MINN — NSP
NORTHERN TR CORP — NTRS
NORTHPOINT COMMUNICATIONS — NPNT
NORTHROP GRUMMAN CORP — NOC
NORTHWEST AIRLS CORP — NWAC
NORTHWEST NAT GAS CO — NWNG
NORTHWESTERN CORP — NOR
NOVA CORP GA — NIS
NOVELL INC — NOVL
NOVELLUS SYS INC — NVLS
NSTAR — NST
NTL INC — NTLI
NU SKIN ENTERPRISES INC — NUS
NUCOR CORP — NUE

NVIDIA CORP — NVDA
O M GROUP INC — OMP
O REILLY AUTOMOTIVE INC — ORLY
OAK INDS INC — OAK
OCCIDENTAL PETE CORP — OXY
OCEAN ENERGY INC — OEI
OFFICE DEPOT INC — ODP
OFFICEMAX INC — OMX
OGDEN CORP — OG
OGE ENERGY CORP — OGE
OHIO CAS CORP — OCAS
OLD KENT FINL CORP — OK
OLD NATL BANCORP IND — OLDB
OLD REP INTL CORP — ORI
OLIN CORP — OLN
OLSTEN CORP — OLS
OMNICARE INC — OCR
OMNICOM GROUP INC — OMC
OMNIPOINT CORP — OMPT
ONE VY BANCORP WEST VA INC — OV
ONEOK INC NEW — OKE
ONYX SOFTWARE CORP — ONXS
OPEN MKT INC — OMKT
OPTICAL CABLE CORP — OCCF
OPTICAL COATING LAB INC — OCLI
ORACLE CORP — ORCL
ORBITAL SCIENCES CORP — ORB
ORTEL CORP — ORTL
ORTHODONTIC CTRS AMER INC — OCA
OUTBACK STEAKHOUSE INC — OSSI
OWENS CORNING — OWC

Company	Symbol	Company	Symbol
OWENS ILL INC	OI	PENNZOIL-QUAKER ST	PZL
OXFORD HEALTH PLANS INC	OXHP	PENTAIR INC	PNR
P P & L RES INC	PPL	PENTON MEDIA INC	PME
PAC WEST TELECOMM	PACW	PEOPLES BK BRIDGEPORT CONN	PBCT
PACCAR INC	PCAR	PEOPLES ENERGY CORP	PGL
PACIFIC CAP BANCORP	SABB	PEOPLES HERITAGE FINL GROUP	PHBK
PACIFIC CENTY FINL CORP	BOH	PEOPLESOFT INC	PSFT
PACIFIC SUNWEAR CALIF INC	PSUN	PEP BOYS MANNY MOE & JACK	PBY
PACIFICARE HEALTH SYS INC CL A	PHSY	PEPSI BOTTLING GROUP INC	PBG
PACKETEER INC	PKTR	PEPSICO INC	PEP
PACTIV CORP	PTV	PEREGRINE SYS INC	PRGN
PAINE WEBBER GROUP INC	PWJ	PERKINELMER INC	PKI
PAIRGAIN TECHNOLOGIES INC	PAIR	PEROT SYS CORP	PER
PALL CORP	PLL	PERRIGO CO	PRGO
PANAMSAT CORP NEW	SPOT	PETSMART INC	PETM
PAPA JOHNS INTL INC	PZZA	PFIZER INC	PFE
PARAMETRIC TECHNOLOGY CORP	PMTC	PFSWEB INC	PFSW
PARK NATL CORP	PRK	PG&E CORP	PCG
PARK PL ENTMT CORP	PPE	PHARMACIA & UPJOHN INC	PNU
PARKER HANNIFIN CORP	PH	PHARMACYCLICS INC	PCYC
PATTERSON DENTAL CO	PDCO	PHELPS DODGE CORP	PD
PAXSON COMMUNICATIONS CORP	PAX	PHILADELPHIA SUBN CORP	PSC
PAYCHEX INC	PAYX	PHILIP MORRIS COS INC	MO
PAYLESS SHOESOURCE INC	PSS	PHILLIPS PETE CO	P
PC TEL INC	PCTI	PHONE COM INC	PHCM
PE CORP - CELERA GENOMICS	CRA	PHOTRONICS INC	PLAB
PE CORP BIOSYSTEMS	PEB	PIEDMONT NAT GAS INC	PNY
PECO ENERGY CO	PE	PIER 1 IMPORTS INC	PIR
PEGASUS COMMUNICATIONS CORP	PGTV	PIERCE LEAHY CORP	PLH
PEGASUS SYS INC	PEGS	PINNACLE HLDGS INC	BIGT
PENNEY J C INC	JCP	PINNACLE SYS INC	PCLE

PINNACLE WEST CAP CORP	PNW
PIONEER NAT RES CO	PXD
PITNEY BOWES INC	PBI
PITTSTON BRINKS GROUP	PZB
PITTWAY CORP CL A	PRYA
PIXAR	PIXR
PLANETRX COM INC	PLRX
PLANTRONICS INC NEW	PLT
PLAYBOY ENTERPRISES INC	PLA
PLAYTEX PRODS INC	PYX
PLEXUS CORP	PLXS
PLUG PWR INC	PLUG
PMI GROUP INC	PMA
PNC BANK CORP	PNC
POGO PRODUCING CO	PPP
POLAROID CORP	PRD
POLICY MGMT SYS CORP	PMS
POLYCOM INC	PLCM
POLYMER GROUP INC	PGI
PORTAL SOFTWARE INC	PRSF
POST PPTYS INC	PPS
POTLATCH CORP	PCH
POTOMAC ELEC PWR CO	POM
POWER INTEGRATIONS INC	POWI
POWER-ONE INC	PWER
POWERTEL INC	PTEL
POWERWAVE TECHNOLOGIES INC	PWAV
PPG INDS INC	PPG
PRAXAIR INC	PX
PRE PAID LEGAL SVCS INC	PPD
PRECISION CASTPARTS CORP	PCP
PREDICTIVE SYS INC	PRDS
PREMIER PKS INC	PKS
PRENTISS PPTYS TR	PP
PRESIDENTIAL LIFE CORP	PLFE
PREVIEW TRAVEL INC	PTVL
PRI AUTOMATION INC	PRIA
PRICE COMUNICATIONS CORP	PR
PRICE T ROWE ASSOC INC	TROW
PRICELINE COM INC	PCLN
PRIDE INTL INC	PDE
PRIMARK CORP	PMK
PRIMEDIA INC	PRM
PRIMUS KNOWLEDGE SOLUTIONS INC	PKSI
PRIMUS TELECOMMUNICATIONS	PRTL
PRIORITY HEALTHCARE CORP	PHCC
PRISON REALTY TRUST	PZN
PROBUSINESS SVCS INC	PRBZ
PROCTER & GAMBLE CO	PG
PRODIGY COMMUNICATIONS CORP	PRGY
PROFIT RECOVERY GROUP INTL INC	PRGX
PROGRESS SOFTWARE CORP	PRGS
PROGRESSIVE CORP OHIO	PGR
PROJECT SOFTWARE & DEV INC	PSDI
PROLOGIS TR	PLD
PROTECTIVE LIFE CORP	PL
PROTEIN DESIGN LABS INC	PDLI
PROVIDENT FINL GROUP INC	PFGI
PROVIDIAN FINL CORP	PVN
PROXICOM INC	PXCM
PROXIM INC	PROX
PS BUSINESS PKS INC CALIF	PSB

RMBS	RAMBUS INC DEL
RRRR	RARE MEDIUM GROUP INC
RATL	RATIONAL SOFTWARE CORP
RJF	RAYMOND JAMES FINL INC
RYN	RAYONIER INC
ROV	RAYOVAC CORP
RTNB	RAYTHEON CO CL B
RAZF	RAZORFISH INC
RCNC	RCN CORP
RDA	READERS DIGEST ASSN INC
RNWK	REALNETWORKS INC
O	REALTY INCOME CORP
RA	RECKSON ASSOCS RLTY CORP
RHAT	RED HAT INC
RBAK	REDBACK NETWORKS INC
REG	REGENCY REALTY CORP
RGBK	REGIONS FINL CORP
RGIS	REGIS CORP MINN
RGA	REINSURANCE GROUP AMER INC
REL	RELIANCE GROUP HLDGS INC
RS	RELIANCE STL & ALUM CO
REI	RELIANT ENERGY INC
RLR	RELIASTAR FINL CORP
RMDY	REMEDY CORP
RCGI	RENAL CARE GROUP INC
RBNC	REPUBLIC BANCORP INC
RSG	REPUBLIC SVCS INC
RMD	RESMED INC
RETK	RETEK INC
RXSD	REXALL SUNDOWN INC
REY	REYNOLDS & REYNOLDS CO

PSIX	PSINET INC
PSSI	PSS WORLD MED INC
PGS	PUBLIC SVC CO N C INC
PNM	PUBLIC SVC CO N MEX
PEG	PUBLIC SVC ENTERPRISE GROUP
PSD	PUGET SOUND ENERGY INC
PTZ	PULITZER INC
PHM	PULTE CORP
PUMA	PUMA TECHNOLOGY INC
PPRO	PURCHASEPRO COM INC
PIM	PUTNAM MASTER INTER INCOME TR
QLGC	QLOGIC CORP
QRSI	QRS CORP
OAT	QUAKER OATS CO
QCOM	QUALCOMM INC
PWR	QUANTA SVCS INC
QCSB	QUEENS CNTY BANCORP INC
DGX	QUEST DIAGNOSTICS INC
QSFT	QUEST SOFTWARE INC
STR	QUESTAR CORP
QTRN	QUINTILES TRANSNATIONAL CORP
QNTS	QUINTUS CORP
QHGI	QUORUM HEALTH GROUP INC
Q	QWEST COMMUNICATIONS INTL INC
RHD	R H DONNELLEY CORP
FLC	R&B FALCON CORP
RDN	RADIAN GROUP INC
RADS	RADIANT SYS INC
ROIA	RADIO ONE INC
RSYS	RADISYS CORP
RAL	RALSTON PURINA CO

Company	Ticker	Company	Ticker
REYNOLDS METALS CO	RLM	SAFEWAY INC	SWY
REYNOLDS R J TOB HLDGS INC	RJR	SAGA SYSTEMS INC	AGS
RF MICRO DEVICES INC	RFMD	SAGENT TECHNOLOGY INC	SGNT
RGS ENERGY GROUP INC	RGS	SAKS INC	SKS
RICHMOND CNTY FINL CORP	RCBK	SALESLOGIX CORP	SLGX
RITE AID CORP	RAD	SALOMON BROS FD INC	SBF
ROBERT HALF INTL INC	RHI	SANCHEZ COMPUTER ASSOCS INC	SCAI
ROBERTS PHARMACEUTICAL CORP	RPC	SANDISK CORP	SNDK
ROCK-TENN CO	RKT	SANMINA CORP	SANM
ROCKWELL INTL CORP NEW	ROK	SANTA FE SNYDER CORP	SFS
ROHM & HAAS CO	ROH	SAPIENT CORP	SAPE
ROLLINS TRUCK LEASING CORP	RLC	SARA LEE CORP	SLE
ROMAC INTL INC	ROMC	SAWTEK INC	SAWS
ROPER INDS INC NEW	ROP	SBC COMMUNICATIONS INC	SBC
ROSLYN BANCORP INC	RSLN	SCANA CORP	SCG
ROSS STORES INC	ROST	SCHEIN HENRY INC	HSIC
ROWAN COS INC	RDC	SCHERING PLOUGH CORP	SGP
RUBY TUESDAY INC	RI	SCHLUMBERGER LTD	SLB
RUDDICK CORP	RDK	SCHOLASTIC CORP	SCHL
RURAL CELLULAR CORP	RCCC	SCHWAB CHARLES CORP NEW	SCH
RUSS BERRIE & CO INC	RUS	SCI SYS INC	SCI
RYDER SYS INC	R	SCIENT CORP	SCNT
S & T BANCORP INC	STBA	SCIENTIFIC ATLANTA INC	SFA
S1 CORP COM	SONE	SCM MICROSYSTEMS INC	SCMM
S3 INC	SIII	SCOTTS CO	SMG
SAATCHI & SAATCHI PLC NEW	SSA	SCRIPPS E W CO OHIO	SSP
SABRE HLDGS CORP	TSG	SDL INC	SDLI
SAFECO CORP	SAFC	SEACOR SMIT, INC	CKH
SAFEGUARD SCIENTIFICS INC	SFE	SEAGATE TECHNOLOGY	SEG
SAFESKIN CORP	SFSK	SEALED AIR CORP	SEE
SAFETY KLEEN CORP	SK	SEARS ROEBUCK & CO	S

Company	Symbol	Company	Symbol
SECTOR SPDR TR - BASIC INDUS	XLB	SILICON IMAGE INC	SIMG
SECTOR SPDR TR - CONS. SVCS	XLV	SILICON STORAGE TECHNOLOGY INC	SSTI
SECTOR SPDR TR - ENERGY	XLE	SILICON VY BANCSHARES	SIVB
SECTOR SPDR TR - FINANCIAL	XLF	SILICONIX INC	SILI
SECTOR SPDR TR - INDUSTRIAL	XLI	SILKNET SOFTWARE INC	SILK
SECTOR SPDR TR - TECH	XLK	SILVERSTREAM SOFTWARE INC	SSSW
SECTOR SPDR TR - UTILITIES	XLU	SIMON PPTY GROUP INC NEW	SPG
SECTOR SPDR TR CONS. STAPLE	XLP	SIMPSON MFG INC	SSD
SECTOR SPDR TR CYCL/TRANS	XLY	SINCLAIR BROADCAST GROUP INC	SBGI
SECURITY CAP GROUP INC	SCZ	SIRIUS SATELLITE RADIO INC	CDRD
SEI INVTS CO	SEIC	SKY FINL GROUP INC	SKYF
SEMPRA ENERGY	SRE	SKYWEST INC	SKYW
SEMTECH CORP	SMTC	SLM HLDG CORP	SLM
SENSORMATIC ELECTRS CORP	SRM	SMARTDISK CORP	SMDK
SEPRACOR INC	SEPR	SMITH INTL INC	SII
SEQUA CORP CLASS A	SQAA	SMITHFIELD FOODS INC	SFD
SERENA SOFTWARE INC	SRNA	SMURFIT-STONE CONTAINER CORP	SSCC
SERVICE CORP INTL	SRV	SNAP ON INC	SNA
SERVICEMASTER CO	SVM	SNYDER COMMUNICATIONS INC	SNC
SFX ENTMT INC	SFX	SODEXHO MARRIOTT SVCS INC	SDH
SHARED MEDICAL SYSTEMS	SMS	SOFTWARE COM INC	SWCM
SHAW INDS INC	SHX	SOLECTRON CORP	SLR
SHERWIN WILLIAMS CO	SHW	SOMERA COMMUNICATIONS INC	SMRA
SHOPKO STORES INC	SKO	SONICWALL INC	SNWL
SHOPNOW COM INC	SPNW	SONOCO PRODS CO	SON
SHURGARD STORAGE CENTERS	SHU	SOTHEBYS HLDGS INC	BID
SIEBEL SYS INC	SEBL	SOUTHDOWN INC	SDW
SIERRA PAC RES	SRP	SOUTHERN CO	SO
SIGCORP INC	SIG	SOUTHERN PERU COPPER CORP	PCU
SIGMA ALDRICH CORP	SIAL	SOUTHERN UN CO NEW	SUG
SILICON GRAPHICS INC	SGI	SOUTHTRUST CORP	SOTR

Company	Ticker	Company	Ticker
SOUTHWEST AIRLINES	LUV	STERIS CORP	STE
SOUTHWEST BANCORPORATION TEX	SWBT	STERLING COMM INC	SE
SOUTHWEST GAS CORP	SWX	STERLING SOFTWARE INC	SSW
SPANISH BROADCASTING SYS INC	SBSA	STEWART ENTERPRISES INC	STEI
SPARTECH CORP	SEH	STILLWATER MNG CO	SWC
SPDR TR - S&P 500 INDEX	SPY	STONE ENERGY CORP	SGY
SPEEDWAY MOTORSPORTS INC	TRK	STORAGE TECHNOLOGY CORP	STK
SPIEGEL INC	SPGLA	STORAGE USA INC	SUS
SPIEKER PROPERTIES INC	SPK	STUDENT ADVANTAGE INC	STAD
SPORTSLINE COM INC	SPLN	STUDENT LN CORP	STU
SPRINGS INDS INC	SMI	SUIZA FOODS CORP	SZA
SPRINT FON GROUP	FON	SUMMIT BANCORP	SUB
SPRINT PCS GROUP	PCS	SUMMIT PPTYS INC	SMT
SPX CORP	SPW	SUMMIT TECHNOLOGY INC	BEAM
ST JOE CO	JOE	SUN COMMUNITIES INC	SUI
ST JUDE MED INC	STJ	SUN MICROSYSTEMS INC	SUNW
ST PAUL COS INC	SPC	SUNGARD DATA SYS INC	SDS
STAMPS COM INC	STMP	SUNGLASS HUT INTL INC	RAYS
STANCORP FINL GROUP INC	SFG	SUNOCO INC	SUN
STANDARD REGISTER CO	SR	SUNRISE TECHNOLOGIES INTL INC	SNRS
STANLEY WKS	SWK	SUNTRUST BKS INC	STI
STAPLES INC	SPLS	SUPERGEN INC	SUPG
STARBUCKS CORP	SBUX	SUPERIOR INDS INTL INC	SUP
STARMEDIA NETWORK INC	STRM	SUPERVALU INC	SVU
STARTEK INC	SRT	SUSQUEHANNA BANCSHARES INC PA	SUSQ
STARWOOD HOTELS & RESORTS CL B	HOT	SWIFT TRANSN INC	SWFT
STATE STR CORP	STT	SYBRON INTL CORP	SYB
STATEN IS BANCORP INC	SIB	SYCAMORE NETWORKS INC	SCMR
STATION CASINOS INC	STN	SYKES ENTERPRISES INC	SYKE
STEEL DYNAMICS INC	STLD	SYLVAN LEARNING SYS INC	SLVN
STEELCASE INC	SCS	SYMANTEC CORP	SYMC

SYMBOL TECHNOLOGIES INC	SBL
SYNOPSYS INC	SNPS
SYNOVUS FINL CORP	SNV
SYSCO CORP	SYY
T-HQ INC	THQI
TALBOTS INC	TLB
TALK.COM INC	TALK
TANDY CORP	TAN
TANNING TECHNOLOGY CORP	TANN
TAUBMAN CTRS INC	TCO
TCF FINL CORP	TCB
TD WATERHOUSE GROUP INC	TWE
TECH DATA CORP	TECD
TECHNE CORP	TECH
TECHNITROL INC	TNL
TECHNOLOGY SOLUTIONS CO	TSCC
TECO ENERGY INC	TE
TECUMSEH PRODS CO	TECUA
TEKELEC	TKLC
TEKTRONIX INC	TEK
TELEBANC FINL CORP	TBFC
TELECORP PCS INC	TLCP
TELEFLEX INC	TFX
TELEPHONE & DATA SYS INC	TDS
TELETECH HLDGS INC	TTEC
TELIGENT INC	TGNT
TELLABS INC	TLAB
TEMPLE-INLAND INC	TIN
TEMPLETON GLOBAL INCOME	GIM
TENET HEALTHCARE CORP	THC
TENFOLD CORP	TENF
TERAYON COMMUNICATION SYS	TERN
TEREX CORP NEW	TEX
TETRA TECH INC NEW	WATR
TEXACO INC	TX
TEXAS INDUSTRIES INC	TXI
TEXAS INSTRS INC	TXN
TEXAS UTILS CO	TXU
TEXTRON INC	TXT
THERMO ELECTRON CORP	TMO
THERMO INSTR SYS INC	THI
THERMO OPTEK CORP	TOC
THERMOQUEST CORP	TMQ
THOMAS & BETTS CORP	TNB
TIBCO SOFTWARE INC	TIBX
TICKETMASTER ONLINE-CITYSEARCH	TMCS
TICKETS COM INC	TIXX
TIDEWATER INC	TDW
TIFFANY & CO NEW	TIF
TIMBERLAND CO	TBL
TIME WARNER INC	TWX
TIME WARNER TELECOM INC	TWTC
TIMES MIRROR CO NEW	TMC
TIMKEN CO	TKR
TITAN CORP	TTN
TIVO INC	TIVO
TJ INTL INC	TJCO
TJX COS INC NEW	TJX
TMP WORLDWIDE INC	TMPW
TNP ENTERPRISES INC	TNP
TOLL BROS INC	TOL
TOOTSIE ROLL INDS INC	TR

TOPPS INC	TOPP
TORCHMARK CORP	TMK
TOSCO CORP	TOS
TOTAL RENAL CARE HLDGS INC	TRL
TOTAL SYS SVCS INC	TSS
TOWER AUTOMOTIVE INC	TWR
TOYS R US INC	TOY
TRANS WORLD ENTMT CORP	TWMC
TRANSACTION SYS ARCHITECTS INC	TSAI
TRANSATLANTIC HLDGS INC	TRH
TRANSKARYOTIC THERAPIES INC	TKTX
TRANSOCEAN OFFSHORE INC	RIG
TRANSWITCH CORP	TXCC
TRAVELERS PPTY CAS CORP	TAP
TREDEGAR CORP	TG
TRI CONTL CORP	TY
TRIANGLE BANCORP INC	TGL
TRIANGLE PHARMACEUTICALS INC	VIRS
TRIBUNE CO NEW	TRB
TRICON GLOBAL RESTAURANTS INC	YUM
TRIGON HEALTHCARE INC	TGH
TRINITY INDS INC	TRN
TRIQUINT SEMICONDUCTOR INC	TQNT
TRITON PCS HLDGS INC	TPCS
TRUE NORTH COMMUNICATIONS INC	TNO
TRUSTCO BK CORP N Y	TRST
TRUSTMARK CORP	TRMK
TRW INC	TRW
TSI INTL SOFTWARE LTD	TSFW
TUBOSCOPE INC	TBI
TUESDAY MORNING CORP	TUES
TUMBLEWEED COMMUNICATIONS CORP	TMWD
TUPPERWARE CORP	TUP
TV GUIDE INC	TVGIA
TYCO INTERNATIONAL INC	TYC
TYSON FOODS INC	TSN
U S FOODSERVICE	UFS
U S INDS INC NEW	USI
U S INTERACTIVE INC	USIT
U S TR CORP NEW	UTC
U S WEST INC NEW	USW
UAL CORP	UAL
UCAR INTL INC	UCR
UGI CORP NEW	UGI
ULTRAMAR DIAMOND SHAMROCK CORP	UDS
UMB FINL CORP	UMBF
UNICOM CORP	UCM
UNIFI INC	UFI
UNIGRAPHICS SOLUTIONS INC	UGS
UNION CARBIDE CORP	UK
UNION PAC CORP	UNP
UNION PAC RES GROUP INC	UPR
UNIONBANCAL CORP	UB
UNISYS CORP	UIS
UNITED ASSET MGMT CORP	UAM
UNITED DOMINION RLTY TR INC	UDR
UNITED HEALTHCARE CORP	UNH
UNITED ILLUM CO	UIL
UNITED PARCEL SVC CL B	UPS
UNITED RENTALS INC	URI
UNITED STATES CELLULAR CORP	USM
UNITED STATIONERS INC	USTR

Company	Symbol	Company	Symbol
UNITED TECHNOLOGIES CORP	UTX	VARCO INTL INC	VRC
UNITED TELEVISION INC	UTVI	VARIAN INC	VARI
UNIVERSAL HEALTH SVCS INC	UHS	VARIAN MED SYS INC	VAR
UNIVISION COMMUNICATIONS INC	UVN	VARIAN SEMICONDUCTOR	VSEA
UNOCAL CORP	UCL	VASTAR RES INC	VRI
UNOVA INC	UNA	VEECO INSTRS INC DEL	VECO
UNUMPROVIDENT CORP	UNM	VENATOR GROUP INC	Z
US AIRWAYS GROUP INC	U	VERIO INC	VRIO
US BANCORP DEL	USB	VERISIGN INC	VRSN
US LEC CORP	CLEC	VERITAS SOFTWARE CORP	VRTS
USA NETWORKS INC	USAI	VERITY INC	VRTY
USEC INC	USU	VERTEX PHARMACEUTICALS INC	VRTX
USFREIGHTWAYS CORP	USFC	VERTICALNET INC	VERT
USG CORP	USG	VIACOM INC CL B	VIAB
USINTERNETWORKING INC	USIX	VIAD CORP	VVI
UST CORP	USTB	VIADOR INC	VIAD
UST INC	UST	VIANT CORP	VIAN
USWEB CORP	USWB	VIATEL INC	VYTL
USX-MARATHON GROUP	MRO	VICOR CORP	VICR
USX-U S STL GROUP	X	VIGNETTE CORP	VIGN
UTILICORP UTD INC	UCU	VINTAGE PETE INC	VPI
V F CORP	VFC	VISHAY INTERTECHNOLOGY INC	VSH
VAIL RESORTS INC	MTN	VISIO CORP	VSIO
VALASSIS COMMUNICATIONS INC	VCI	VISUAL NETWORKS INC	VNWK
VALERO ENERGY CORP NEW	VLO	VISX INC DEL	VISX
VALHI INC NEW	VHI	VOICESTREAM WIRELESS CORP	VSTR
VALLEY NATL BANCORP	VLY	VORNADO RLTY TR	VNO
VALSPAR CORP	VAL	VULCAN MATLS CO	VMC
VALUE AMER INC	VUSA	WACHOVIA CORP NEW	WB
VALUE CITY DEPT STORES INC	VCD	WADDELL & REED FINL INC	WDR
VALUEVISION INTL INC CL-A	VVTV	WAL-MART STORES INC	WMT

WEBS INDEX FD INC - SWITZERLAN	EWL
WEBS INDEX FD INC AUSTRALIA	EWA
WEBSTER FINL CORP WATERBURY	WBST
WEBTRENDS CORP	WEBT
WEBVAN GROUP INC	WBVN
WEINGARTEN RLTY INVS	WRI
WEIS MKTS INC	WMK
WELLMAN INC	WLM
WELLPOINT HEALTH NETWORKS INC	WLP
WELLS FARGO & CO NEW	WFC
WENDYS INTL INC	WEN
WERNER ENTERPRISES INC	WERN
WESCO FINL CORP	WSC
WESLEY JESSEN VISIONCARE INC	WJCO
WEST PHARMACEUTICAL SVCS INC	WST
WEST TELESERVICES CORP	WTSC
WESTAMERICA BANCORPORATION	WABC
WESTERN RES INC	WR
WESTERN WIRELESS CORP	WWCA
WESTFIELD AMER INC	WEA
WESTPOINT STEVENS INC	WXS
WESTVACO CORP	W
WESTWOOD ONE INC	WON
WEYERHAEUSER CO	WY
WFS FINL INC	WFSI
WHIRLPOOL CORP	WHR
WHITMAN CORP	WH
WHITNEY HLDG CORP	WTNY
WHITTMAN-HART INC	WHIT
WHOLE FOODS MKT INC	WFMI
WICOR INC	WIC

WALDEN RESIDENTIAL PPTYS INC	WDN
WALGREEN CO	WAG
WALLACE COMPUTER SVCS INC	WCS
WALTER INDS INC	WLT
WARNACO GROUP INC	WAC
WARNER LAMBERT CO	WLA
WASHINGTON FED INC	WFSL
WASHINGTON GAS LT CO	WGL
WASHINGTON MUT INC	WM
WASHINGTON POST CO CL B	WPO
WASHINGTON REAL ESTATE INVT TR	WRE
WASTE MANAGEMENT INC	WMI
WATERS CORP	WAT
WATSON PHARMACEUTICAL INC	WPI
WAUSAU-MOSINEE PAPER CORP	WMO
WAVE SYS CORP	WAVX
WEATHERFORD INTL INC NEW	WFT
WEBS INDEX FD INC - AUSTRIA	EWO
WEBS INDEX FD INC - BELGIUM	EWK
WEBS INDEX FD INC - CANADA	EWC
WEBS INDEX FD INC - FRANCE	EWQ
WEBS INDEX FD INC - GERMANY	EWG
WEBS INDEX FD INC - HONG KONG	EWH
WEBS INDEX FD INC - ITALY	EWI
WEBS INDEX FD INC - JAPAN	EWJ
WEBS INDEX FD INC - MALAYSIA	EWM
WEBS INDEX FD INC - MEXICO	EWW
WEBS INDEX FD INC - NETHERLAND	EWN
WEBS INDEX FD INC - SINGAPORE	EWS
WEBS INDEX FD INC - SPAIN	EWP
WEBS INDEX FD INC - SWEDEN	EWD

WILD OATS MKTS INC	OATS	WPS RES CORP	WPS
WILEY JOHN & SONS INC CL A	JWA	WRIGLEY WM JR CO	WWY
WILLAMETTE INDS INC	WLL	WYNDHAM INTL INC CL A	WYN
WILLIAMS COMMUNICATIONS GROUP	WCG	XCEED INC	XCED
WILLIAMS COS INC	WMB	XEROX CORP	XRX
WILLIAMS SONOMA INC	WSM	XILINX INC	XLNX
WILMINGTON TR CORP	WL	XIRCOM	XIRC
WIND RIV SYS INC	WIND	XTRA CORP	XTR
WINK COMMUNICATIONS INC	WINK	YAHOO INC	YHOO
WINN DIXIE STORES INC	WIN	YANKEE CANDLE INC	YCC
WINSTAR COMMUNICATIONS INC	WCII	YORK INTL CORP NEW	YRK
WIRELESS FACS INC	WFII	YOUNG & RUBICAM INC	YNR
WISCONSIN CENT TRANSN CORP	WCLX	YOUNG BROADCASTING INC	YBTVA
WISCONSIN ENERGY CORP	WEC	ZALE CORP	ZLC
WIT CAPITAL GROUP	WITC	ZEBRA TECHNOLOGIES CORP	ZBRA
WOMEN COM NETWORKS INC	WOMN	ZIFF-DAVIS INC	ZD
WORLD ACCESS INC	WAXS	ZIONS BANCORPORATION	ZION
WORLD WRESTLING FEDN ENTMT INC	WWFE	ZIXIT CORP	ZIXI
WORLDGATE COMMUNICATIONS INC	WGAT	ZOMAX INC MINN	ZOMX
WORTHINGTON INDS INC	WTHG		

Historical Returns of Large-Cap U.S. Stocks

Large-Cap U.S. Stocks (As of January 2000)					
Company Name	**Ticker Symbol**	**1 Year Return**	**3 Year Average Return**	**5 Year Average Return**	**10 Year Average Return**
3Com	COMS	4.9	-13.8	12.8	29.9
Abbott Laboratories	ABT	-24.8	14.5	19.5	17.9
AES	AES	57.8	47.6	50.3	NA
AFLAC	AFL	8.2	31.2	36.0	27.3
Albertson's	ABS	-48.6	-1.8	3.7	10.4
Alcoa	AA	125.9	39.8	33.2	18.8
Allstate	ALL	-36.4	-4.6	17.2	NA
Alltel	AT	40.7	41.7	26.0	19.4
Amazon.com	AMZN	42.2	NA	NA	NA
America Online	AOL	95.2	231.7	144.1	NA
American Express	AXP	63.4	44.6	43.3	21.5
American General	AGC	-0.6	26.0	25.9	22.1
American Home Products	AHP	-29.2	12.4	23.2	15.1
American International Group	AIG	40.2	41.5	36.4	24.0
AMFM	AFM	63.5	84.3	68.1	NA
Amgen	AMGN	129.8	64.1	52.1	50.3
Analog Devices	ADI	196.4	54.1	51.4	39.9
Anheuser-Busch Companies	BUD	9.8	23.5	26.2	17.0
Apple Computer	AAPL	151.1	70.1	21.8	12.1
Applied Materials	AMAT	196.8	91.8	64.4	53.2
Associates First Capital A	AFS	-34.9	8.2	NA	NA
AT&T	T	2.4	25.5	20.3	13.2
AT&T - Liberty Media Group A	LMG.A	146.7	107.6	NA	NA
Atlantic Richfield	ARC	37.1	13.5	15.9	9.2
Automatic Data Processing	AUD	35.4	37.1	31.0	25.5
AXA Financial	AXF	17.9	40.8	31.1	NA
Bank of America	BAC	-14.0	3.5	20.7	11.6
Bank of New York	BK	1.0	35.9	43.6	27.7
Bank One	ONE	-34.8	-3.3	12.7	10.8
Baxter International	BAX	-0.6	17.6	21.9	13.4
BEA Systems	BEAS	1041.8	NA	NA	NA
Bell Atlantic	BEL	17.0	28.1	24.7	13.3
BellSouth	BLS	-4.5	35.4	31.0	13.7

Large-Cap U.S. Stocks
(As of January 2000)

Company Name	Ticker Symbol	1 Year Return	3 Year Average Return	5 Year Average Return	10 Year Average Return
Berkshire Hathaway B	BRK.B	-22.1	18.1	NA	NA
BestFoods	BFO	0.7	15.6	18.7	14.6
Biogen	BGEN	103.6	63.4	51.9	35.1
BMC Software	BMCS	79.4	56.9	62.3	41.2
Boeing	BA	28.7	-6.9	13.5	9.6
Bristol-Myers Squibb	BMY	-2.8	35.0	37.9	20.3
Broadcom	BRCM	351.1	NA	NA	NA
BroadVision	BVSN	1494.3	301.6	NA	NA
Burlington Northern Santa Fe	BNI	-28.1	-4.2	10.3	11.2
Campbell Soup	CPB	-28.2	2.0	15.1	13.1
Cardinal Health	CAH	-36.8	7.4	18.6	24.3
Carnival	CCL	0.5	44.0	36.7	27.4
Caterpillar	CAT	4.7	10.0	13.7	14.6
CBS	CBS	94.9	48.2	40.2	8.0
Cendant	CD	37.5	3.1	12.4	30.0
Charles Schwab	SCH	36.3	75.8	72.3	56.8
Chase Manhattan	CMB	11.7	23.0	37.6	22.9
Chevron	CHV	7.4	13.3	18.0	14.1
Cigna	CI	5.7	23.0	33.5	19.6
Cisco Systems	CSCO	130.8	96.4	94.0	NA
Citigroup	C	70.1	41.8	52.6	35.1
Citrix Systems	CTXS	153.4	111.4	NA	NA
Clear Channel Communications	CCU	63.8	70.3	69.7	64.3
Clorox	CLX	-12.5	28.2	30.6	20.4
CMGI	CMGI	939.9	418.3	213.1	NA
Coca-Cola	KO	-12.2	4.4	19.0	21.3
Colgate-Palmolive	CL	41.7	43.3	35.1	26.1
Columbia/HCA Healthcare	COL	25.2	-8.6	5.2	15.9
Comcast	CMCSK	72.4	78.8	45.7	25.7
Compaq Computer	CPQ	-35.4	22.3	28.1	26.2
Computer Associates International	CA	64.3	28.4	37.5	34.8
Computer Sciences	CSC	47.3	32.1	30.0	25.7
Compuware	CPWR	-4.6	81.2	52.6	NA
Comverse Technology	CMVT	205.8	79.1	78.8	47.8
ConAgra	CAG	-26.0	-0.8	10.3	11.5
Conoco A	COC.A	22.5	NA	NA	NA
Corning	GLW	189.7	51.5	41.4	24.5

Large-Cap U.S. Stocks
(As of January 2000)

Company Name	Ticker Symbol	1 Year Return	3 Year Average Return	5 Year Average Return	10 Year Average Return
Costco Wholesale	COST	26.4	53.7	47.9	24.6
Cox Communications A	COX	49.0	64.5	NA	NA
CVS	CVS	-27.1	25.3	26.8	10.7
Dayton Hudson	DH	36.2	56.7	46.2	23.5
Dell Computer	DELL	39.4	148.6	140.0	97.0
DoubleClick	DCLK	1037.4	NA	NA	NA
Dow Chemical	DOW	51.5	23.7	19.4	11.2
Du Pont De Nemours E.I.	DD	26.9	14.3	21.6	15.9
Duke Energy	DUK	-19.4	6.5	9.7	10.8
Eastman Kodak	EK	-5.6	-3.8	9.4	14.1
eBay	EBAY	55.7	NA	NA	NA
EchoStar Communications	DISH	706.2	160.7	NA	NA
Electronic Data Systems	EDS	34.8	17.3	13.2	18.8
Eli Lilly & Company	LLY	-24.2	23.7	34.8	17.5
EMC	EMC	157.1	136.3	81.9	95.2
Emerson Electric	EMR	-3.1	8.0	14.9	12.3
Enron	ENE	57.7	29.6	26.3	23.2
Estee Lauder A	EL	18.5	26.3	NA	NA
Excite@Home	ATHM	15.5	NA	NA	NA
Exodus Communications	EXDS	1005.7	NA	NA	NA
ExxonMobil	XOM	12.6	21.0	25.3	16.9
Fannie Mae	FNM	-14.3	20.4	30.7	24.9
FDX	FDX	-8.2	22.5	22.1	13.6
Fifth Third Bancorp	FITB	4.3	39.8	41.0	28.4
First Data	FDC	55.0	10.8	16.0	NA
First Union	FTU	-43.5	-0.6	13.6	16.8
Firstar	FSR	-30.6	29.6	42.2	27.9
FleetBoston Financial	FBF	-19.9	14.9	20.5	14.7
Ford Motor	F	-6.2	41.9	30.5	21.5
Fox Entertainment Group A	FOX	-0.7	NA	NA	NA
Freddie Mac	FRE	-26.2	20.8	31.9	25.9
Gannett	GCI	28.0	31.4	27.2	16.7
Gap	GPS	23.2	73.5	60.2	38.7
Gateway	GTW	181.6	75.2	67.9	NA
Gemstar International Group	GMST	397.8	153.5	NA	NA
General Electric	GE	53.6	48.4	46.1	28.4
General Instrument	GIC	150.5	NA	NA	NA

Large-Cap U.S. Stocks
(As of January 2000)

Company Name	Ticker Symbol	1 Year Return	3 Year Average Return	5 Year Average Return	10 Year Average Return
General Mills	GIS	-5.5	7.1	12.3	13.0
General Motors	GM	26.5	22.9	21.4	12.8
General Motors H	GMH	141.9	45.9	38.0	21.2
Gillette	G	-12.8	3.0	18.4	22.6
GTE	GTE	11.5	19.8	23.1	12.4
Guidant	GDT	-14.6	49.0	63.9	NA
Halliburton	HAL	37.7	11.6	22.6	9.6
Heinz HJ	HNZ	-27.5	6.5	13.5	8.8
Hewlett-Packard	HWP	67.7	32.5	36.7	26.7
Home Depot	HD	69.0	84.0	46.9	44.3
Honeywell International	HON	31.8	21.5	29.6	23.6
Household International	HI	-4.4	8.2	26.9	19.3
I2 Technologies	ITWO	542.0	116.8	NA	NA
IBM	IBM	17.6	42.7	43.7	19.3
Illinois Tool Works	ITW	17.6	20.3	26.6	21.1
Immunex	IMNX	248.1	182.2	96.7	45.0
Infinity Broadcasting A	INF	32.2	NA	NA	NA
Intel	INTC	39.1	36.2	59.8	44.2
International Paper	IP	28.5	14.0	10.8	9.8
Interpublic Group of Companies	IPG	45.9	55.4	41.8	28.6
Intimate Brands	IBI	53.5	41.0	NA	NA
Intuit	INTU	148.0	78.7	40.1	NA
J.P. Morgan & Co.	JPM	24.3	12.7	21.9	15.5
JDS Uniphase	JDSU	830.1	190.8	181.9	NA
Johnson & Johnson	JNJ	12.5	24.9	29.6	22.3
Kellogg	K	-7.2	0.4	3.6	8.8
Kimberly-Clark	KMB	22.3	13.3	23.7	16.3
Kohl's	KSS	17.5	54.4	48.7	NA
Kroger	KR	-37.6	17.5	25.6	17.7
Level 3 Communications	LVLT	89.9	NA	NA	NA
Lexmark International	LXK	80.1	87.1	NA	NA
Liberty Digital A	LDIG	1483.8	NA	NA	NA
Linear Technology	LLTC	60.2	48.8	42.6	49.9
Lowe's Companies	LOW	17.0	50.3	28.6	33.3
Lucent Technologies	LU	36.6	87.0	NA	NA
Marsh & McLennan Companies	MMC	67.7	44.1	33.4	17.6
Masco	MAS	-10.3	13.9	19.9	10.1

Large-Cap U.S. Stocks
(As of January 2000)

Company Name	Ticker Symbol	1 Year Return	3 Year Average Return	5 Year Average Return	10 Year Average Return
Maxim Integrated Products	MXIM	116.0	63.4	60.9	57.1
May Department Stores	MAY	-18.0	3.4	12.4	11.8
MBNA	KRB	11.0	15.1	44.9	NA
McDonald's	MCD	5.4	21.8	23.2	17.6
McGraw-Hill Companies	MHP	22.9	41.6	33.0	19.5
MCI Worldcom	WCOM	10.9	45.1	52.3	52.9
MediaOne Group	UMG	63.4	61.1	NA	NA
Medtronic	MDT	-1.5	29.5	39.9	34.2
Mellon Financial	MEL	1.3	27.4	39.3	26.4
Merck	MRK	-7.5	21.0	31.2	20.6
Merrill Lynch & Company	MER	26.6	28.6	38.2	31.7
Metromedia Fiber Network A	MFNX	186.2	NA	NA	NA
Micron Technology	MU	54.5	38.9	28.9	44.9
Microsoft	MSFT	68.4	78.1	72.5	57.9
Minnesota Mining & Manufacturing	MMM	41.1	8.3	16.9	13.3
Monsanto	MTC	-25.2	0.5	24.2	16.0
Morgan Stanley Dean Witter & Co.	MWD	103.1	64.7	55.1	NA
Motorola	MOT	142.5	35.0	21.4	27.0
National City	NCC	-32.5	5.0	17.0	14.0
Network Appliance	NTAP	270.5	135.5	NA	NA
Nextlink Communications A	NXLK	506.0	NA	NA	NA
Nike	NKE	23.3	-5.3	22.7	23.6
Northern Trust	NTRS	22.7	44.8	45.8	28.7
Novell	NOVL	120.4	61.6	18.5	26.3
NTL	NTLI	176.3	83.5	49.6	NA
Omnicom Group	OMC	73.8	65.3	52.7	34.8
Oracle	ORCL	289.8	82.1	66.7	47.4
PE Corp - PE Biosystems	PEB	148.0	61.2	58.3	28.9
PepsiCo	PEP	-12.5	11.0	18.0	15.5
Pfizer	PFE	-21.5	34.1	40.1	29.9
Pharmacia & Upjohn	PNU	-19.0	6.9	NA	NA
Philip Morris Companies	MO	-54.7	-11.5	8.4	9.7
Phillips Petroleum	P	13.5	5.1	10.9	10.3
Pitney Bowes	PBI	-25.6	23.2	27.8	17.8
PMC-Sierra	PMCS	407.9	177.5	111.2	NA
PNC Bank	PNC	-15.0	9.2	20.8	12.8
PPG Industries	PPG	10.2	6.1	13.8	15.4

Company Name	Ticker Symbol	1 Year Return	3 Year Average Return	5 Year Average Return	10 Year Average Return
Large-Cap U.S. Stocks					
(As of January 2000)					
Procter & Gamble	PG	21.6	28.5	30.8	22.5
Providian Financial	PVN	21.7	38.9	34.9	18.1
Qualcomm	QCOM	2619.2	230.5	126.8	NA
Qwest Communications International	QWST	72.0	NA	NA	NA
Safeway	SWY	-41.3	18.7	35.0	NA
Sara Lee	SLE	-20.1	7.9	14.3	12.8
SBC Communications	SBC	-7.4	26.4	22.7	16.0
Schering-Plough	SGP	-22.6	39.5	37.9	25.7
Schlumberger	SLB	38.0	9.6	22.5	12.1
Sears Roebuck	S	-26.8	-11.2	8.6	22.5
Siebel Systems	SEBL	395.0	131.7	NA	NA
Solectron	SLR	104.7	92.5	69.1	70.4
Southern	SO	-15.0	6.8	9.0	11.5
Sprint	FON	61.6	52.3	45.7	19.4
Sprint PCS Group	PCS	343.2	NA	NA	NA
State Street	STT	5.0	32.4	40.1	23.9
Sun Microsystems	SUNW	261.7	129.3	103.5	53.3
SunTrust Banks	STI	-8.2	13.7	26.0	22.6
Sysco	SYY	45.6	36.2	27.2	19.0
Tellabs	TLAB	87.2	50.5	55.9	66.5
Teradyne	TER	211.5	75.6	50.8	37.4
Texaco	TX	5.7	6.7	16.8	11.0
Texas Instruments	TXN	126.3	83.2	60.7	37.6
Textron	TXT	2.6	19.6	27.3	23.1
Time Warner	TWX	16.9	57.6	33.6	17.9
Travelers Property Casualty A	TAP	12.1	0.0	NA	NA
Tribune	TRB	68.3	42.4	33.9	18.6
TV Guide	TVGIA	264.0	114.2	70.3	NA
Union Pacific	UNP	-1.5	-8.3	10.4	9.8
United Technologies	UTX	21.0	27.0	35.2	20.1
US Bancorp	USB	-31.3	3.7	19.4	19.4
US West	USW	15.9	37.0	35.3	22.0
VeriSign	VRSN	1191.7	NA	NA	NA
Veritas Software	VRTS	616.4	168.8	177.8	NA
Viacom A	VIA	64.3	51.9	23.8	NA
Wachovia	WB	-20.3	9.0	19.4	16.4
Wal-Mart Stores	WMT	70.4	83.5	46.4	29.3

Large-Cap U.S. Stocks
(As of January 2000)

Company Name	Ticker Symbol	1 Year Return	3 Year Average Return	5 Year Average Return	10 Year Average Return
Walgreen	WAG	0.4	43.7	41.3	27.6
Walt Disney	DIS	-1.7	8.7	14.6	12.8
Warner-Lambert	WLA	10.2	50.3	47.6	26.9
Washington Mutual	WM	-30.8	-1.5	21.2	19.7
Waste Management	WMI	-63.1	-18.6	8.6	27.1
Wells Fargo	WFC	3.3	25.5	31.4	25.3
Weyerhaeuser	WY	45.2	18.5	17.6	14.0
Williams Companies	WMB	-0.5	20.0	32.6	20.6
Xerox	XRX	-60.8	-3.2	8.7	12.6
Xilinx	XLNX	179.3	70.3	55.9	NA
Yahoo!	YHOO	265.2	434.5	NA	NA

Historical Performance of Mid-Cap U.S. Stocks

Mid-Cap U.S. Stocks (As of January 2000)					
Company Name	Ticker Symbol	1 Year Return	3 Year Average Return	5 Year Average Return	10 Year Average Return
Abercrombie & Fitch A	ANF	-24.6	47.9	NA	NA
Abgenix	ABGX	715.4	NA	NA	NA
ACTV	IATV	1098.2	141.4	66.0	NA
Acxiom	ACXM	-22.6	0.0	28.2	24.8
Adaptec	ADPT	184.0	7.6	33.4	36.5
ADC Telecommunications	ADCT	108.8	32.6	42.2	41.2
Adelphia Business Solutions	ABIZ	227.6	NA	NA	NA
Adelphia Communications A	ADLAC	43.4	125.2	50.1	9.1
Adobe Systems	ADBE	188.4	54.4	36.1	30.4
Adolph Coors B	RKY	-5.8	42.5	28.2	16.4
Adtran	ADTN	180.9	7.4	17.6	NA
Advanced Fibre Communication	AFCI	308.6	17.1	NA	NA
Advanced Micro Devices	AMD	-0.2	4.0	3.1	13.9
Aerial Communications	AERL	936.2	95.7	NA	NA
Aetna	AET	-28.2	-10.4	5.6	4.0
Affiliated Computer Services	ACS	2.2	15.6	33.7	NA
Affymetrix	AFFX	596.2	103.3	NA	NA
AG Edwards	AGE	-12.2	14.7	24.2	20.1
Air Products and Chemicals	APD	-14.3	0.8	10.5	13.1
AK Steel Holding	AKS	-17.7	0.8	6.2	NA
Allegheny Energy	AYE	-17.5	1.7	10.7	9.6
Allegheny Technologies	ATI	-35.3	-15.2	-5.5	0.5
Allegiance Telecom	ALGX	660.8	NA	NA	NA
Allergan	AGN	54.6	43.0	30.6	21.0
Alliance Capital Management Holding LP	AC	25.3	41.1	36.7	33.2
Alliant Energy	LNT	-8.6	6.2	7.0	8.1
Allmerica Financial	AFC	-3.5	18.9	NA	NA
Altera	ALTR	62.8	39.7	56.8	50.0
Alza	AZA	-33.7	11.0	14.5	4.9
AMB Property	AMB	-3.1	NA	NA	NA
Ambac Financial Group	ABK	-12.7	17.2	24.1	NA
Amdocs	DOX	101.5	NA	NA	NA

Mid-Cap U.S. Stocks
(As of January 2000)

Company Name	Ticker Symbol	1 Year Return	3 Year Average Return	5 Year Average Return	10 Year Average Return
Amerada Hess	AHC	15.3	0.4	5.6	2.7
Ameren	AEE	-18.0	1.2	5.1	8.3
American Eagle Outfitters	AEOS	35.1	195.2	72.5	NA
American Electric Power	AEP	-27.4	-2.6	5.6	6.7
American Power Conversion	APCC	8.9	24.6	26.4	53.6
American Standard Companies	ASD	27.4	6.3	NA	NA
American Tower A	AMT	3.4	NA	NA	NA
American Water Works	AWK	-35.2	4.1	13.3	13.1
AmeriTrade Holding	AMTD	313.1	NA	NA	NA
Amkor Technology	AMKR	161.3	NA	NA	NA
AMR	AMR	12.8	15.0	20.3	8.7
AmSouth Bancorporation	ASO	-34.6	13.4	24.3	19.9
Anadarko Petroleum	APC	11.2	2.3	12.8	7.1
Ancor Communications	ANCR	1596.9	69.3	64.6	NA
Aon	AOC	10.7	15.5	26.0	16.0
Apache	APA	47.1	2.6	9.1	8.5
Apartment Investment & Management	AIV	14.0	19.2	26.8	NA
Applied Micro Circuits	AMCC	649.2	NA	NA	NA
Archer Daniels Midland	ADM	-24.6	-12.9	-4.6	3.3
Archstone Communities Trust	ASN	8.6	2.8	13.0	18.2
Arrow Electronics	ARW	-4.9	-1.7	7.2	29.3
Ashland	ASH	-30.0	-6.9	1.7	1.0
Aspect Communication	ASPT	126.8	7.2	36.1	NA
Aspect Development	ASDV	54.6	71.3	NA	NA
Associated Banc-Corp	ASBC	3.5	9.6	15.9	16.6
Associated Group A	AGRPA	112.2	81.1	50.7	NA
Atmel	ATML	286.1	21.3	28.7	NA
Autodesk	ADSK	-20.3	7.2	-2.5	6.5
Autoliv	ALV	-20.4	NA	NA	NA
AutoNation	AN	-37.8	-33.3	35.8	NA
AutoZone	AZO	-1.9	5.5	5.9	NA
AvalonBay Communities	AVB	7.5	4.1	18.2	NA
Avery Dennison	AVY	64.6	29.5	35.3	19.3
Avnet	AVT	1.3	2.4	11.6	8.6
Avon Products	AVP	-24.1	6.9	19.8	17.4
AVX	AVX	198.3	34.3	NA	NA

| Mid-Cap U.S. Stocks | | | | | |
| (As of January 2000) | | | | | |

Company Name	Ticker Symbol	1 Year Return	3 Year Average Return	5 Year Average Return	10 Year Average Return
B.F. Goodrich	GR	-20.7	-9.5	8.4	7.2
Baker Hughes	BHI	21.7	-13.9	4.6	-0.1
BancWest	BWE	-16.3	7.1	14.5	8.5
Bausch & Lomb	BOL	15.9	27.7	17.9	10.0
BB&T	BBT	-30.7	17.4	27.0	18.7
Bear Stearns Companies	BSC	27.7	22.9	31.2	23.6
Becton Dickinson	BDX	-36.2	8.6	18.9	14.9
Bed Bath & Beyond	BBBY	1.8	42.0	35.9	NA
Belo AH	BLC	-3.1	4.2	7.4	8.6
Bemis	BMS	-5.6	0.4	10.2	9.8
Best Buy	BBY	63.7	166.4	45.1	58.6
BHC Communications	BHC	32.3	17.4	17.4	13.0
Biomet	BMET	-0.2	38.9	23.8	19.5
Bisys Group	BSYS	26.4	20.8	24.2	NA
BJ Services	BJS	167.6	17.9	37.7	NA
BJ's Wholesale Club	BJ	57.6	NA	NA	NA
Black & Decker	BDK	-5.9	21.4	18.4	12.3
Boise Cascade	BCC	32.8	10.4	10.6	1.7
Boston Properties	BXP	7.8	NA	NA	NA
Boston Scientific	BSX	-18.4	-10.0	20.3	NA
Bowater Incorporated	BOW	33.2	15.0	17.5	10.3
Broadwing	BRW	142.1	47.0	66.4	29.3
Brown-Forman B	BF.B	-22.9	9.9	16.2	9.9
Brunswick	BC	-8.2	-0.6	5.5	7.3
Burlington Resources	BR	-6.3	-11.9	0.2	-0.8
Burr-Brown	BBRC	131.2	67.4	68.4	36.3
C-Cube Microsystems	CUBE	129.5	19.0	45.6	NA
Cabletron Systems	CS	210.5	-7.9	2.3	30.1
Cadence Design Systems	CDN	-19.3	6.7	39.3	17.7
Calpine	CPN	406.9	85.7	NA	NA
Capital One Financial	COF	26.0	59.7	56.4	NA
Carolina Power & Light	CPL	-32.0	-1.2	8.1	8.8
Catalina Marketing	POS	69.3	28.1	33.0	NA
CCB Financial	CCB	-21.8	10.8	23.3	16.4
CDW Computer Centers	CDWC	63.9	38.4	47.2	NA
Central and South West	CSR	-21.6	-1.0	4.6	3.5
Centurytel	CTL	5.7	52.2	30.4	17.3

Mid-Cap U.S. Stocks

(As of January 2000)

Company Name	Ticker Symbol	1 Year Return	3 Year Average Return	5 Year Average Return	10 Year Average Return
Ceridian	CEN	-38.2	2.1	9.9	9.1
Champion International	CHA	53.6	13.2	11.7	7.8
Charter One Financial	CF	-26.0	3.8	22.4	22.5
Checkfree Holdings	CKFR	347.1	82.7	NA	NA
Chiron	CHIR	61.8	31.5	16.1	19.5
Chris-Craft Industries	CCN	54.2	24.1	19.4	10.3
Chubb	CB	-11.1	3.5	10.0	11.4
Ciena	CIEN	293.2	NA	NA	NA
Cincinnati Financial	CINF	-12.9	15.2	17.4	16.5
Cinergy	CIN	-26.2	-5.4	6.3	8.1
Cintas	CTAS	-24.4	22.4	25.1	22.3
Circuit City Group	CC	80.8	44.5	32.7	24.0
CIT Group	CIT	-32.6	NA	NA	NA
Citadel Communications	CITC	150.7	NA	NA	NA
Citizens Utilities	CZN	77.4	11.9	6.7	NA
Clarify	CLFY	415.6	38.0	NA	NA
CMS Energy	CMS	-33.4	0.7	10.0	0.9
CNA Financial	CNA	-3.3	3.0	12.5	1.8
CNET	CNET	326.3	98.6	NA	NA
Coastal	CGP	1.6	14.0	23.5	9.1
Coca-Cola Enterprises	CCE	-43.4	8.1	27.9	14.6
Columbia Energy Group	CG	11.3	15.9	33.7	6.8
Comair Holdings	COMR	4.3	30.7	47.8	36.6
Comdisco	CDO	121.9	53.1	49.9	23.2
Comerica	CMA	-29.8	12.8	27.1	20.1
Commerce Bancshares	CBSH	-15.0	10.0	21.2	16.8
CommScope	CTV	139.8	NA	NA	NA
Compass Bancshares	CBSS	-9.2	11.2	21.7	23.5
Concord EFS	CEFT	-8.9	27.1	50.9	46.6
Conexant Systems	CNXT	692.5	NA	NA	NA
Conseco	CNC	-40.2	-16.4	11.7	27.7
Consolidated Edison	ED	-31.4	11.7	12.6	8.5
Consolidated Natural Gas	CNG	24.4	9.3	17.3	6.9
Consolidated Papers	CDP	19.5	12.6	10.6	7.0
Consolidated Stores	CNS	-19.5	-14.3	6.4	20.7
Constellation Energy Group	CEG	-0.4	8.8	12.2	9.1
Continental Airlines B	CAL	32.5	16.2	57.2	NA

Company Name	Ticker Symbol	1 Year Return	3 Year Average Return	5 Year Average Return	10 Year Average Return
Convergys	CVG	37.4	NA	NA	NA
Cooper Cameron	CAM	99.8	8.6	NA	NA
Cooper Industries	CBE	-12.8	1.3	6.6	3.5
Cornerstone Properties	CPP	1.3	NA	NA	NA
Countrywide Credit Industries	CCR	-49.2	-3.2	15.6	23.8
Cox Radio	CXR	136.1	78.6	NA	NA
CR Bard	BCR	8.8	26.1	16.7	11.4
Credence Systems	CMOS	367.6	62.6	40.7	NA
Cree Research	CREE	256.7	163.1	110.6	NA
Crescent Real Estate Equities	CEI	-11.3	-3.4	15.0	NA
Crown Castle International	TWRS	41.1	NA	NA	NA
Crown Cork & Seal	CCK	-24.8	-23.7	-8.1	3.4
CSG Systems International	CSGS	1.0	73.1	NA	NA
CSX	CSX	-22.3	-7.2	0.3	8.5
CTS	CTS	247.6	121.1	76.7	37.4
Cummins Engine	CUM	39.4	3.9	3.6	8.8
Cypress Semiconductor	CY	289.5	31.9	22.9	20.7
Dallas Semiconductor	DS	58.8	41.6	31.7	26.3
Dana	DCN	-24.3	-0.1	8.1	9.5
Danaher	DHR	-11.1	27.6	30.1	29.1
Darden Restaurants	DRI	1.1	28.2	NA	NA
Deere & Company	DE	34.9	4.4	16.9	10.9
Delhaize America B	DZB	-29.6	-10.3	8.1	0.6
Delta Air Lines	DAL	-4.0	12.2	14.8	4.6
Deluxe	DLX	-21.5	-1.4	5.5	1.8
Devon Energy	DVN	7.6	-1.3	13.1	9.7
Dial (New)	DL	-14.9	20.2	NA	NA
Diamond Offshore Drilling	DO	31.3	3.5	NA	NA
Diamond Technology Partners	DTPI	574.0	NA	NA	NA
Digital Lightwave	DIGL	2667.0	NA	NA	NA
DII Group	DIIG	208.6	82.8	40.7	NA
Dillard's	DDS	-28.4	-12.7	-5.0	-1.2
Dollar General	DG	20.9	30.1	30.1	40.8
Dollar Tree Stores	DLTR	10.9	41.8	NA	NA
Dominion Resources	D	-11.0	7.2	8.5	9.1
Donaldson, Lufkin & Jenrette	DLJ	18.6	40.1	NA	NA
Dover	DOV	25.3	23.0	30.2	19.9

Mid-Cap U.S. Stocks
(As of January 2000)

Mid-Cap U.S. Stocks
(As of January 2000)

Company Name	Ticker Symbol	1 Year Return	3 Year Average Return	5 Year Average Return	10 Year Average Return
Dow Jones & Company	DJ	43.9	28.7	19.7	10.1
DPL	DPL	-15.8	7.9	10.6	13.4
DQE	DQE	-18.0	10.6	17.0	13.5
DST Systems	DST	33.7	34.5	NA	NA
DTE Energy Holding	DTE	-22.5	5.1	10.5	8.9
Duke-Weeks Realty	DRE	-10.3	6.5	13.4	12.5
Dun & Bradstreet	DNB	-4.3	10.6	13.6	14.9
Dynegy	DYN	122.9	1.8	18.7	NA
E*Trade Group	EGRP	123.4	108.7	NA	NA
E-Tek Dynamics	ETEK	403.3	NA	NA	NA
Eastman Chemical	EMN	10.6	-1.7	1.9	NA
Eaton	ETN	5.1	3.6	10.6	12.9
Ecolab	ECL	9.3	29.3	32.2	20.9
Edison International	EIX	-2.9	13.7	17.5	8.8
El Paso Energy	EPG	17.4	19.3	25.0	NA
Electronic Arts	ERTS	49.7	41.0	34.3	43.4
Electronics for Imaging	EFII	45.3	12.2	53.3	NA
Emmis Communications A	EMMS	187.3	56.1	56.0	NA
Emulex	EMLX	1025.0	205.7	101.6	75.5
Energy East	NEG	-23.9	29.8	23.0	10.5
Engelhard	EC	-1.2	1.6	7.1	15.1
Ensco International	ESV	115.4	-1.4	30.3	10.3
Entergy	ETR	-13.9	3.3	9.8	6.9
Entrust Technologies	ENTU	151.1	NA	NA	NA
EOG Resources	EOG	2.5	-10.9	-0.7	4.1
Equifax	EFX	-30.3	-3.6	16.6	15.3
Equity Office Properties Trust	EOP	18.3	NA	NA	NA
Equity Residential Properties Trust	EQR	13.5	7.6	14.6	NA
Erie Indemnity A	ERIE	5.3	2.9	NA	NA
EW Scripps	SSP	-8.8	9.9	20.5	14.0
Expeditors International of WA	EXPD	109.3	56.7	52.4	30.0
Express Scripts	ESRX	-4.7	52.8	28.4	NA
Family Dollar Stores	FDO	-25.1	35.6	33.8	27.3
Federated Department Stores	FD	16.1	14.0	21.3	NA
Federated Investors B	FII	11.7	NA	NA	NA
Finova Group	FNV	-33.1	4.8	19.3	NA

Mid-Cap U.S. Stocks
(As of January 2000)

Company Name	Ticker Symbol	1 Year Return	3 Year Average Return	5 Year Average Return	10 Year Average Return
First Security	FSCO	12.1	22.4	34.5	23.7
First Tennessee National	FTN	-23.3	17.7	26.2	25.9
First Virginia Banks	FVB	-5.8	13.4	18.5	16.4
FirstEnergy	FE	-26.6	NA	NA	NA
FirstMerit	FMER	-12.0	12.0	16.8	16.6
Fiserv	FISV	11.7	32.9	32.0	29.6
Flextronics International	FLEX	114.9	87.9	64.6	NA
Florida Progress	FPC	-0.7	15.8	12.2	7.2
Fluor	FLR	10.4	-8.2	2.8	3.5
FMC	FMC	2.3	-6.5	-0.2	5.0
Forest Laboratories	FRX	15.5	55.4	21.4	19.3
Fort James	FJ	-30.3	-4.6	10.0	3.0
Fortune Brands	FO	7.1	4.5	11.9	10.4
FPL Group	FPL	-27.7	1.3	8.2	7.3
Franklin Resources	BEN	0.9	12.7	22.8	22.0
Freeport-McMoRan Copper & Gold A	FCX.A	91.6	-11.5	-0.6	16.9
Galileo International	GLC	-30.6	NA	NA	NA
General Dynamics	GD	-9.2	16.4	22.1	32.8
Gentex	GNTX	38.8	40.2	35.6	33.1
Genuine Parts	GPC	-23.1	-2.8	3.9	6.2
Genzyme Corporation General Division	GENZ	-8.1	29.5	24.5	20.6
Georgia-Pacific - Timber Group	TGP	7.8	NA	NA	NA
Georgia-Pacific Group	GP	75.4	27.2	15.7	11.8
Getty Images	GETY	184.4	NA	NA	NA
Gilead Sciences	GILD	31.8	29.4	41.6	NA
Global Marine	GLM	84.7	-6.9	35.6	16.5
Global Telesystems Group	GTS	24.7	NA	NA	NA
GO2Net	GNET	883.7	NA	NA	NA
Golden State Bancorp	GSB	3.8	-4.3	16.2	3.7
Golden West Financial	GDW	10.2	17.5	24.1	14.8
Goodyear Tire & Rubber	GT	-43.0	-16.5	-1.4	5.1
GPU	GPU	-28.9	1.4	8.6	8.4
Great Lakes Chemical	GLK	-3.8	-1.0	-4.1	7.3
GreenPoint Financial	GPT	-30.3	2.1	20.9	NA
H & R Block	HRB	-0.6	17.2	6.1	12.4

Mid-Cap U.S. Stocks
(As of January 2000)

Company Name	Ticker Symbol	1 Year Return	3 Year Average Return	5 Year Average Return	10 Year Average Return
Hannaford Bros	HRD	32.3	28.5	24.0	17.1
Harcourt General	H	-8.9	2.9	8.1	9.9
Harley-Davidson	HDI	35.6	40.3	36.2	39.0
Harmonic	HLIT	912.7	131.1	NA	NA
Harrah's Entertainment	HET	68.5	10.0	3.7	NA
Harris	HRS	-12.5	-0.7	10.8	10.3
Hartford Financial Services Group	HIG	-12.5	13.9	NA	NA
Hartford Life	HLI	-23.9	NA	NA	NA
Hasbro	HAS	-20.6	4.1	9.0	14.0
Health Management Associates	HMA	-38.2	10.2	22.1	NA
Healthsouth	HRC	-65.2	-34.7	-10.0	6.5
Hearst-Argyle Television	HTV	-19.3	NA	NA	NA
Heller Financial	HF	-30.2	NA	NA	NA
Hercules	HPC	6.2	-11.1	-3.9	11.6
Herman Miller	MLHR	-13.8	18.3	29.9	18.8
Hershey Foods	HSY	-22.3	4.4	16.6	12.6
Hertz	HRZ	10.3	NA	NA	NA
Hillenbrand Industries	HB	-43.2	-2.9	4.5	5.3
Hilton Hotels	HLT	-24.6	-17.1	-1.7	-0.9
Hispanic Broadcasting	HBCCA	87.3	80.2	79.1	NA
HNC Software	HNCS	161.5	49.9	NA	NA
Homestake Mining	HM	-13.7	-17.4	-13.6	-7.6
Hormel Foods	HRL	26.3	17.1	12.8	11.4
Host Marriott	HMT	-35.1	-15.5	2.3	15.3
Howmet International	HWM	12.0	NA	NA	NA
Hubbell B	HUB.B	-25.7	-11.7	4.5	6.9
Human Genome Sciences	HGSI	329.2	55.3	59.6	NA
Huntington Bancshares	HBAN	-10.2	9.2	19.9	17.9
ICN Pharmaceuticals	ICN	13.1	25.9	19.3	23.7
IDEC Pharmaceuticals	IDPH	318.1	102.3	147.3	NA
Illinova	ILN	45.8	13.5	14.8	10.2
IMC Global	IGL	-22.0	-24.2	-4.6	1.1
IMS Health	RX	-19.6	NA	NA	NA
Incyte Pharmaceuticals	INCY	60.5	32.6	54.0	NA
Informix	IFMX	15.8	-17.5	-6.6	19.5
InfoSpace.com	INSP	1022.6	NA	NA	NA

Mid-Cap U.S. Stocks
(As of January 2000)

Company Name	Ticker Symbol	1 Year Return	3 Year Average Return	5 Year Average Return	10 Year Average Return
Ingersoll-Rand	IR	17.9	24.6	23.2	14.8
Ingram Micro	IM	-62.9	-17.1	NA	NA
Inktomi	INKT	174.4	NA	NA	NA
Integrated Device Technology	IDTI	373.5	28.6	14.4	21.7
InterDigital Communications	IDC	1543.7	132.9	59.0	29.0
International Flavors & Fragrances	IFF	-11.4	-2.4	-0.9	8.5
International Game Tech	IGT	-16.3	4.1	5.9	29.2
International Speedway A	ISCA	24.5	35.2	NA	NA
Ipalco Enterprises	IPL	-36.6	9.8	13.9	9.8
ISS Group	ISSX	158.6	NA	NA	NA
ITT Industries	IIN	-14.5	13.0	17.9	23.2
Ivax	IVX	107.0	35.9	6.4	17.3
Jabil Circuit	JBL	96.0	94.0	135.9	NA
JC Penney	JCP	-55.2	-22.5	-11.2	-1.9
JD Edwards & Company	JDEC	5.3	NA	NA	NA
Jefferson-Pilot	JP	-7.3	24.4	27.3	21.9
Johns Manville	JM	-13.8	11.1	22.5	13.2
Johnson Controls	JCI	-2.0	13.2	20.8	16.6
Jones Apparel Group	JNY	22.9	13.2	33.3	NA
Jones Intercable	JOIN	97.9	87.0	42.4	16.2
Jones Pharma	JMED	79.2	21.6	86.6	40.4
Kansas City Southern Industries	KSU	52.2	71.5	49.5	36.3
Keane	KEA	-19.6	26.5	40.2	35.0
Keebler Foods	KBL	-25.3	NA	NA	NA
Kemet	KEM	300.6	24.7	24.9	NA
Kerr-McGee	KMG	68.7	-1.5	9.5	5.4
KeyCorp	KEY	-28.6	-1.3	16.1	13.9
Keyspan	KSE	-20.2	-3.6	6.1	6.5
Kimco Realty	KIM	-8.6	4.9	12.2	NA
Kinder Morgan Energy Partners	KMP	22.6	54.1	37.9	NA
King Pharmaceuticals	KING	218.9	NA	NA	NA
KLA-Tencor	KLAC	156.8	46.4	35.4	38.2
Kmart	KM	-34.3	-1.0	-4.1	-2.7
Knight-Ridder	KRI	18.4	17.8	20.9	9.8
Knight/Trimark Group	NITE	284.3	NA	NA	NA
Lafarge	LAF	-30.5	12.9	11.2	6.9
Lam Research	LRCX	526.3	58.3	24.5	41.0

Mid-Cap U.S. Stocks
(As of January 2000)

Company Name	Ticker Symbol	1 Year Return	3 Year Average Return	5 Year Average Return	10 Year Average Return
Lamar Advertising A	LAMR	62.6	55.3	NA	NA
Lattice Semiconductor	LSCC	105.3	27.0	41.3	36.3
Lear	LEA	-16.9	-2.1	10.1	NA
Legato Systems	LGTO	108.7	103.6	NA	NA
Legg Mason	LM	15.8	37.2	37.0	27.5
Leggett & Platt	LEG	-1.0	8.9	21.5	21.2
Lehman Brothers Holdings	LEH	93.4	40.1	42.9	NA
LG&E Energy	LGE	-34.6	-6.0	4.2	8.4
Limited	LTD	59.7	39.2	23.4	12.3
Lincare Holdings	LNCR	-14.5	19.2	19.1	NA
Lincoln National	LNC	0.2	18.3	21.9	14.7
Litton Industries	LIT	-23.6	1.6	6.2	11.5
Liz Claiborne	LIZ	20.7	0.2	18.8	6.0
Lockheed Martin	LMT	-46.9	-20.2	NA	NA
Loews	LTR	-37.4	-12.7	8.1	0.8
Loral Space & Communications	LOR	36.5	9.8	NA	NA
LSI Logic	LSI	318.6	36.1	27.4	34.2
Lycos	LCOS	186.4	211.8	NA	NA
M & T Bank	MTB	-19.4	13.9	26.2	21.8
Macromedia	MACR	117.1	59.6	41.8	NA
Mallinckrodt	MKG	5.2	-8.6	3.1	7.9
Mandalay Resort Group	MBG	77.9	-16.3	-2.7	0.8
Manpower	MAN	50.4	5.6	6.6	NA
Marriott International A	MAR	9.6	NA	NA	NA
Marshall & Ilsley	MI	9.1	24.0	29.6	21.5
Martin Marietta Materials	MLM	-33.4	22.3	20.1	NA
Mattel	MAT	-43.2	-21.2	-3.0	10.3
Maytag	MYG	-22.0	36.7	29.0	12.6
MBIA	MBI	-18.2	2.8	15.2	14.4
McClatchy A	MNI	23.6	17.0	21.9	11.6
McCormick	MKC	-10.0	10.5	12.8	11.0
McKesson HBOC	MCK	-71.3	-6.1	8.2	NA
McLeodUSA A	MCLD	276.8	66.5	NA	NA
MCN Energy Group	MCN	31.3	-2.5	10.1	22.3
Mead	MEA	50.8	16.6	14.5	11.6
Medical Manager	MMGR	91.5	20.2	34.5	27.9
MedImmune	MEDI	233.6	169.2	148.5	NA

Mid-Cap U.S. Stocks
(As of January 2000)

Company Name	Ticker Symbol	1 Year Return	3 Year Average Return	5 Year Average Return	10 Year Average Return
Mercantile Bankshares	MRBK	-14.7	17.5	23.1	14.8
Mercury Interactive	MERQ	241.3	155.1	74.7	NA
Meredith	MDP	11.0	17.5	30.3	18.8
Metro-Goldwyn-Mayer	MGM	78.7	NA	NA	NA
MGIC Investment	MTG	51.5	16.8	29.8	NA
MGM Grand	MGG	85.5	13.0	15.8	12.5
Micrel	MCRL	107.1	93.1	73.5	NA
Microchip Technology	MCHP	85.0	26.4	30.1	NA
Micromuse	MUSE	771.8	NA	NA	NA
MicroStrategy	MSTR	566.7	NA	NA	NA
Midamerican Energy Holdings	MEC	-2.8	0.1	16.6	10.8
Millennium Pharmaceuticals	MLNM	371.5	91.5	NA	NA
Millipore	MIL	38.2	-1.0	11.1	12.7
MiniMed	MNMD	39.9	65.6	NA	NA
MIPS Technologies	MIPS	62.5	NA	NA	NA
Mirage Resorts	MIR	1.3	-11.2	8.1	10.7
Molex	MOLX	48.9	31.5	26.5	33.3
Montana Power	MTP	30.7	57.1	33.0	20.2
Murphy Oil	MUR	43.3	8.3	12.2	8.0
Mylan Laboratories	MYL	-19.5	15.7	7.8	12.9
Nabisco Group Holdings	NGH	-42.2	-15.0	-2.2	NA
Nabisco Holding	NA	-22.6	-5.1	NA	NA
Nabors Industries	NBR	129.2	17.1	36.6	24.4
National Commerce Bancorp	NCBC	22.6	35.6	34.6	27.9
National Fuel Gas	NFG	7.2	8.3	17.8	10.7
National Instruments Corp	NATI	68.1	39.1	NA	NA
National Semiconductor	NSM	217.1	20.5	17.0	19.4
Nationwide Financial Services	NFS	-45.6	NA	NA	NA
Navistar International	NAV	64.9	72.7	25.5	2.0
NCR	NCR	-9.3	4.1	NA	NA
Network Associates	NETA	-59.7	-3.1	46.2	NA
Network Solutions	NSOL	232.5	NA	NA	NA
New Century Energies	NCE	-33.7	-2.6	6.7	8.6
New England Electric Systems	NES	12.6	20.5	16.8	13.0
New York Times A	NYT	43.3	38.9	36.8	16.2
Newell Rubbermaid	NWL	-28.3	-1.0	8.6	12.1
Newmont Mining	NEM	35.1	-17.6	-6.6	-3.2

Mid-Cap U.S. Stocks
(As of January 2000)

Company Name	Ticker Symbol	1 Year Return	3 Year Average Return	5 Year Average Return	10 Year Average Return
Niagara Mohawk Holdings	NMK	-13.6	12.2	1.2	0.5
NiSource	NI	-39.4	0.3	8.0	11.3
Noble Drilling	NE	153.1	18.1	41.0	13.5
Nordstrom	JWN	-23.4	15.2	5.7	4.6
Norfolk Southern	NSC	-33.5	-8.9	3.0	7.4
North Fork Bancorporation	NFB	-25.4	16.6	34.1	15.2
Northeast Utilities	NU	29.1	17.1	2.8	5.0
Northern States Power	NSP	-25.0	0.2	3.4	6.0
Northrop Grumman	NOC	-24.2	-11.5	7.6	16.1
Northwest Airlines	NWAC	-13.0	-17.2	7.2	NA
Nova Corp GA	NIS	-9.0	12.6	NA	NA
Novellus Systems	NVLS	147.5	65.4	37.4	43.0
Nstar	NST	3.2	21.0	18.1	14.7
Nucor	NUE	28.1	3.4	0.6	14.5
Oak Industries	OAK	203.2	66.5	35.9	35.7
Occidental Petroleum	OXY	34.8	1.9	7.0	2.2
Office Depot	ODP	-55.5	-2.6	-6.9	15.2
Old Kent Financial	OK	-18.6	22.2	27.7	20.2
Old Republic International	ORI	-37.5	-6.7	9.7	13.2
Open Market	OMKT	286.1	49.5	NA	NA
Optical Coating Laboratory	OCLI	1039.9	203.7	118.8	47.1
Outback Steakhouse	OSSI	-2.4	13.3	10.6	NA
Owens-Illinois	OI	-18.2	3.3	17.9	NA
Paccar	PCAR	13.6	14.6	21.3	12.2
PacifiCare Health Systems	PHSY	-27.2	-13.3	-4.0	15.3
PaineWebber Group	PWJ	1.6	29.1	33.4	25.4
Pall	PLL	-12.2	-2.9	5.4	8.7
PanAmSat	SPOT	52.5	28.5	NA	NA
Parametric Tech	PMTC	66.5	1.8	25.7	40.9
Park Place Entertainment	PPE	96.1	NA	NA	NA
Parker Hannifin	PH	59.2	27.7	22.5	19.2
Paychex	PAYX	17.6	39.0	50.7	43.8
PECO Energy	PE	-14.7	16.6	12.7	10.0
Pegasus Communications A	PGTV	294.2	93.0	NA	NA
PeopleSoft	PSFT	12.5	-3.8	35.2	NA
Peregrine Systems	PRGN	263.1	NA	NA	NA
Perkinelmer	PKI	52.6	30.4	27.4	12.2

Mid-Cap U.S. Stocks

(As of January 2000)

Company Name	Ticker Symbol	1 Year Return	3 Year Average Return	5 Year Average Return	10 Year Average Return
PG & E Corp	PCG	-32.0	3.6	2.1	5.4
Phelps Dodge	PD	37.3	3.2	5.0	12.5
PIMCO Advisors Holdings LP	PA	30.2	33.0	38.4	23.5
Pinnacle West Capital	PNW	-25.4	2.0	13.1	13.2
Pittway A	PRY.A	36.1	30.8	35.4	NA
Plum Creek Timber Company	PCL	4.1	6.3	12.7	21.7
PMI Group	PMA	48.9	10.2	NA	NA
Polycom	PLCM	186.2	135.5	NA	NA
Popular	BPOP	-16.1	20.5	34.8	22.0
Potomac Electric Power	POM	-7.0	2.9	12.0	6.8
Powertel	PTEL	640.1	101.6	56.0	NA
PP and L Resources	PPL	-14.7	5.7	10.7	7.5
Praxair	PX	44.6	4.1	21.0	NA
Premier Parks	PKS	-4.6	21.6	57.6	NA
Progressive	PGR	-56.7	3.0	16.3	19.7
ProLogis Trust	PLD	-1.1	2.0	8.4	NA
Protective Life	PL	-19.0	18.5	23.3	26.0
PSINet	PSIX	207.6	80.7	NA	NA
Public Service Enterprise Group	PEG	-8.0	15.9	12.9	9.3
Public Storage	PSA	-8.7	-5.3	15.0	14.9
Puma Technology	PUMA	3770.4	96.4	NA	NA
Qlogic	QLGC	388.6	191.8	148.5	NA
Quaker Oats	OAT	12.3	22.4	19.4	12.5
Quantum Corp-Dlt & Storage	DSS	-28.8	1.9	14.9	15.4
Quintiles Transnational	QTRN	-65.0	-17.4	20.6	NA
R&B Falcon	FLC	75.2	-12.3	NA	NA
Radian Group	RDN	4.2	9.4	27.4	NA
Ralston Purina	RAL	-12.0	7.1	16.1	14.7
Rational Software	RATL	85.4	7.5	69.9	35.6
Raytheon B	RTN.B	-49.2	-16.5	-1.9	6.7
RCN	RCNC	174.2	NA	NA	NA
Reader's Digest Association A	RDA	16.9	-7.6	-7.0	NA
RealNetworks	RNWK	570.7	NA	NA	NA
Reckson Services Industries	RSII	1412.1	NA	NA	NA
Regions Financial	RGBK	-35.7	1.7	13.3	16.1
Reliant Energy	REI	-25.7	5.9	11.3	9.8
ReliaStar Financial	RLR	-13.9	12.5	24.4	18.5

Mid-Cap U.S. Stocks
(As of January 2000)

Company Name	Ticker Symbol	1 Year Return	3 Year Average Return	5 Year Average Return	10 Year Average Return
Republic New York	RNB	60.8	23.0	28.7	18.1
Republic Services A	RSG	-22.7	NA	NA	NA
Reynolds & Reynolds	REY	0.0	-3.0	14.3	24.9
Reynolds Metals	RLM	49.2	13.5	12.0	6.4
RF Micro Devices	RFMD	490.3	NA	NA	NA
Rite Aid	RAD	-77.1	-16.1	1.1	5.4
Robert Half International	RHI	-35.8	7.9	29.0	25.8
Rockwell International	ROK	21.5	5.1	17.9	15.8
Rohm and Haas	ROH	37.7	16.7	19.1	16.3
Rowan Companies	RDC	119.6	-1.4	28.3	6.8
Royal Caribbean Cruises	RCL	34.6	63.5	30.1	NA
RR Donnelley & Sons	DNY	-41.8	-5.4	-1.3	1.8
RSA Security	RSAS	237.0	35.0	75.5	NA
S1	SONE	412.3	148.0	NA	NA
Sabre Holdings	TSG	15.2	22.5	NA	NA
SAFECO	SAFC	-40.6	-11.9	1.9	5.8
Safeguard Scientifics	SFE	494.1	78.2	102.4	56.1
Saks	SKS	-50.7	-5.5	6.9	16.5
SanDisk	SNDK	581.4	114.5	NA	NA
Sanmina	SANM	59.8	52.3	71.1	NA
Santa Fe International	SDC	79.5	NA	NA	NA
Sapient	SAPE	403.4	137.4	NA	NA
Sawtek	SAWS	660.7	49.8	NA	NA
Scana	SCG	-12.2	5.7	11.0	10.7
SCI Systems	SCI	42.3	54.4	55.6	34.3
Scientific-Atlanta	SFA	145.3	55.4	22.0	22.2
SDL	SDLI	1000.3	155.1	NA	NA
Seagate Technology	SEG	53.9	5.6	31.2	20.0
Sealed Air	SEE	1.5	7.6	23.4	26.1
SEI Investments	SEIC	20.0	75.8	48.2	30.5
Sempra Energy	SRE	-26.2	-2.3	5.3	4.3
Sepracor	SEPR	12.6	81.4	88.9	NA
Service Corp International	SRV	-81.3	-36.3	-11.8	4.8
ServiceMaster	SVM	-43.0	4.0	14.1	20.8
SFX Entertainment A	SFX	-1.1	NA	NA	NA
Shaw Industries	SHX	-35.7	10.6	2.4	8.8
Sherwin-Williams	SHW	-27.1	-7.7	6.4	11.0

Mid-Cap U.S. Stocks

(As of January 2000)

Company Name	Ticker Symbol	1 Year Return	3 Year Average Return	5 Year Average Return	10 Year Average Return
Sigma-Aldrich	SIAL	3.4	-0.4	13.7	8.4
Silicon Graphics	SGI	-24.8	-27.6	-20.8	2.9
Simon Property Group	SPG	-13.0	-3.1	6.1	NA
SLM Holding	SLM	-10.8	18.3	37.9	14.2
Smith International	SII	97.3	3.5	32.1	14.8
Smurfit-Stone Container	SSCC	54.9	15.1	7.6	NA
Sonoco Products	SON	-20.9	1.4	6.3	6.2
Sotheby's Holdings A	BID	-5.1	19.3	23.4	6.0
Southdown	SDW	-11.8	19.5	30.1	7.3
Southtrust	SOTR	4.7	20.2	28.9	22.7
Southwest Airlines	LUV	6.7	35.4	26.8	26.4
Spieker Properties	SPK	12.5	6.5	19.5	NA
SPX	SPW	20.6	27.9	38.5	13.2
St. Joe	JOE	3.8	8.8	9.2	NA
St. Jude Medical	STJ	10.1	-10.2	3.0	7.0
St. Paul	SPC	0.0	7.7	11.7	12.2
Stanley Works	SWK	11.9	6.2	13.9	7.6
Staples	SPLS	-28.8	37.2	33.5	34.6
Starbucks	SBUX	-13.6	19.2	28.7	NA
Starwood Hotels & Resorts Worldwide	HOT	6.0	-10.6	19.9	2.0
Steelcase	SCS	-22.7	NA	NA	NA
Sterling Commerce	SE	-24.4	-1.2	NA	NA
Sterling Software	SSW	16.4	25.8	36.5	34.3
Storage Technology	STK	-48.3	-8.3	4.9	12.1
Stryker	SYK	26.7	32.9	30.7	27.6
Summit Bancorp	SUB	-27.6	4.6	17.2	13.6
SunGard Data Systems	SDS	-40.2	6.3	19.8	14.9
Sunoco	SUN	-32.6	1.8	-0.5	-0.8
SuperValu	SVU	-26.8	15.0	13.6	6.1
Sybron International	SYB	-9.2	14.4	23.4	NA
Sykes Enterprises	SYKE	43.9	20.6	NA	NA
Symantec	SYMC	169.5	59.3	27.4	22.4
Symbol Technologies	SBL	49.3	69.4	47.4	29.5
Synopsys	SNPS	23.0	13.0	25.0	NA
Synovus Financial	SNV	-15.7	13.3	32.2	22.3
T Rowe Price Associates	TROW	9.2	20.7	39.4	28.1

Mid-Cap U.S. Stocks
(As of January 2000)

Company Name	Ticker Symbol	1 Year Return	3 Year Average Return	5 Year Average Return	10 Year Average Return
Tandy	TAN	140.0	66.2	33.1	19.4
TCF Financial	TCB	5.7	7.0	22.0	25.3
TECO Energy	TE	-30.2	-3.6	3.2	7.4
Tektronix	TEK	31.5	6.0	12.9	15.0
Telephone and Data Systems	TDS	182.2	52.9	23.4	11.5
TeleTech Holdings	TTEC	228.7	9.0	NA	NA
Teligent A	TGNT	114.8	NA	NA	NA
Temple-Inland	TIN	13.5	9.2	10.4	9.0
Tenet Healthcare	THC	-10.5	2.4	10.7	3.7
Texas Utilities	TXU	-19.3	1.0	8.4	7.3
Thermo Electron	TMO	-11.4	-28.6	-5.5	5.2
Thomas & Betts	TNB	-24.5	-8.2	1.7	6.3
Ticketmaster Online-City Search B	TMCS	-31.4	NA	NA	NA
Tidewater	TDW	58.7	-5.7	16.2	11.1
Tiffany	TIF	245.6	70.6	56.7	23.4
Times Mirror	TMC	21.2	11.7	26.7	14.5
Titan	TTN	760.2	141.1	49.3	34.9
TJX Companies	TJX	-29.2	20.6	41.2	20.5
TMP Worldwide	TMPW	238.1	123.3	NA	NA
Tommy Hilfiger	TOM	-22.1	-0.9	15.7	NA
Torchmark	TMK	-16.8	11.6	16.6	9.0
Tosco	TOS	6.2	2.0	24.3	15.8
Total System Services	TSS	-30.4	-2.9	23.7	22.5
Toys "R" Us	TOY	-15.5	-21.8	-14.1	-5.0
Transatlantic Holdings	TRH	4.0	14.0	16.7	NA
Transocean Sedco Forex	RIG	26.2	2.9	31.2	NA
TranSwitch	TXCC	179.5	174.7	NA	NA
Tricon Global Restaurants	YUM	-22.9	NA	NA	NA
Triquint Semiconductor	TQNT	766.9	85.0	91.4	NA
True North Commumications	TNO	69.4	29.8	18.7	15.5
TRW	TRW	-4.8	4.1	12.3	9.1
Tyson Foods A	TSN	-23.0	-10.2	3.3	7.3
UAL	UAL	30.0	7.5	28.8	10.4
Ultramar Diamond Shamrock	UDS	-1.9	-6.8	1.7	NA
Unicom	UCM	-9.3	13.0	12.8	5.4
Union Carbide	UK	59.7	19.8	20.0	38.8

Mid-Cap U.S. Stocks

(As of January 2000)

Company Name	Ticker Symbol	1 Year Return	3 Year Average Return	5 Year Average Return	10 Year Average Return
Union Pacific Resources Group	UPR	42.8	-23.0	NA	NA
Union Planters	UPC	-9.9	3.8	17.6	17.7
UnionBanCal	UB	18.3	33.5	38.0	22.5
Unisys	UIS	-7.3	67.9	29.9	8.4
United HealthCare	UNH	23.4	5.8	3.4	33.2
United States Cellular	USM	165.6	53.6	25.3	12.5
UnitedGlobalCom	UCOMA	633.8	125.9	51.8	NA
Unitrin	UNIT	9.1	15.0	16.5	NA
Univision Communications	UVN	183.9	76.8	NA	NA
Unocal	UCL	17.5	-4.3	6.7	3.8
Unumprovident	UNM	-44.3	-2.7	13.0	12.1
US Airways Group	U	-38.3	11.1	49.8	-0.4
USA Networks	USAI	66.8	66.9	59.4	NA
USG	USG	-6.7	12.0	19.6	NA
UST, Inc.	UST	-23.5	-2.8	3.3	9.7
USWeb	USWB	68.5	NA	NA	NA
USX-Marathon Group	MRO	-15.6	3.9	11.9	NA
USX-US Steel Group	X	48.8	5.2	1.9	NA
UtiliCorp United	UCU	-16.3	8.3	7.9	9.1
Valassis Communications	VCI	22.8	44.2	33.4	NA
Valspar	VAL	13.7	15.4	21.7	22.2
ValueVision International A	VVTV	715.2	120.1	64.6	NA
Vastar Resources	VRI	37.4	16.6	19.8	NA
Verio	VRIO	312.8	NA	NA	NA
VF	VFC	-34.5	-1.9	6.6	9.4
Viad	VVI	-7.1	21.2	25.3	31.3
Vishay Intertechnology	VSH	172.6	23.3	14.6	21.9
Visual Networks	VNWK	111.3	NA	NA	NA
VISX	VISX	136.7	110.7	81.5	31.4
Vitesse Semiconductor	VTSS	129.9	90.5	127.8	NA
Vornado Realty Trust	VNO	2.1	12.8	19.0	22.8
Vulcan Materials	VMC	-7.3	27.8	21.6	13.3
Washington Post	WPO	-2.9	19.6	19.6	8.7
Waters	WAT	21.5	51.7	NA	NA
Watson Pharmaceuticals	WPI	-43.0	16.8	22.2	NA
Weatherford International	WFT	106.1	16.2	45.8	20.0
Weis Markets	WMK	15.0	14.1	15.8	6.6

Mid-Cap U.S. Stocks
(As of January 2000)

Company Name	Ticker Symbol	1 Year Return	3 Year Average Return	5 Year Average Return	10 Year Average Return
Wellpoint Health Networks	WLP	-24.2	24.3	12.4	NA
Wendy's International	WEN	-3.7	1.6	8.6	16.7
Wesco Financial	WSC	-30.7	9.8	16.9	15.7
Western Wireless A	WWCA	390.9	98.2	NA	NA
Westvaco	W	25.7	7.6	7.7	8.3
Westwood One	WON	149.2	66.0	50.8	24.1
Whirlpool	WHR	20.2	14.4	7.9	9.9
Whitman	WH	-46.8	-0.2	7.0	11.8
Whittman-Hart	WHIT	94.1	61.2	NA	NA
Willamette Industries	WLL	41.0	12.1	16.5	15.4
Williams-Sonoma	WSM	14.1	36.3	25.1	27.1
Winn-Dixie Stores	WIN	-45.1	-6.3	1.3	6.9
Wisconsin Energy	WEC	-34.8	-5.1	-0.3	4.5
Wm. Wrigley Jr.	WWY	-5.9	15.7	12.9	19.0
WW Grainger	GWW	16.5	7.4	12.1	13.0
Xcelera.com	XLA	11060.0	476.0	219.8	52.0
Xircom	XIRC	120.6	51.1	33.4	NA
Young & Rubicam	YNR	118.9	NA	NA	NA
Zebra Technologies	ZBRA	103.5	35.8	24.5	NA
Zions Bancorporation	ZION	-4.4	33.1	48.1	36.1

Historical Performance of Small-Cap U.S. Stocks

			3 Year	5 Year	10 Year
Company Name	**Ticker Symbol**	**1 Year Return**	**Average Return**	**Average Return**	**Average Return**

Selected Small-Cap U.S. Stocks
(As of January 2000)

Company Name	Ticker Symbol	1 Year Return	3 Year Average Return	5 Year Average Return	10 Year Average Return
4Front Technologies	FFTI	20.9	45.1	NA	NA
99 Cents Only Stores	NDN	-22.1	54.0	NA	NA
Aaron Rents	RNT	17.6	14.6	24.6	NA
ACNielsen	ART	-12.8	17.3	NA	NA
Adaptive Broadband	ADAP	687.3	70.6	15.1	25.3
Advance ParadigM	ADVP	23.2	27.6	NA	NA
Advanced Digital Information	ADIC	507.8	81.6	NA	NA
Advanced Energy Industries	AEIS	97.0	109.3	NA	NA
Advent Software	ADVS	105.1	47.1	NA	NA
Agnico-Eagle Mines	AEM	81.1	-18.6	-6.3	-0.1
Air Express International	AEIC	50.4	15.6	20.4	28.1
Airborne Freight	ABF	-38.7	24.2	17.6	10.7
Alaska Air Group	ALK	-20.6	18.7	18.6	5.8
Alexion Pharmaceuticals	ALXN	125.2	51.4	NA	NA
Align-Rite International	MASK	88.7	25.9	NA	NA
Alkermes	ALKS	121.4	28.3	87.4	NA
Alleghany	Y	-1.2	12.9	14.9	12.8
Allied Capital	ALLC	15.0	15.5	21.5	NA
Alpha Industries	AHAA	138.8	121.8	68.9	38.2
Alpharma	ALO	-12.5	29.2	9.5	10.1
Alpine Group	AGI	-14.2	23.3	31.7	25.8
Alterra Healthcare	ALI	-75.6	-16.7	NA	NA
America Service Group	ASGR	15.4	13.5	24.6	NA
American Classic Voyages	AMCV	98.6	38.7	21.2	NA
American Freightways	AFWY	40.4	13.3	-4.0	15.8
American Pacific	APFC	7.9	8.7	4.0	-2.4
American Woodmark	AMWD	-28.8	20.4	40.7	15.0
Americredit	ACF	33.9	21.8	43.9	12.9
Ames Department Stores	AMES	6.7	88.3	63.1	NA
Anaren Microwave	ANEN	156.2	105.4	85.0	34.1
Antec	ANTC	81.4	59.5	14.7	NA
Applebee's International	APPB	43.5	2.8	17.5	21.6
Applied Science and Technology	ASTX	224.1	77.7	54.7	NA
AptarGroup	ATR	-9.9	13.3	12.6	NA

Selected Small-Cap U.S. Stocks

(As of January 2000)

Company Name	Ticker Symbol	1 Year Return	3 Year Average Return	5 Year Average Return	10 Year Average Return
Ardent Software	ARDT	69.6	73.3	17.1	NA
Arkansas Best	ABFS	105.3	40.0	-0.2	NA
Armor Holdings	AH	14.8	17.3	NA	NA
Arthrocare	ARTC	180.5	103.4	NA	NA
Arthur J. Gallagher & Co.	AJG	51.3	32.1	18.9	13.4
Arvin Industries	ARV	-30.2	7.2	7.1	9.2
Astec Industries	ASTE	-32.4	58.2	24.2	24.0
Asyst Technologies	ASYT	221.8	97.1	41.0	NA
Atlantic Coast Airlines Holdings	ACAI	-5.0	57.1	90.9	NA
ATS Medical	ATSI	113.4	24.5	29.4	NA
Atwood Oceanics	ATW	127.2	6.8	45.7	16.2
AVT	AVTC	62.1	97.2	41.2	NA
Aware	AWRE	33.8	53.2	NA	NA
Aztar	AZR	114.8	14.5	12.6	2.8
Aztec Manufacturing	AZZ	35.3	14.6	26.9	9.6
Badger Meter	BMI	-13.6	18.3	23.1	15.2
Ball	BLL	-12.7	16.4	6.5	5.7
Bally Total Fitness Holding	BFT	7.3	49.8	NA	NA
Bangor Hydro-Electric	BGR	31.8	21.2	15.1	6.0
Banta	BN	-15.5	1.6	4.2	10.2
Basin Exploration	BSNX	40.3	41.3	9.9	NA
Beckman Coulter	BEC	-5.0	11.3	14.0	11.7
Ben & Jerry's Homemade A	BJICA	11.2	31.8	21.2	12.2
Bindley Western Industries	BDY	-22.5	38.5	27.6	18.0
Biomatrix	BXM	-33.9	34.0	61.5	NA
Bowne	BNE	-23.3	4.4	10.8	11.0
Bradley Real Estate Trust	BTR	-7.8	6.5	11.0	7.5
Briggs & Stratton	BGG	9.8	9.3	13.1	18.6
Brinker International	EAT	-16.5	14.7	5.9	14.0
Brown & Brown	BRO	11.2	31.2	23.5	21.6
Brush Wellman	BW	-0.7	3.5	1.7	0.2
Buckhead America	BUCK	17.1	-2.5	9.7	NA
Buffets	BOCB	-16.2	3.1	0.3	6.2
Butler International	BUTL	-37.6	17.2	22.4	14.9
C & D Technologies	CHP	55.5	41.0	36.6	32.6
C-Cor.net	CCBL	457.3	79.5	19.8	28.2
California Amplifier	CAMP	1257.7	62.6	49.7	46.9
Cambrex	CBM	44.1	28.7	32.4	24.7
Camden Property Trust	CPT	15.6	6.4	10.2	NA

Selected Small-Cap U.S. Stocks
(As of January 2000)

Company Name	Ticker Symbol	1 Year Return	3 Year Average Return	5 Year Average Return	10 Year Average Return
Carver Bancorp	CNY	27.1	10.8	12.4	NA
Castle Energy	CECX	50.3	37.3	19.3	4.2
Catalyst International	CLYS	6.3	40.2	NA	NA
Catherine's Stores	CATH	93.1	56.3	19.1	NA
Cato A	CACOA	31.1	39.0	14.2	19.6
CEC Entertainment	CEC	52.7	32.7	52.8	24.1
Celestial Seasonings	CTEA	-33.2	23.5	20.5	NA
CenterPoint Properties	CNT	13.7	9.2	20.8	NA
Centex	CTX	-44.9	10.0	17.4	13.2
Central Newspapers A	ECP	11.7	23.0	24.8	15.3
Central Parking	CPC	-40.9	-4.9	NA	NA
Charles E. Smith Residential Realty	SRW	17.6	13.9	15.0	NA
Chattem	CHTT	-60.3	28.3	31.3	NA
Cheesecake Factory	CAKE	18.0	42.6	27.2	NA
Chico's FAS	CHCS	61.0	106.9	49.7	NA
Childtime Learning Centers	CTIM	-15.4	9.7	NA	NA
Chittenden	CHZ	-4.6	19.5	26.5	23.6
Cima Labs	CIMA	397.6	28.7	5.0	NA
City National	CYN	-19.4	17.1	27.9	5.0
Civic Bancorp	CIVC	22.8	18.6	25.5	NA
Clarcor	CLC	-7.7	9.6	7.8	9.7
Cleco	CNL	-1.6	10.9	12.9	12.5
CMP Group	CTP	52.1	41.0	22.6	10.3
CNF Transportation	CNF	-7.2	17.0	14.2	5.5
Cognex	CGNX	95.0	28.2	24.8	31.5
Coherent	COHR	115.1	8.2	25.6	13.9
Colorado MEDtech	CMED	-39.6	38.7	51.6	7.7
Comarco	CMRO	-2.1	8.8	22.9	22.9
Commonwealth Telephone Enterprises	CTCO	57.8	73.7	44.9	19.3
Computer Network Technology	CMNT	83.5	66.2	27.5	21.8
Conmed	CNMD	-21.6	8.1	14.3	29.9
Continental Materials	CUO	26.0	29.4	31.7	10.9
Cooper Companies	COO	46.0	20.5	34.9	12.0
Copart	CPRT	168.7	87.8	37.6	NA
COR Therapeutics	CORR	102.8	39.6	19.6	NA
Cordant Technologies	CDD	-11.1	15.0	20.4	19.8

Selected Small-Cap U.S. Stocks
(As of January 2000)

Company Name	Ticker Symbol	1 Year Return	3 Year Average Return	5 Year Average Return	10 Year Average Return
Core Laboratories	CLB	4.6	33.7	NA	NA
Corvel	CRVL	33.3	17.5	11.1	NA
Cost Plus	CPWM	155.5	61.2	NA	NA
Courier	CRRC	-0.2	35.4	19.2	8.5
Cousins Properties	CUZ	10.6	11.7	20.3	13.1
Craftmade International	CRFT	-56.0	39.6	11.3	NA
Crossmann Communities	CROS	-43.9	11.0	34.7	NA
Cullen/Frost Bankers	CFR	-3.7	18.5	30.5	28.2
Cuno	CUNO	27.3	11.6	NA	NA
Curtiss-Wright	CW	-1.9	15.4	17.3	11.2
Cutter & Buck	CBUK	-39.1	25.0	NA	NA
Cyberonics	CYBX	18.1	65.8	35.4	NA
Cybex Computer Products	CBXC	37.9	85.6	NA	NA
Cytyc	CYTC	137.1	31.3	NA	NA
D & K Healthcare Resources	DKWD	-46.3	57.4	16.3	NA
Daisytek International	DZTK	22.7	4.4	NA	NA
Datascope	DSCP	74.1	26.0	18.7	13.7
Dean Foods	DF	-0.4	9.3	8.9	8.3
Decorator Industries	DII	-29.5	-7.2	12.4	20.7
Del Webb	WBB	-9.5	15.7	8.0	12.8
Dendrite International	DRTE	103.5	131.0	NA	NA
DeVRY	DV	-38.8	16.9	37.1	NA
Diodes	DIO	330.0	43.7	33.9	27.6
Dionex	DNEX	12.5	33.0	34.3	19.9
Dixie Group	DXYN	-9.2	-1.1	1.4	-5.5
Dominion Homes	DHOM	-43.2	12.6	4.6	NA
Donaldson	DCI	17.4	14.0	16.3	22.0
Doral Financial	DORL	-43.3	23.4	37.3	35.5
Duff & Phelps Credit Rating	DCR	62.6	54.9	56.0	NA
Dycom Industries	DY	15.7	92.6	92.5	18.7
Eagle USA Airfreight	EUSA	164.0	35.1	NA	NA
Eastern Enterprises	EFU	36.6	22.5	22.0	10.3
EastGroup Properties	EGP	8.9	8.0	17.7	13.1
Eaton Vance	EV	84.2	49.2	54.0	35.3
Ebix.com	EBIX	31.6	21.4	24.4	-10.5
Echelon International Corp	EIN	3.1	13.8	NA	NA
Education Management	EDMC	-40.7	10.1	NA	NA
El Paso Electric	EE	12.2	14.7	3.8	-19.4
Elcor	ELK	41.0	48.4	35.8	20.0
Engineered Support Systems	EASI	-19.1	7.1	35.4	17.1

Selected Small-Cap U.S. Stocks
(As of January 2000)

Company Name	Ticker Symbol	1 Year Return	3 Year Average Return	5 Year Average Return	10 Year Average Return
Engle Homes	ENGL	-20.1	13.9	11.6	NA
Enzon	ENZN	225.8	145.3	90.0	27.7
Equitable Resources	EQT	19.0	8.1	8.5	5.7
Essex Property Trust	ESS	22.2	11.6	26.2	NA
Ethan Allen Interiors	ETH	17.9	36.3	32.1	NA
Evergreen Resources	EVER	11.3	33.8	30.3	23.0
EW Blanch Holdings	EWB	30.2	46.7	26.2	NA
Exar	EXAR	265.1	56.0	19.2	27.8
EXCO Resources	EXCO	0.0	9.7	NA	NA
Farm Family Holdings	FFH	24.3	29.4	NA	NA
Farr	FARC	-3.7	9.7	29.1	11.7
Federal Screw Works	FSCR	-12.2	17.8	22.2	18.4
FEI	FEIC	103.3	18.3	NA	NA
Financial Federal	FIF	-7.8	26.9	23.3	NA
Financial Security Assurance Holdings	FSA	-3.1	17.7	21.2	NA
First American Financial	FAF	-60.6	12.3	28.7	19.3
First Health Group	FHCC	62.3	8.3	9.5	34.9
Firstbank	FBP	-30.1	18.6	30.7	33.3
Florida East Coast Industries	FLA	19.0	24.5	20.9	10.9
Florida Rock Industries	FRK	12.1	29.4	21.8	9.9
Foremost Corp of America	FOM	37.3	14.3	21.3	12.8
Forest City Enterprises A	FCE.A	7.5	12.2	23.6	8.5
Forrester Research	FORR	57.4	38.8	NA	NA
Forward Air	FWRD	362.7	105.5	41.1	NA
Fossil	FOSL	20.7	56.8	31.7	NA
Fred's	FRED	7.8	34.0	19.2	NA
Frontier Oil	FTO	36.7	29.3	7.3	-4.8
Funco	FNCO	-36.1	10.1	13.3	NA
G & K Services A	GKSRA	-39.1	-4.8	14.5	14.1
Garan	GAN	8.1	20.5	18.3	11.8
Garden Fresh Restaurant	LTUS	19.1	19.2	NA	NA
Gardner Denver	GDI	13.1	13.5	38.0	NA
GATX	GMT	-8.0	15.1	12.5	11.0
Gehl	GEHL	17.1	18.3	23.6	2.8
Genesco	GCO	128.6	12.0	43.7	5.7
Genlyte Group	GLYT	14.0	19.6	38.1	7.4
Geon	GON	43.9	20.9	5.7	NA
Gleason	GLE	30.1	13.5	27.6	12.9
Gorman-Rupp Company	GRC	8.5	12.5	3.1	9.9

Selected Small-Cap U.S. Stocks
(As of January 2000)

Company Name	Ticker Symbol	1 Year Return	3 Year Average Return	5 Year Average Return	10 Year Average Return
Graco	GGG	23.4	31.9	32.4	25.5
Granite Construction	GVA	-44.1	15.2	17.4	NA
GZA GeoEnvironmental	GZEA	2.9	10.1	0.0	-10.6
Haemonetics	HAE	4.7	8.1	6.7	NA
Handleman	HDL	-3.6	15.8	3.3	-4.3
Hanger Orthopedic Group	HGR	-55.6	15.4	27.2	19.0
Harding Lawson Associates Group	HRDG	26.5	3.5	6.6	-8.3
Haverty Furniture	HVT	22.0	32.9	19.1	17.0
Helix Technology	HELX	251.5	50.9	44.3	44.2
Herley Industries	HRLY	26.6	25.5	45.3	32.1
Highland Bancorp	HBNK	22.3	31.9	NA	NA
Hilb Rogal & Hamilton	HRH	46.5	33.3	23.1	8.0
Home Federal Bancorp	HOMF	3.2	11.3	18.1	24.7
Home Products International	HPII	4.4	7.9	19.3	2.8
Home Properties of NY	HME	14.9	14.9	15.7	NA
Hooper Holmes	HH	79.1	82.0	74.8	34.2
ICU Medical	ICUI	-30.7	24.6	-0.3	NA
Idex	IEX	26.7	6.5	12.1	16.1
IHOP	IHP	-16.4	12.2	4.1	NA
Imation	IMN	91.8	6.1	NA	NA
Imax	IMAX	-13.4	20.9	45.1	NA
Information Resource Engineering	IREG	120.1	31.6	27.6	NA
Inhale Therapuetic Systems	INHL	29.0	41.2	35.7	NA
Insight Enterprises	NSIT	19.8	69.8	NA	NA
Insituform Technologies A	INSUA	94.8	56.5	19.4	13.3
Insteel Industries	III	91.8	4.2	8.5	5.1
Insurance Auto Auctions	IAAI	32.6	18.4	-12.4	NA
Intelligent Systems	INS	137.0	10.1	13.5	5.9
InterContinental Life	ILCO	-7.5	11.1	12.0	5.3
Interim Services	IS	5.9	11.7	15.0	NA
International Airline Support Group	YLF	-18.9	7.7	12.2	NA
InterTAN	ITN	349.4	75.0	26.3	-7.3
InterVoice-Brite	INTV	34.8	56.0	27.6	21.5
Investment Technology Group	ITG	44.8	53.4	58.4	39.7
Investors Financial Services	IFIN	54.5	49.4	NA	NA
Iron Mountain	IRM	9.0	24.9	NA	NA
Isle of Capris Casinos	ISLE	232.3	60.5	10.5	NA

Selected Small-Cap U.S. Stocks

(As of January 2000)

Company Name	Ticker Symbol	1 Year Return	3 Year Average Return	5 Year Average Return	10 Year Average Return
IT Group	ITX	-18.0	2.9	-6.1	-10.4
ITI Technologies	ITII	-3.2	25.6	5.8	NA
J&J Snack Foods	JJSF	-8.4	14.9	12.0	5.2
J. Jill Group	JILL	-78.3	18.2	5.4	NA
Jack Henry & Associates	JKHY	8.9	32.2	54.1	67.8
Jack In The Box	JBX	-6.2	32.6	37.2	NA
Jacobs Engineering Group	JEC	-20.3	11.2	11.9	16.9
Jakks Pacific	JAKK	160.8	51.9	NA	NA
Javelin Systems	JVLN	-38.8	20.5	NA	NA
K-Swiss	KSWS	38.5	56.1	14.1	NA
K-Tron International	KTII	-27.0	9.6	4.7	3.6
Kaneb Services	KAB	9.4	10.4	15.5	-1.3
Kaufman & Broad Home	KBH	-14.8	25.1	15.4	8.0
Kaydon	KDN	-32.2	5.6	18.9	14.5
Kellwood	KWD	-20.1	1.4	1.2	6.1
Kenan Transport	KTCO	1.7	20.5	14.3	10.6
Kenneth Cole Productions	KCP	144.0	43.5	34.2	NA
Koala	KARE	61.1	27.5	33.9	NA
Kollmorgen	KOL	-18.7	4.4	17.2	1.4
Koss	KOSS	35.2	30.1	6.7	13.0
Kronos	KRON	103.1	41.2	39.0	NA
Labor Ready	LRW	-7.6	44.7	NA	NA
Landstar System	LSTR	5.1	22.6	5.5	NA
Laser Vision Centers	LVCI	-4.7	57.8	21.8	NA
LB Foster A	FSTR	-26.4	9.1	8.5	2.0
Learning Tree International	LTRE	209.0	-1.7	NA	NA
Lennar	LEN	-35.5	16.1	23.1	22.3
Liberty Property Trust	LRY	9.3	6.1	13.2	NA
Lindsay Manufacturing	LNN	24.2	-3.7	15.8	20.3
Linens 'N Things	LIN	-25.2	44.5	NA	NA
LSI Industries	LYTS	-2.0	19.7	26.1	10.7
LTX	LTXX	773.0	56.2	40.7	23.9
Lubrizol	LZ	24.9	3.2	1.3	8.4
M/I Schottenstein Homes	MHO	-28.4	13.1	17.8	NA
MacDermid	MRD	5.2	65.3	59.6	38.1
Mail-Well	MWL	18.0	35.2	NA	NA
Manitowoc	MTW	16.1	25.1	42.4	23.0
Manor Care	HCR	-45.5	-17.6	-4.4	NA
Manufactured Home Communities	MHC	3.4	7.6	10.8	NA

Selected Small-Cap U.S. Stocks
(As of January 2000)

Company Name	Ticker Symbol	1 Year Return	3 Year Average Return	5 Year Average Return	10 Year Average Return
Marten Transport	MRTN	-2.8	12.0	-0.7	16.4
Mastech Corp	MAST	-13.5	37.6	NA	NA
Matthews International A	MATW	-12.1	25.7	33.2	NA
Maverick Tube	MAVK	343.8	57.0	39.8	NA
MDC Holdings	MDC	-25.8	23.4	27.3	28.5
Medco Research	MRE	15.6	42.0	21.5	7.4
Media General A	MEG.A	-0.7	21.4	14.5	7.0
Medical Assurance	MAI	-35.9	15.3	16.2	NA
Medicis Pharmaceuticals A	MRX	6.6	29.6	97.2	NA
MedQuist	MEDQ	-34.7	46.3	60.6	NA
MemberWorks	MBRS	12.5	29.6	NA	NA
Mercury Air Group	MAX	1.6	12.8	12.3	7.6
Meridian Gold	MDG	19.8	18.2	15.4	-4.4
Meristar Hospitality	MHX	-3.5	-1.4	NA	NA
Meritage	MTH	-10.8	13.2	30.1	6.8
Metris Companies	MXT	42.0	43.9	NA	NA
Metro One Telecommunications	MTON	-1.9	18.2	NA	NA
Michael Foods	MIKL	-16.9	26.0	21.7	12.2
Michaels Stores	MIKE	57.5	33.4	-3.9	18.7
Micros Systems	MCRS	125.1	68.8	31.4	44.4
Mid-Atlantic Realty Trust	MRR	-9.8	5.0	14.0	NA
Midwest Express Holdings	MEH	21.1	25.8	NA	NA
Mobile Mini	MINI	100.0	90.2	42.8	NA
Mohawk Industries	MHK	-37.3	21.6	25.4	NA
Molecular Devices	MDCC	139.1	49.5	NA	NA
Monaco Coach	MNC	44.7	74.5	41.4	NA
Moore Products	MORP	64.4	31.3	21.7	4.5
Morrison Management Specialists	MHI	14.0	16.8	NA	NA
MS Carriers	MSCA	-27.5	14.3	1.9	8.6
Myers Industries	MYE	-38.9	5.3	9.6	11.3
MYR Group	MYR	158.0	57.9	45.5	27.2
Nanometrics	NANO	157.6	61.8	104.7	27.7
National Computer System	NLCS	2.3	44.7	38.9	26.6
National RV Holdings	NVH	-25.2	25.5	41.8	NA
NCO Group	NCOG	-33.1	38.9	NA	NA
Netegrity	NETE	1220.2	208.6	134.1	NA
Netopia	NTPA	697.2	104.2	NA	NA
Network Event Theater	NETS	129.9	81.2	NA	NA

Selected Small-Cap U.S. Stocks
(As of January 2000)

Company Name	Ticker Symbol	1 Year Return	3 Year Average Return	5 Year Average Return	10 Year Average Return
New England Business Services	NEB	-35.8	7.3	9.1	6.8
New Jersey Resources	NJR	3.3	15.3	17.4	13.0
Newport	NEWP	171.6	73.2	43.1	17.9
Newport News Shipbuilding	NNS	-17.3	23.2	NA	NA
NICE-Systems ADR	NICE	127.5	39.8	NA	NA
Nortek	NTK	1.4	11.9	18.7	17.7
Novoste	NOVT	-41.9	7.6	NA	NA
NS Group	NSS	71.8	19.2	13.1	-3.7
Nu Horizons Electronics	NUHC	171.5	20.6	11.0	27.7
NVR	NVR	0.1	54.3	54.1	NA
O'Charley's	CHUX	-7.1	14.8	10.9	NA
O'Reilly Automotive	ORLY	-9.0	39.0	28.3	NA
OM Group	OMP	-4.6	9.6	17.9	NA
On Assignment	ASGN	-13.4	26.5	30.2	NA
Oneida	OCQ	49.6	24.6	23.3	11.9
OnHealth Network	ONHN	78.8	41.0	-4.9	NA
Ortel	ORTL	1271.4	71.0	35.5	NA
Orthofix International	OFIX	2.2	20.2	4.5	NA
Oshkosh Truck	OTRKB	34.3	64.4	36.5	20.9
Osteotech	OSTE	-56.9	42.0	35.6	NA
Pacific Bank NA	PBSF	29.1	29.7	35.0	NA
Pacific Gulf Properties	PAG	10.0	9.7	16.2	NA
Pacific Sunwear	PSUN	192.0	61.1	59.8	NA
Parlex	PRLX	163.1	54.3	25.4	25.7
Patterson Dental	PDCO	-2.0	31.3	25.2	NA
Payless ShoeSource	PSS	-0.8	7.8	NA	NA
Pentair	PNR	-1.8	7.8	14.4	17.9
Performance Food Group	PFGC	-13.3	16.3	23.9	NA
Performance Technologies	PTIX	98.6	59.4	NA	NA
Perry Ellis International	PERY	-3.1	6.3	12.3	NA
Pharmacyclics	PCYC	61.8	37.1	NA	NA
Philadelphia Consolidated Holding	PHLY	-35.9	7.6	18.8	NA
Photon Dynamics	PHTN	656.1	71.9	NA	NA
Pinnacle Systems	PCLE	127.6	97.9	40.2	NA
Pitt-Des Moines	PDM	5.5	24.8	22.4	13.4
Plantronics	PLT	-16.8	47.1	36.7	NA
Plexus	PLXS	29.9	73.8	59.6	34.6
PolyMedica	PLMD	151.7	82.4	45.8	NA

Selected Small-Cap U.S. Stocks
(As of January 2000)

Company Name	Ticker Symbol	1 Year Return	3 Year Average Return	5 Year Average Return	10 Year Average Return
Polymer Group	PGI	83.8	9.6	NA	NA
Powerwave Technologies	PWAV	213.4	58.6	NA	NA
PRI Automation	PRIA	158.2	43.4	52.8	NA
Price Communications	PR	252.7	174.4	102.8	NA
Primex Technologies	PRMX	-0.9	28.8	NA	NA
Primus Telecommunications Group	PRTL	131.8	44.2	NA	NA
Professionals Group	PICM	-16.8	8.8	23.2	NA
Profit Recovery Group International	PRGX	6.4	35.5	NA	NA
Progress Software	PRGS	68.2	62.1	35.2	NA
Protein Design Labs	PDLI	202.7	24.2	34.8	NA
Providence & Worcester Railroad	PWX	-35.2	1.6	4.6	0.9
Proxim	PROX	312.2	68.5	91.7	NA
PS Business Parks A	PSB	-0.5	10.1	15.7	NA
Pulte	PHM	-18.5	14.3	15.2	16.0
QRS	QRSI	228.1	76.8	65.7	NA
Quaker City Bancorp	QCBC	1.6	10.2	27.6	NA
Quest Diagnostics	DGX	71.6	26.4	NA	NA
Quiksilver	ZQK	-22.5	29.6	25.0	9.3
Quixote	QUIX	26.3	19.4	9.4	11.5
RailAmerica	RAIL	0.7	20.7	24.4	NA
Ralcorp Holdings	RAH	9.3	21.3	11.0	NA
Rare Hospitality International	RARE	54.5	4.6	20.5	NA
Rayonier	RYN	8.4	11.1	12.9	NA
RCM Technologies	RCMT	-34.9	25.4	41.0	-3.9
Reckson Associates Realty	RA	-1.0	4.9	NA	NA
Regis	RGIS	-28.8	20.9	23.6	NA
RehabCare Group	RHB	13.7	16.6	19.7	NA
Reinsurance Group of America	RGA	-40.2	10.4	21.2	NA
RenaissanceRe Holdings	RNR	16.0	10.7	NA	NA
Renal Care Group	RCGI	-18.9	18.5	NA	NA
Rent-A-Center	RCII	-37.6	11.0	NA	NA
Rent-Way	RWY	-23.1	24.8	22.6	NA
Res-Care	RSCR	-48.4	3.0	11.7	NA
ResMed	RMD	-8.0	56.0	NA	NA
Rex Stores	RSC	159.3	62.7	16.6	25.5

Selected Small-Cap U.S. Stocks
(As of January 2000)

Company Name	Ticker Symbol	1 Year Return	3 Year Average Return	5 Year Average Return	10 Year Average Return
RLI	RLI	3.9	10.0	23.1	22.9
Roanoke Electric Steel	RESC	13.5	16.3	20.9	13.6
Rogers	ROG	28.0	12.1	9.0	12.7
Rollins Truck Leasing	RLC	-17.5	14.1	10.3	18.3
Roper Industries	ROP	87.3	25.7	25.6	NA
Ruby Tuesday	RI	-14.0	25.2	9.0	13.9
Rural Cellular A	RCCC	786.4	113.1	NA	NA
Ryan's Family Steak House	RYAN	-31.3	7.3	2.5	1.1
Ryland Group	RYL	-19.6	20.9	11.7	4.9
Safety-Kleen	SK	-19.9	17.4	-10.8	-14.5
ScanSource	SCSC	88.7	38.2	36.7	NA
Scott Technologies	SCTT	14.2	16.3	25.2	-0.3
SCP Pool	POOL	71.5	41.2	NA	NA
Sea Containers A	SCR.A	-7.7	23.5	19.5	0.6
Semtech	SMTC	190.6	130.0	139.8	60.2
Sharper Image	SHRP	6.9	49.3	13.9	5.1
Shoe Carnival	SCVL	-9.6	23.3	16.2	NA
Shorewood Packaging	SWD	-7.6	13.4	6.9	9.0
Silicon Valley Bancshare	SIVB	190.7	45.3	49.0	27.3
Simpson Industries	SMPS	20.6	4.8	8.0	10.5
Simpson Manufacturing	SSD	16.9	23.9	32.4	NA
SkyWest	SKYW	-13.9	60.3	36.2	30.3
Sonic	SONC	14.6	18.8	25.9	NA
Source Information Management Company	SORC	44.1	83.2	NA	NA
Spartech	SEH	47.8	44.3	48.0	27.7
Specialty Equipment	SEC	-11.6	24.2	18.8	NA
Spectrian	SPCT	119.4	53.9	0.1	NA
Standard Pacific	SPF	-20.9	24.1	13.3	0.7
Stanley Furniture	STLY	0.7	22.7	29.7	NA
Station Casinos	STN	174.0	30.4	11.5	NA
Steiner Leisure	STNR	-47.9	23.1	NA	NA
Steven Madden	SHOO	124.3	54.9	32.8	NA
Stillwater Mining	SWC	19.5	38.2	28.5	NA
Stone Energy	SGY	23.9	6.0	13.1	NA
Strattec Security	STRT	7.9	21.1	NA	NA
Strayer Education	STRA	-43.5	9.5	NA	NA
Suiza Foods	SZA	-22.2	25.1	NA	NA
Sunglass Hut International	RAYS	60.7	15.8	-0.4	NA
Sunrise Assisted Living	SNRZ	-73.5	-21.0	NA	NA

Selected Small-Cap U.S. Stocks
(As of January 2000)

Company Name	Ticker Symbol	1 Year Return	3 Year Average Return	5 Year Average Return	10 Year Average Return
Superior Industries International	SUP	-2.4	6.3	1.2	18.6
Suprema Specialties	CHEZ	57.5	20.5	19.8	NA
Swift Transportation	SWFT	-5.7	19.1	14.1	NA
Syncor International	SCOR	6.9	29.6	33.0	14.0
Taco Cabana	TACO	4.8	3.3	-2.0	NA
Tandy Brands Accessories	TBAC	-17.2	32.2	1.3	NA
Techne	TECH	160.7	61.8	60.8	55.0
Tejon Ranch	TRC	19.7	18.5	14.9	-5.7
Tekelec	TKLC	35.8	78.8	40.5	35.7
Terex	TEX	-2.9	39.9	31.7	4.7
Terra Nova Bermuda Holdings	TNA	19.8	12.7	NA	NA
Tetra Tech	WATR	-29.0	15.0	21.5	NA
Texas Industries	TXI	59.5	20.0	20.3	15.7
Thomas Industries	TII	5.9	15.4	18.4	7.4
Thor Industries	THO	19.7	22.3	19.1	21.7
THQ	THQI	24.2	77.2	40.9	NA
TLC Laser Eye Center	TLCV	-36.3	38.9	NA	NA
TNP Enterprises	TNP	12.4	18.8	27.5	13.7
Topps	TOPP	107.5	37.4	15.2	0.1
Toro	TTC	32.8	2.2	6.9	6.1
Trans World Entertainment	TWMC	-44.9	64.0	32.4	2.3
Transkaryotic Therapies	TKTX	51.7	27.7	NA	NA
Transportation Technologies	TTII	37.6	60.4	2.0	NA
Triad Guaranty	TGIC	3.1	16.5	39.9	NA
U.S. Can	USC	11.2	5.6	0.9	NA
Ultimate Electronics	ULTE	312.5	83.6	11.7	NA
United Industrial	UIC	-2.5	20.4	17.9	1.5
United Payors & United Providers	UPUP	-41.9	21.8	NA	NA
United Retail Group	URGI	-23.3	36.4	0.9	NA
United Stationers	USTR	9.9	43.1	54.1	23.9
Universal Electronics	UEIC	327.9	103.0	60.1	NA
Universal Health Services B	UHS	-30.6	7.9	24.1	22.8
Uno Restaurant	UNO	55.4	22.7	3.9	2.8
Urban Shopping Centers	URB	-10.7	4.7	14.7	NA
URS	URS	-7.2	34.1	32.2	13.3
USFreightways	USFC	65.9	21.8	14.9	NA
UST Corporation	USTB	37.7	17.9	27.5	9.8

Selected Small-Cap U.S. Stocks
(As of January 2000)

Company Name	Ticker Symbol	1 Year Return	3 Year Average Return	5 Year Average Return	10 Year Average Return
UTI Energy	UTI	218.1	25.1	83.7	NA
Vallen	VALN	23.1	14.0	12.4	7.5
Ventana Medical Systems	VMSI	15.0	19.7	NA	NA
Verity	VRTY	221.2	76.9	NA	NA
VICorp Restaurants	VRES	4.0	6.8	-1.9	-0.7
Webster Financial	WBST	-12.7	10.4	23.0	22.5
Weingarten Realty	WRI	-6.4	5.2	7.3	8.8
Westpoint Stevens	WXS	-44.5	5.5	19.5	NA
Weyco Group	WEYS	3.6	26.4	18.8	12.9
Whitehall Jewellers	WHJI	104.9	46.9	NA	NA
Whole Foods Market	WFMI	-4.1	27.3	35.2	NA
WHX	WHX	-10.6	0.5	-7.4	NA
Wild Oats Markets	OATS	5.7	39.2	NA	NA
WMS Industries	WMS	78.0	70.6	39.8	35.2
Zale	ZLC	50.0	36.0	32.2	NA
Zoll Medical	ZOLL	330.3	52.6	27.1	NA
Zomax	ZOMX	456.9	154.4	NA	NA
Zoran	ZRAN	218.6	45.8	NA	NA

Web Site Addresses for Frugal Forty Mutual Funds

Frugal Forty Funds (listed alphabetically)	Internet (Web) Address	Phone Number
Alleghany/Montag & Caldwell Growth	www.alleghanyfunds.com	800-992-8151
Ariel Appreciation	www.arielfunds.com	800-292-7435
Columbia International Stock	www.columbiafunds.com	800-547-1707
Columbia Real Estate Equity	www.columbiafunds.com	800-547-1707
Eclipse Small Cap Value	www.eclipsefund.com	800-872-2710
Excelsior Value & Restructuring	www.excelsiorfunds.com	800-446-1012
Fasciano	www.fascianofunds.com	800-848-6050
Fremont Global	www.fremontfunds.com	800-548-4539
Fremont U.S. Micro-Cap	www.fremontfunds.com	800-548-4539
Homestead Value	n/a	800-258-3030
Invesco Dynamics	www.invesco.com	800-525-8085
Invesco European	www.invesco.com	800-525-8085
Invesco Health Sciences	www.invesco.com	800-525-8085
Invesco Total Return	www.invesco.com	800-525-8085
Legg Mason Spec Investment Prime	www.leggmason.com	800-577-8589
Legg Mason Total Return Prime	www.leggmason.com	800-577-8589
Legg Mason Value Prime	www.leggmason.com	800-577-8589
Preferred Asset Allocation	n/a	800-662-4769
Preferred International	n/a	800-662-4769
Preferred Value	n/a	800-662-4769
Safeco Equity No Load	www.safecofunds.com	800-426-6730
Spectra	www.algerfunds.com	800-711-6141
Strong American Utilities	www.strongfunds.com	800-368-1030
Strong Asset Allocation	www.strongfunds.com	800-368-1030
Strong Growth	www.strongfunds.com	800-368-1030
Strong Opportunity	www.strongfunds.com	800-368-1030
Strong Total Return	www.strongfunds.com	800-368-1030
T. Rowe Price Blue Chip Growth	www.troweprice.com	800-638-5660
T. Rowe Price Equity Index 500	www.troweprice.com	800-638-5660
T. Rowe Price Equity-Income	www.troweprice.com	800-638-5660
T. Rowe Price European Stock	www.troweprice.com	800-638-5660
T. Rowe Price International	www.troweprice.com	800-638-5660
T. Rowe Price International Stock	www.troweprice.com	800-638-5660
T. Rowe Price Mid-Cap Growth	www.troweprice.com	800-638-5660
T. Rowe Price Personal Strategy	www.troweprice.com	800-638-5660
T. Rowe Price Science & Technology	www.troweprice.com	800-638-5660
T. Rowe Price Small Cap Stock	www.troweprice.com	800-638-5660
T. Rowe Price Spectrum Growth	www.troweprice.com	800-638-5660
T. Rowe Price Value	www.troweprice.com	800-638-5660
USAA Growth & Income	www.usaa.com	800-382-8722

Web Site Addresses for Thrifty Stock Funds with Low Expense Ratios

Fund Name (Listed by Expense Ratio)	Internet (Web) Address	1999 Annual Expense Ratio	Phone Number
SSgA S&P 500 Index	www.ssgafunds.com	0.17	800-647-7327
Orbitex Focus 30 Dow	www.orbitex.com	0.18	800-445-2763
Vanguard 500 Index	www.vanguard.com	0.18	800-662-7447
Fidelity Spartan Market Index	www.fidelity.com	0.19	800-544-8888
Vanguard Tax-Mgd Balanced	www.vanguard.com	0.19	800-662-7447
Vanguard Tax-Mgd Cap App	www.vanguard.com	0.19	800-662-7447
Vanguard Tax-Mgd Gr&Inc	www.vanguard.com	0.19	800-662-7447
California Invmt S&P 500 Index	www.caltrust.com	0.20	800-225-8778
Vanguard Tot Stk Market Index	www.vanguard.com	0.20	800-662-7447
Vanguard Balanced Index	www.vanguard.com	0.21	800-662-7447
Vanguard Growth Index	www.vanguard.com	0.22	800-662-7447
Vanguard Value Index	www.vanguard.com	0.22	800-662-7447
Vanguard Extend Mkt Index	www.vanguard.com	0.23	800-662-7447
Vanguard Small Cap Index	www.vanguard.com	0.24	800-662-7447
Montgomery Balanced R	www.montgomeryfunds.com	0.25	800-572-3863
Vanguard Windsor	www.vanguard.com	0.27	800-662-7447
Vanguard LifeStrat Income	www.vanguard.com	0.28	800-662-7447
Vanguard LifeStrat Cons Growth	www.vanguard.com	0.29	800-662-7447
Vanguard LifeStrat Growth	www.vanguard.com	0.29	800-662-7447
Vanguard LifeStrat Mod Growth	www.vanguard.com	0.29	800-662-7447
Vanguard Wellesley Income	www.vanguard.com	0.31	800-662-7447
Vanguard Wellington	www.vanguard.com	0.31	800-662-7447
Vanguard Growth & Income	www.vanguard.com	0.36	800-662-7447
Vanguard Health Care	www.vanguard.com	0.36	800-662-7447
Vanguard STAR	www.vanguard.com	0.37	800-662-7447
Vanguard Energy	www.vanguard.com	0.38	800-662-7447
Vanguard Utilities Income	www.vanguard.com	0.38	800-662-7447
Vanguard Equity-Income	www.vanguard.com	0.39	800-662-7447
California Invmt S&P MidCap	www.caltrust.com	0.40	800-225-8778
Galaxy II Small Co Index Ret	www.galaxyfunds.com	0.40	800-628-0414
Galaxy II Utility Index Ret	www.galaxyfunds.com	0.40	800-628-0414
T. Rowe Price Equity Index 500	www.troweprice.com	0.40	800-638-5660
Vanguard U.S. Growth	www.vanguard.com	0.41	800-662-7447
Vanguard Windsor II	www.vanguard.com	0.41	800-662-7447
Vanguard Morgan Growth	www.vanguard.com	0.44	800-662-7447
Schwab 1000 Inv	www.schwab.com	0.46	800-435-4000
Galaxy II Large Co Index Return	www.galaxyfunds.com	0.47	800-628-0414
Schwab Small Cap Index Inv	www.schwab.com	0.49	800-435-4000
Vanguard Asset Allocation	www.vanguard.com	0.49	800-662-7447
Dreyfus MidCap Index	www.dreyfus.com	0.50	800-373-9387
Dreyfus S&P 500 Index	www.dreyfus.com	0.50	800-373-9387

Examples of Direct Stock Purchase Plan Applications

GE STOCK DIRECT

Direct Stock Purchase Plan
New Account Application

GE STOCK DIRECT
c/o The Bank of New York
P.O. Box 19552
Newark, NJ 07195-0552
Email: ge-shareowners@bankofny.com
Website: http://www.ge.com
1-800-STOCK-GE

❶ Account Ownership
Complete only one part of this section (A, B or C).
Please use a pen and print clearly in CAPITAL LETTERS.

A. Individual or Joint Account

Owner's Name (first, middle initial, last):

Owner's Social Security Number (used for tax reporting):

☐☐☐ - ☐☐ - ☐☐☐☐   or

Joint Owner's Name if applicable (first, middle initial, last):

B. Gift Transfers to a Minor (UGMA UTMA)

Custodian's Name, one name only (first, middle initial, last):

As Custodian for Minor's Name (first, middle initial, last):

or

Under the ☐☐ Uniform Gifts/Transfers to Minors Act
        (State)

Minor's Social Security Number

☐☐☐ - ☐☐ - ☐☐☐☐

C. Trust

Trustee's Name (first, middle initial, last):

and Co-Trustee's Name if applicable (first, middle initial, last):

As Trustees of (Name of Trust):

For the Benefit of:

Trust's Taxpayer Identification Number

☐☐ - ☐☐☐☐☐☐☐

Date of Trust (month, day, year)

☐☐ - ☐☐ - ☐☐

Individual/Joint: Joint accounts will be presumed to be joint tenants with rights of survivorship unless restricted by applicable state law or otherwise indicated. Only one social security number is required.
Gifts/Transfers to a minor UGMA/UTMA: A minor is the beneficial owner of the account with an adult as custodian, managing the account until the minor becomes of age, as specified in the uniform gift transfers to minor act in the minor's state of residence.
Trust: An account established in accordance with the provisions of a trust agreement.

❷ Address & Citizenship

Street Address and Apartment or Box Number:

City

State   Zip Code

Citizenship of Owner, Minor or Trust Beneficiary:
☐ U.S. Citizen   ☐ Resident Alien   ☐ Non-Resident Alien

Country of Citizenship:

❸A Investment Information for Initial Purchase
This Section Must Be Completed

A check must be included with this application for the initial investment ($250 minimum to a maximum $10,000, plus a one-time fee of $7.50). Thereafter, subsequent payments may be a minimum $10 to $10,000 maximum per investment plus a $3.00 fee. Please make your check payable to GE Stock Direct. Note that GE Stock Direct cannot accept foreign checks. Checks must be drawn on a U.S. Bank and payable in U.S. Dollars.

$ ☐☐ , ☐☐☐ . ☐☐

❸B Automatic Monthly Deductions - Electronic Funds Transfer (EFT)

This feature is optional. Complete this section if you want future monthly investments electronically deducted from your designated Bank Account. In addition to your initial investment made by check, you can elect to have future invested amounts deducted from your designated Bank Account. Deductions may be a minimum $10 to $10,000 maximum per investment as indicated below and will be automatically withdrawn from your checking or savings account on the 25th day each month. Enter amount to be withdrawn monthly (include $1.00 fee), and complete EFT information below.

$ ☐☐ , ☐☐☐ . ☐☐   monthly deduction

Electronic Funds Transfer (EFT) Information:
Bank Routing (ABA) Number:

Account Number:

You must check one of the following boxes:
☐ Checking Account (please attach voided check to this application) or
☐ Savings Account (please attach deposit slip to this application)

❹ Dividend Reinvest Enrollment Election
Taxpayer ID Certification

Check One
☐ Reinvest dividends.
☐ Pay cash dividends.
☐ Reinvest dividends on _____ shares and pay cash dividends on remaining shares.

I certify that I have received and read the prospectus for GE Stock Direct, and I agree to the terms and conditions of the prospectus.

Under penalties of perjury, I certify that:
1. The number shown on this form is my correct taxpayer identification number (or I am waiting for a number to be issued to me), and
2. I am not subject to backup withholding because: (a) I am exempt from backup withholding, or (b) I have not been notified by the Internal Revenue Service that I am subject to backup withholding as a result of a failure to report all interest or dividends, or (c) the IRS has notified me that I am no longer subject to backup withholding.

Certification Instructions - You must cross out item 2 above if you have been notified by the IRS that you are currently subject to backup withholding because of underreporting interest or dividends on your tax return. If I am a Non-Resident Alien, as I've indicated above, I certify under penalties of perjury that I am not a U.S. Citizen or Resident Alien, and that I am an "exempt foreign person" as defined under IRS regulations.

Please make sure that all owners sign the application as required.

Signature of Owner, Custodian or Trustee   Date
X

Signature of Joint Tenant or Co-Trustee if applicable   Date
X

Telephone Number: _____

20512(1-98)
(Rev. 10/98)

MDU RESOURCES GROUP, INC.
AUTOMATIC DIVIDEND REINVESTMENT AND STOCK PURCHASE PLAN
ACCOUNT AUTHORIZATION FORM

Please print all items except signatures. QUESTIONS? Call toll-free 1-888-291-3713 from 7:30 a.m. to 7 p.m. Central Time, Monday through Friday. Mail your completed Account Authorization form in the courtesy envelope to Shareholder Services℠, P.O. Box 64863, St. Paul, MN 55164-0863.

A. Enrolling in the Plan

I AM A CURRENT STOCKHOLDER – MY MDU ACCOUNT NUMBER IS: __ __ __ __ __ __ __ __ __ __

❑ I **AM** a current stockholder and wish to enroll by having $ _____ ($50.00 minimum/$5,000.00 maximum) automatically withdrawn from my checking or savings account each month. **Complete sections B, C, D, E, F, and G.**

❑ I **AM** a current stockholder and wish to enroll by making an initial investment of $ _____ ($50.00 minimum/$5,000.00 maximum). Make check payable to Shareowner Services℠. **Complete sections B, C, D, F and G.**

❑ I **AM** a current stockholder and would like my dividends reinvested. I DO NOT wish to make an additional cash investment at this time. **Complete sections B, C, D, F and G.**

NOTE: Cash dividends on shares credited to the participant's account under the Plan will be automatically reinvested in additional shares of Common Stock.

I AM NOT A CURRENT STOCKHOLDER

❑ I **AM NOT** a current stockholder and wish to enroll by having $ _____ ($50.00 minimum/$5,000.00 maximum) automatically withdrawn from my checking or savings account each month. **Complete sections B, C, E, F and G.**

❑ I **AM NOT** a current stockholder and wish to enroll by making an initial investment of $ _____ ($50.00 minimum/$5,000.00 maximum). Make check payable to Shareowner Services℠. **Complete sections B, C, F and G.**

NOTE: Cash dividends on shares credited to the participant's account under the Plan will be automatically reinvested in additional shares of Common Stock.

MY MDU SHARES ARE HELD BY MY STOCKBROKER

❑ I would like information on how to enroll by transferring common or preferred stock held by my broker (or other agent). Please send me a broker transfer form. **Complete section B.**

B. Account Mailing Address

We require a complete address to process your enrollment.

First Name _____ MI _____ Last Name _____

Street or P.O. Box _____ Apt. # _____

City _____ State _____ Zip _____

Please provide your day and evening phone numbers to assist us in processing your enrollment.

Daytime Phone: (_____) _____ - _____

Evening Phone: (_____) _____ - _____

I am a citizen of: ❑ the United States or
                              ❑ Other (please specify)
_____

C. Account Registration

TYPE OF ACCOUNT: Please check one (1) box and provide all requested information.

❑ **INDIVIDUAL OR JOINT** – Joint accounts will be presumed to be joint tenants unless restricted by applicable state law or otherwise indicated. Only one (1) Social Security Number is required for tax reporting.

Owner's First Name _____ MI _____ Last Name _____ Owner's Social Security Number _____   Joint Owner's First Name _____ MI _____ Last Name _____

❑ **CUSTODIAL** – A minor is the beneficial owner of the account with an adult Custodian managing the account until the minor reaches legal age, as specified in the Uniform Gift/Transfer to Minor's Act in the minor's state of residence.

Custodian's First Name _____ MI _____ Last Name _____ Minor's First Name _____ MI _____ Last Name _____ Minor's Social Security No. _____ Minor's State of Residence _____

❑ **TRUST** – Account is established in accordance with provisions of a trust agreement.

Trustee Name _____ Name of Trust _____ Beneficiary _____ Trust Date _____ Tax ID Number _____

❑ **CORPORATION, PARTNERSHIP, OR OTHER ENTITY** – Please contact us if you have questions regarding proper registration.

Business Name _____ Tax ID Number _____

D. Dividends

Choose only one option: 1) Full Dividend Reinvestment, 2) Partial Dividend Reinvestment or 3) Cash Payments Only.
If you do not check any box then FULL DIVIDEND REINVESTMENT will be assumed.

NOTE: Cash dividends on shares credited to the participant's account under the Plan will be automatically reinvested in additional shares of Common Stock.

❑ 1) **Full Dividend Reinvestment** *(Internal use only - RD)*
   I wish to reinvest all dividends from shares registered in my name that I hold.

❑ 2) **Partial Dividend Reinvestment** *(Internal use only - RP)*
   I wish to reinvest only a portion of dividends from shares registered in my name that I hold.
   ❑ Common   ❑ Preferred   Reinvest the cash dividend on _____ (number) of shares that I hold.

❑ 3) **Cash Payments Only** *(Internal use only - RV)*
   All cash dividends from shares registered in my name will be paid directly to me in cash. The dividend on shares held in the Plan will be reinvested.

   ❑ I am interested in having my cash dividends automatically deposited to my bank account.
   Please send me an ACH Dividend Deposit Authorization Card.

E. Automatic Cash Withdrawal and Investment (ACH)

In order to have your cash investment automatically withdrawn from your checking or savings account each month, complete the information below. The Automatic Cash Withdrawal is a minimum of $50.00 and a maximum of $5,000.00 per month.

BANK ACCOUNT INFORMATION:
❑ Checking   ❑ Savings

Please attach a voided check or account deposit slip for account verification.

_____
Name of Financial Institution

_____
ABA Routing Number *(Number always begins with a 0, 1, 2, or 3)*

_____
Bank Account Number   Bank Telephone

_____
Mailing Address of Bank

_____
City   State   Zip

AUTHORIZATION:

I (We) authorize Norwest Bank Minnesota, N.A. to electronically withdraw from my (our) account

$ _____ .00 per month ($50.00 minimum / $5,000.00 maximum)

and to apply amounts so deducted to the purchase of Common Stock as defined by the terms and conditions of the Plan. This authority remains in effect until I cancel in writing. I have attached a voided check or deposit slip.

DISCONTINUE/CHANGE AUTHORIZATION:
❑ Please discontinue withdrawing funds from my checking/savings account.
❑ Please change my monthly deduction to $ _____ .00.

Please verify authorization by signing below in Section G.
A signature guarantee is necessary if the name(s) on the bank account is/are different from the name(s) on your stockholder account.

F. Telephone Privileges

❑ By checking here, I hereby authorize Shareholder Services℠ to establish telephone privileges for my account as defined by the terms and conditions of the Plan. For security purposes, I would like my 4-digit PIN set to _____ – _____ – _____ – _____ . *(PIN must be numeric digits.)*

G. Signatures   *IMPORTANT: All joint owners must sign.*

By completing and signing this form, I certify that I have received and read the prospectus describing the MDU Resources Group, Inc. Automatic Dividend Reinvestment and Stock Purchase Plan and hereby request that the above account be enrolled in the Plan. I understand that the account's participation is subject to the terms and conditions of the Plan as set forth in the prospectus that accompanied this Account Authorization Form, and that enrollment may be discontinued at any time by written notice to Norwest Bank Minnesota, N.A. I further understand that all dividends paid on the shares registered in my name or held in my Plan account will be reinvested as selected above. I hereby appoint Norwest Bank Minnesota, N.A. as agent for applying dividends and any investments I may make to the purchase of shares under the Plan.

For joint owner: I understand that if Section F is completed above, Norwest Bank Minnesota, N.A. will be authorized to effect transactions in my Plan account (including sales of shares held in the account) pursuant to the telephone instructions of the other joint owner of the account without any approval or other action on my part.

Under penalties of perjury, I certify that: A. The number shown on this form is my/our correct Social Security Number or Tax ID Number; B. I am not subject to backup withholding, either because (1) I have not been notified by the Internal Revenue Service (IRS) that I am subject to backup withholding as a result of failure to report all interest or dividends, or (2) the IRS has notified me that I am no longer subject to backup withholding. ❑ Check this box if you have been notified by the IRS that you are subject to backup withholding because of underreporting of interest or dividends on your tax returns.

_____   _____
Stockholder Signature   Date   Stockholder Signature   Date

STOCK PURCHASE INITIAL INVESTMENT FORM

WALMART 06973
7171

⌐

|||I||I||I||I||I||I||I||I||I||I||I||I||I||I||I||I||I||I||I||I||

Please check only one box below (☒).

If you do not check any box, then **FULL DIVIDEND REINVESTMENT** will be assumed.

☐ **FULL DIVIDEND REINVESTMENT**
Reinvest all dividends for this account.

☐ **PARTIAL DIVIDEND REINVESTMENT**
Send any dividends in cash on _____ * whole shares and reinvest any remaining dividends.
* Cannot be greater than the total number of certificated and/or book-entry shares that may hereafter be registered in your name.

☐ **CASH PAYMENTS ONLY (NO DIVIDEND REINVESTMENT)**
All dividends will be paid in cash.

The name and address above are for mailing purposes only. **Please complete one of the boxes below (ACCOUNT LEGAL REGISTRATION) to show the exact name in which the account will be established.**

Under each of the options above, participants may make additional cash investments by check or money order at any time and/or by automatic deductions from their U.S. bank or financial institution.

ACCOUNT LEGAL REGISTRATION (CHOOSE ONE):

☐ SINGLE/JOINT ACCOUNT	☐ CUSTODIAL ACCOUNT	☐ TRUST ACCOUNT
Name	Custodian's Name (only one custodian permitted)	Trust Name or Beneficiary
Joint Owner (if any)	Minor's Name	Trustee Name
Joint Owner (if any)	Minor's State of Residence	Date of Trust
| — | | — | | | | | |	| | | — | | — | | | | |	| | | — | | | | | | |
TIN (Social Security Number)	Minor's TIN (Social Security Number)	TIN (Employer Identification Number)

ACCOUNT ADDRESS _____

Street   Apt. No.

City   State   Zip Code   ( ) Daytime Phone No.

I (We) hereby warrant that, under penalties of perjury, the U.S. Taxpayer Identification Number (TIN) provided above is correct.

SIGNATURE(s) _____

All joint owners must sign. . . . This form will be rejected if it is not properly signed.

To enroll, you may make your initial investment by either check or automatic deductions from your U.S. bank or financial institution. If you enroll by check, you may also authorize automatic deductions for future purchases of shares.

☐ **Enclosed is a check for** $ _____   *(Check must be payable in U.S. Dollars.)*

☐ **I (We) authorize automatic deductions of funds from my (our) U.S. bank or financial institution as indicated on the reverse.**

PLEASE REFER TO THE ENCLOSED PLAN DESCRIPTION FOR THE MINIMUM AMOUNT OF THE INITIAL INVESTMENT.

This form, when completed and signed, should be mailed with your check or money order (if applicable) in the enclosed envelope. If you do not have the envelope, mail your payment (if applicable) and the form to Investment Plan Services, P.O. Box 13517, Newark, NJ 07188-0001.

Participation in the plan is subject to the terms as outlined in the enclosed plan description. For information, participants may write to the plan administrator at the above address or call them at the telephone number listed in the enclosed plan description.

ACCOUNT INFORMATION

1. **SINGLE/JOINT:** Joint account will be presumed to be joint tenants with right of survivorship unless restricted by applicable state law or otherwise indicated. Only one Social Security Number is required.

2. **CUSTODIAL:** A minor is the beneficial owner of the account with an adult custodian managing the account until the minor becomes of age, as specified in the Uniform Gifts or Transfers to Minors Act in the minor's state of residence.

3. **TRUST:** Account is established in accordance with the provisions of a trust agreement.

FC90630 NEW 03/99 (SEE REVERSE)

AUTHORIZATION FORM FOR AUTOMATIC DEDUCTIONS

COMPLETE THE INFORMATION BELOW FOR STOCK PURCHASES USING AUTOMATIC DEDUCTIONS

Deductions can only be made from accounts at U.S. banks and financial institutions.

PLEASE PRINT ALL INFORMATION:

1. Type of Account: ☐ Checking   ☐ Savings
   *If deductions are to be made from a **money market account**, please contact your bank/financial institution to confirm if your account is a checking or a savings account.*

2. ☐☐☐☐☐☐☐☐☐☐☐☐☐☐☐☐☐☐☐☐☐☐☐☐
   Bank Account Number *(see example below)*

3. ☐☐☐☐☐☐☐☐☐
   Bank Routing Number *(see example below)*

4. $ _____
   Amount of automatic deduction. *(Refer to the enclosed plan description for the minimum amount.)*

5. Cycle: ☐ 1st   ☐ 2nd
   Refer to the enclosed plan description for the frequency of automatic deductions. If the plan permits deductions *once* a month, *please check the "1st Cycle" box above.* If the plan permits deductions *twice* per month, *you must indicate your choice of deduction dates,* either the earlier date (1st Cycle) or the later date (2nd Cycle), or both.

6. ☐☐☐☐☐☐☐☐☐☐☐☐☐☐☐☐☐☐☐☐☐☐☐☐☐☐☐☐☐☐☐☐
   Name on Bank Account *(see example below)*

7. ☐☐☐☐☐☐☐☐☐☐☐☐☐☐☐☐☐☐☐☐☐☐☐☐☐☐☐☐☐☐☐☐
   Financial Institution *(see example below)*

   ☐☐☐☐☐☐☐☐☐☐☐☐☐☐☐☐☐☐☐☐☐☐☐☐☐☐☐☐☐☐☐☐
   Branch Name

   ☐☐☐☐☐☐☐☐☐☐☐☐☐☐☐☐☐☐☐☐☐☐☐☐☐☐☐☐☐☐☐☐
   Branch Street Address

   ☐☐☐☐☐☐☐☐☐☐☐☐☐☐☐☐☐☐☐☐☐☐☐☐☐☐☐☐☐☐☐☐
   Branch City, State and Zip Code

Please enclose a copy of a VOIDED check or a savings deposit slip to verify banking information.

I (We) hereby authorize the plan administrator to make monthly deductions from my (our) checking or savings account in the amount stated above. These funds will be used to purchase shares to be held for my (our) account.

Signature(s) _____

Date _____ Daytime Phone Number (_____) _____
                                               Area Code

USE THIS ILLUSTRATION AS A GUIDE TO HELP YOU COMPLETE THE AUTHORIZATION FORM ABOVE

Name on
Bank Account

JOHN A. DOE
MARY B. DOE
123 YOUR STREET
ANYWHERE, U.S.A. 12345

_____ 19 ___

63-858
670

PAY TO THE
ORDER OF _____ $ ☐

_____ DOLLARS

Financial
Institution and
Branch
Information

First National Bank
of Anywhere
123 Main Street
Anywhere, U.S.A. 12345

FOR _____   **SAMPLE (NON-NEGOTIABLE)**

⑈071000013⑈ 123456789⑈

Bank Routing Number   Bank Account Number

Making additional investments through the Johnson Controls Dividend Reinvestment and Stock Purchase Plan can be very easy. The Automatic Cash Investment option provides for automatic monthly transfers from your checking account directly to your Johnson Controls Dividend Reinvestment and Stock Purchase Plan account. You can automatically transfer any amount from $50 to $5,000 per month. With this feature, the funds are automatically withdrawn from your checking account on the 25th of each month (or the following business day if the 25th falls on a weekend or holiday). The investment is made on the last business day of each month.

To sign up: 1) Complete and sign the lower portion of the enclosed statement

2) Attach a voided blank check

3) Return to: **Firstar Bank, N.A.**
                  P.O. Box 3078
                  Milwaukee, WI 53201

The first withdrawal from your checking account will occur in the month following the receipt of your authorization form. Cancellation of the Automatic Cash Investment option must be done by the 15th of the month.

Call our transfer agent, Firstar Bank, N.A., at 800/828-1489 with any questions. You will have to enter the Johnson Controls company code of "5201" and your account number.

✂ --

JOHNSON CONTROLS DIVIDEND REINVESTMENT AND STOCK PURCHASE PLAN
AUTHORIZATION FOR AUTOMATIC DEDUCTION FROM CHECKING ACCOUNT

AMOUNT TO BE DEDUCTED EACH MONTH FROM MY CHECKING
ACCOUNT   *(Minimum, $50.00; Maximum, $5,000 per month)* $_____

NAME OF FINANCIAL INSTITUTION _____

ADDRESS OF FINANCIAL INSTITUTION _____
                                                    STREET

_____   _____   _____
              CITY   STATE   ZIP CODE

CHECKING ACCOUNT NO. _____

ABA TRANSIT ROUTING NUMBER *(usually printed in the lower left corner of your check)* __ __ __ __ __ __ __ __ __

NAME OF SHAREHOLDER _____

ADDRESS OF SHAREHOLDER _____
                                                    STREET

_____   _____   _____
              CITY   STATE   ZIP CODE

JOHNSON CONTROLS 10-DIGIT PLAN ACCT. NO.*(if already have an account)* _____

SOCIAL SECURITY NO. _____

I hereby authorize Firstar Bank, N.A., to withdraw from my checking account on the 25th of each month the amount specified above. The funds will be used to purchase Johnson Controls, Inc., common stock in accordance with the Johnson Controls Automatic Dividend Reinvestment and Common Stock Purchase Plan.

Shareholder ✍_____

Shareholder ✍_____
                          (If joint account, both must sign)

Form 11212   **IMPORTANT: YOU MUST ATTACH A VOIDED CHECK**

	JOHNSON CONTROLS AUTOMATIC DIVIDEND REINVESTMENT AND COMMON STOCK PURCHASE PLAN
	AUTHORIZATION FORM
	Only register one account per application. This form may be duplicated.

NEW ACCOUNT APPLICATION FORM (Own no registered shares at this time)

Please review the guidelines on the reverse side of this form and check the appropriate box for the desired account registration:

☐ INDIVIDUAL ☐ JOINT (Both must sign application) ☐ TOD (Beneficiary need not sign)

☐ TRUST (Trustee(s) must sign) ☐ CUSTODIAL (Custodian must sign) ☐ CORPORATE (Authorized person must sign)

☐ PARTNERSHIP (Same as Corporate) ☐ INVESTMENT CLUB (Same as Corporate) ☐ OTHER_____

Note: Our agent, Firstar Bank, N.A., will not act as a custodian for an IRA registration.

NAME(S) _____   _____

MAILING ADDRESS _____
                              (Street Address)   (Apt. No., Unit No., etc.)

_____   _____   _____
              (City)   (State/Country)   (Zip Code)

SOCIAL SECURITY No. _____ Daytime Phone No. (_____)

I acknowledge receipt of the prospectus describing the details of the Johnson Controls Automatic Dividend Reinvestment and Common Stock Purchase Plan (the "Plan") and hereby request that the above account be enrolled in the Plan. I understand participation is subject to the Terms and Conditions of the Plan as set forth in the prospectus. I hereby authorize Firstar Bank, N.A., as my agent, subject to the description of the Plan, to apply this investment for not less than $50 toward the initial purchase of shares for the above account and understand that all dividends paid on the shares held by the account, whether Plan or registered, will automatically be reinvested and Firstar will apply any supplemental cash investments to the purchase of shares of Johnson Controls common stock.

Enclosed is my check in the amount of $_____

Signature: ✍ _____   Signature: ✍ _____
                                                                                    (If joint account, both must sign)

TAXPAYER IDENTIFICATION - SUBSTITUTE W-9 FORM

Under penalties of perjury, I certify the Social Security/Taxpayer Identification Number indicated above is true and correct and that I am not subject to backup withholding under the Internal Revenue Code. Please note that if a Social Security Number/Taxpayer Identification Number is not provided, backup withholding tax will be imposed on dividend payments and broker exchange transactions. Signature of Taxpayer whose Social Security/Taxpayer Identification Number is indicated above must sign below (signature for a corporation, partnership, etc., should be by the individual authorized by that entity).

Signature: ✍ _____   Date: _____

☐ **I am a U.S. Citizen or Resident Alien**   ☐ **I am a Nonresident Alien-Foreign Tax Status Applies**

SHAREHOLDER ACCOUNT APPLICATION FORM (*CURRENTLY* own registered shares)

CHECK ONE BOX ONLY

☐ **Full Dividend Reinvestment** - I wish to reinvest dividends on *all* shares personally held in certificate form and all Plan shares held by this shareholder account.

☐ **Partial Dividend Reinvestment** - I wish to reinvest dividends on _____ (enter number) shares personally held in certificate form and all Plan shares held by this shareholder account.

Optional Cash Investment - Enclosed is my check in the amount of $_____ to purchase shares of Common Stock.

COMPLETE EXACTLY AS YOUR STOCK IS REGISTERED: ACCOUNT No. (if known)_____

NAME(S)_____   _____

MAILING ADDRESS _____
                              (Street Address)   (Apt. No., Unit No., etc.)

_____   _____   _____
              (City)   (State/Country)   (Zip Code)

SOCIAL SECURITY No. _____ Daytime Phone No. (_____)

I acknowledge receipt of the prospectus describing the details of the Johnson Controls Automatic Dividend Reinvestment and Common Stock Purchase Plan (the "Plan") and hereby request that the above account be enrolled in the Plan. I understand participation is subject to the Terms and Conditions of the Plan as set forth in the prospectus. I hereby authorize Firstar Bank, N.A., as my agent, subject to the description of the Plan, to apply cash dividends and/or supplemental cash investments to the purchase of shares of Johnson Controls Common Stock. Sign below exactly as stock is registered and name(s) are shown:

Signature: ✍ _____   Signature: ✍ _____
                                                                                    (If joint account, both must sign)

TAXPAYER IDENTIFICATION - SUBSTITUTE W-9 FORM

Under penalties of perjury, I certify the Social Security/Taxpayer Identification Number indicated above is true and correct and that I am not subject to backup withholding under the Internal Revenue Code. Please note that if a Social Security Number/Taxpayer Identification Number is not provided, backup withholding tax will be imposed on dividend payments and broker exchange transactions. Signature of Taxpayer whose Social Security/Taxpayer Identification Number is indicated above must sign below (signature for a corporation, partnership, etc., should be by the individual authorized by that entity).

Signature: ✍ _____   Date: _____

☐ I am a U.S. Citizen or Resident Alien   ☐ **I am a Nonresident Alien-Foreign Tax Status Applies**

Form 11211   **Mail the form to: Firstar Bank, N.A., P.O. Box 3078, Milwaukee, WI 53201-3078**

GENERAL GUIDELINES FOR COMMON FORMS OF STOCK REGISTRATION

The manner in which stock may be registered is governed by various state laws. The following are intended as general guidelines indicating some of the more common forms of stock registration. If you have any questions regarding a specific form of registration, we suggest you consult an attorney.

OWNERSHIP OF STOCK BY AN INDIVIDUAL: The given name of an individual must be used. Titles such as "Dr.," "Mrs.," or "Rev." are not used. A married woman should use her given name, not that of her husband. Example:

"SANDRA LARSON SMITH" *not* "MRS. JOHN W. SMITH"

OWNERSHIP OF STOCK BY TWO OR MORE INDIVIDUALS: Most states recognize the registration "As Joint Tenants with Right of Survivorship" and "As Tenants in Common." This form of registration, which is shown as "JT TEN" following the names, provides for vesting of title in the surviving tenant upon the death of the other tenant. The conjunction "OR" *CANNOT* be used in registering stock ownership. Other forms of multiple tenant registration, such as "Tenants in Common," may also be used, but may not provide for survivorship benefits. Should you have any questions about the registration you wish to use, we suggest you consult an attorney. Example:

"JOHN H. WILSON AND SANDRA L. SMITH JT TEN"

TRANSFER ON DEATH (TOD): Transfer on Death (TOD) is a form of stock ownership which enables a shareholder to designate, while retaining all normal rights of ownership, an individual or other entity that will automatically become the shareholder upon death of the owner. This is available to shareholders holding stock in a company registered in the state of Wisconsin or whose transfer agent is located in the state of Wisconsin. Johnson Controls, Inc., is a company registered in the state of Wisconsin and our transfer agent is also located in this state. Therefore, this form of stock ownership is available to all of our shareholders.

Ownership of the stock passes to the designated beneficiary outside of probate. The owners of the stock may be joint, but only one TOD beneficiary may be named per account. TOD registrations must be concluded by the phrase, "SUBJECT TO STA TOD RULES." STA stands for Securities Transfer Association, Inc. Example:

"JOHN W. SMITH TOD SANDRA L. SMITH SUBJECT TO STA TOD RULES"

TRUSTS: There are many forms of trusts and an attorney can assist you in setting up the right trust for your needs. All trust registrations require the name of the trustee(s), the name of the trust, the date it was established, the address and Taxpayer Identification Number for the trust. Example:

"JOHN N. DOE, TRUSTEE, OF THE MARY J. DOE TR UA DTD JULY 1, 1997"

OWNERSHIP OF STOCK BY A MINOR (CUSTODIAL REGISTRATION): It is not common practice to register stock in an individual minor's name, since it may require court action to sell or transfer the shares prior to the minor attaining his/her age of majority. The minor is the legal and beneficial owner and the custodian is merely the supervisor. The state indicated in the registration is the state under which the registration is created. The custodian collects, holds, manages, invests and reinvests the custodial property for the benefit of the minor. *The social security number of the minor must be furnished for the account.* The custodian should sign the substitute W-9 form on behalf of the minor. Example:

"JANE E. DOE, CUSTODIAN FOR AMY L. DOE, _____ (Enter the name of the State where the custodian lives) UNIFORM TRANSFERS TO MINORS ACT"

CORPORATIONS, PARTNERSHIPS OR INVESTMENT CLUBS: A person who is authorized to act on behalf of the entity must sign the form. It is recommended that investment clubs be organized as partnerships and the shares should be registered under a partnership registration. A taxpayer identification number of the entity must be provided and the person who is authorized to act on the entity's behalf must sign the substitute W-9 form. Example:

"THE ABC COMPANY" *or* "BADGER STATE INVESTMENT CLUB, A PARTNERSHIP"

Eastman Kodak
SHARES PROGRAM

A. Enrolling in the Program	☐ I wish to enroll in the Eastman Kodak Shares Program ("Program") by making an initial investment. Enclosed is a check or money order for $_____ ($150 minimum/$120,000 maximum annually) payable to "BKB-Kodak." The timing of your investment is explained in the Prospectus.

Please note any address corrections on this form.

Please provide your day and evening phone numbers to assist us in processing your enrollment.

Daytime phone: (_____) _____

Evening phone: (_____) _____

B. Account registration Please check one box and provide the requested information. Please print clearly.	☐ Check here if you want the name on the account to match the mailing information above. Social Security Number _____ ☐ **Individual or Joint.** Joint accounts will be presumed to be "joint tenants with right of survivorship" and not as "tenants in common" unless restricted by applicable state law or otherwise indicated. Only one Social Security Number (which should be that of the first person named) is required for tax reporting.

Owner's Name: First   M.I.   Last   Owner's Social Security Number   Joint Owner's Name: First   M.I.   Last

☐   **Custodian for a Minor.** An adult custodian manages the account until the minor becomes of age, as specified in the Uniform Gifts/Transfers to Minors Act in the minor's state of residence. One minor per account.

Custodian's Name: First   M.I.   Last

Minor's Name: First   M.I.   Last   Minor's Social Security Number   Minor's State of Residence

☐   **Trust.** Account is established in accordance with a trust agreement.

Trustee Name   Name of Trust   Trust Date   Tax ID Number   Beneficiary

C. Dividend Election Please check one box and provide the requested information.	You may choose to reinvest all, a portion or none of the dividends paid on company stock registered in your name and held for you under the Program. If you do not indicate a choice, all of your dividends will be reinvested. ☐ **Full Dividend Reinvestment.** I wish to reinvest all of my dividends to purchase additional shares of common stock. I may also make optional payments to the Program. (You will not receive a dividend check.) ☐ **Partial Dividend Reinvestment.** I wish to reinvest my dividends on _____ whole shares of common stock and dividends on the rest of my shares will be paid to me in cash. I may also make optional payments to the Program. ☐ **Optional Cash Only.** I wish to make only optional cash payments to the Program. All dividends will be paid to me.

D. Signatures	By signing this form, I request enrollment and certify that I have received and read the Prospectus describing the Eastman Kodak Shares Program and agree to abide by the terms and conditions of the Program. I hereby appoint BankBoston, N.A. as my Program Agent to apply dividends and any investments I may make to the purchase of shares under the Program. I understand that I may revoke this authorization at any time by written notice to BankBoston, N.A. Under penalties of perjury, I also certify that (1) the number shown on this form is my/our correct Social Security Number or Taxpayer Identification Number and (2) that I am not subject to backup withholding. (Check here _____ if you have been notified by the IRS that you are subject to backup withholding.) Names must be signed exactly as shown above. Any individual, all joint owners, the custodian, the trustees and/or an authorized officer must sign.

Signature   Date   Signature   Date

E. Automatic Investment	AUTOMATIC INVESTMENT — You may authorize automatic monthly deductions from your bank account. BankBoston will invest these deductions in company stock and credit your account. To initiate these deductions, please complete the reverse side of this form and check this box. ☐ Your authorized monthly deduction from your bank account must be for at least $50, and cannot exceed $120,000 in a calendar year.

Mail your completed Enrollment Form in the envelope provided to: BankBoston, N.A.   Eastman Kodak Shares Program   P.O. Box 9049 Boston, MA 02205-9838

F. Automatic Investment Application

Please fill out the information requested below to begin monthly deductions from your checking or savings account to purchase common stock of Eastman Kodak Company under the terms and conditions of the Eastman Kodak Shares Program. Please see below for a sample illustration of where the requested information can be found. This form must be received by the end of the month preceding the first applicable date of withdrawal from your bank account. Should your bank account contain insufficient funds to cover the authorized deduction, no withdrawal will be made and no investment will occur. If this happens, you may be charged a fee by your bank for insufficient funds. You must notify BankBoston, N.A. at least four (4) business days prior to the date of withdrawal for any change or cancellation of this authorization to be effective.

ABA Routing Number ☐☐☐☐☐☐☐☐☐   Checking ☐   Savings ☐

Bank Account Number ☐☐☐☐☐☐☐☐☐☐☐☐☐☐☐☐☐

Name on Account (Please Print)

Amount to be Withdrawn $ ☐☐,☐☐☐.☐☐   Minimum $50.00

I hereby authorize BankBoston, N.A. to make monthly automatic withdrawals of funds from my bank account in the amount indicated on this form. These funds will be used to purchase shares of common stock for my account. Note: If this is a joint bank account, both owners must sign.

Name of Financial Institution

Mailing Address of Financial Institution

City   State   Zip Code

Signature   Date   Signature (Joint account only)   Date

John Smith
123 Your Street
Anywhere, USA 12345

63-85/670   0752   19____

PAY TO THE ORDER OF ____ $____

____ DOLLARS

YOUR BANK 000-001 123 Main Street Anywhere, USA 12345

FOR ____   SAMPLE (NON-NEGOTIABLE)

:063000047:   1234567890:   0752:

ABA Routing Number   Bank Account Number   Check Number (Do not include as part of bank account number)

INDEX

ABOUT THE AUTHOR

CRAIG L. ISRAELSEN, PH.D., is one of today's top authorities on investing on a budget. An associate professor of consumer and family economics at University of Missouri, Dr. Israelsen is the author of *Personal and Family Finance Workbook.* He is a regular contributor to *Financial Planning Magazine,* and is regularly quoted in major publications including *The New York Times* and *Christian Science Monitor.*